A Day at a Time

Words to Live By

KEEP IT SIMPLE

DAILY MEDITATIONS FOR TWELVE-STEP BEGINNINGS & RENEWAL

HAZELDEN

MJF BOOKS

NEW YORK

Published by MJF Books
Fine Communications
Two Lincoln Square
60 West 66th Street
New York, NY 10023

A Day at a Time/Keep It Simple
Library of Congress Catalog Card Number 97-75632
ISBN 1-56731-258-6

10 9 8 7 6 5 4 3 2 1

Editor's Foreword

These daily reflections, prayers, and tags of memory-sticking phrases are intended to offer inspiration, comfort, and, above all, hope to those recovering from alcoholism, or from other forms of chemical dependency or compulsive behavior.

The book is based on the solid spiritual foundation of Alcoholics Anonymous (AA), and upon the Twelve Steps and Twelve Traditions. It draws also upon the great body of accumulated human wisdom—from civilization's Golden Age to our not-always-so-golden modern era, from Socrates to Bill W., co-founder of AA. Here, in brief day-by-day messages are some of these available riches, the words of poets, scholars, philosophers, psychologists, which are the verbal sums of centuries of human experience. May those sums and sayings serve as guidelines—a day at a time.

Hazelden Publishing and Education is a division of the Hazelden Foundation, a not-for-profit organization. Since 1949, Hazelden has been a leader in promoting the dignity and treatment of people afflicted with the disease of chemical dependency.

The mission of the Foundation is to improve the quality of life for individuals, families, and communities by providing a national continuum of information, education, and recovery services that are widely accessible; to advance the field through research and training; and to improve quality and effectiveness through continuous improvement and innovation.

Stemming from that, the mission of the Publishing division is to provide quality information and support to people wherever they may be in their personal journey— from education and early intervention, through treatment and recovery, to personal and spiritual growth.

Although our treatment programs do not necessarily use everything Hazelden publishes, our bibliotherapeutic materials support our mission and the Twelve Step philosophy upon which it is based. We encourage your comments and feedback.

The headquarters of the Hazelden Foundation is in Center City, Minnesota. Additional treatment facilities are located in Chicago, Illinois; New York, New York; Plymouth, Minnesota; St. Paul, Minnesota; and West Palm Beach, Florida. At these sites we provide a continuum of care for men and women of all ages. Our Plymouth facility is designed specifically for youth and families.

For more information on Hazelden, please call **1-800-257-7800**, or access our World Wide Web site on the Internet [http://www.hazelden.org].

JANUARY 1

Reflection for the Day

In the old days, I saw everything in terms of *forever*. Endless hours were spent rehashing old mistakes. I tried to take comfort in the forlorn hope that tomorrow "would be different."

As a result, I lived a fantasy life in which happiness was all but nonexistent. No wonder I rarely smiled and hardly ever laughed aloud. *Do I still think in terms of "forever"?*

Today I Pray

May I set my goals for the New Year not at the year-long mark, but one day at a time. My traditional New Year's resolutions have been so grandly stated and so soon broken. Let me not weaken my resolve by stretching it to cover "forever"—or even one long year. May I reapply it firmly each new day. May I learn not to stamp my past mistakes with that indelible word, "forever." Instead, may each single day in each New Year be freshened by my new-found hope.

Today I Will Remember

Happy New Day.

Reflection for the Day

Before I came to the Program, I hadn't the faintest idea of what it was to "Live In The Now." I often became obsessed with the things that happened yesterday, last week, or even five years ago. Worse yet, many of my waking hours were spent clearing away the "wreckage of the future." "To me," Walt Whitman once wrote, "every hour of the day and night is an unspeakably perfect miracle." *Can I truly believe that in my heart?*

Today I Pray

Let me carry only the weight of 24 hours at one time, without the extra bulk of yesterday's regrets or tomorrow's anxieties. Let me breathe the blessings of each new day for itself, by itself, and keep my human burdens contained in daily perspective. May I learn the balance of soul that comes through keeping close to God.

Today I Will Remember

Don't borrow from tomorrow.

Reflection for the Day

My addiction is three-fold in that it affects me physically, mentally, and spiritually. As a chemically dependent person, I was totally out of touch not only with myself, but with reality. Day after miserable day, like a caged animal on a treadmill, I repeated my self-destructive pattern of living. *Have I begun to break away from my old ideas? Just for today, can I adjust myself to what is, rather than try to adjust everything to my own desires?*

Today I Pray

I pray that I may not be caught up again in the downward, destructive spiral which removed me from myself and from the realities of the world around me. I pray that I may adjust to people and situations as they are instead of always trying, unsuccessfully and with endless frustration, to bend them to my own desires.

Today I Will Remember

I can only change myself.

Reflection for the Day

For a good part of my life, I saw things mostly in negative terms. *Everything* was serious, heavy, or just plain awful. Perhaps now I can truly change my attitude, searching out the winners in the Program who have learned how to live comfortably in the real world—without numbing their brains with mood-altering chemicals. *If things get rough today, can I take a quiet moment and say to myself, as the philosopher Homer once said, "Bear patiently, my heart—for you have suffered heavier things...*"?

Today I Pray

May the peace of God that passes all human understanding fill the place within me that once harbored my despair. May an appreciation for living—even for life's trails—cancel out my old negative attitudes. During heart-heavy moments, help to remind me that my heart was once much heavier still.

Today I Will Remember

I, too, am a winner.

Reflection for the Day

"Vision is, I think, the ability to make good estimates," wrote Bill W., the co-founder of Alcoholics Anonymous. "Some might feel this sort of striving to be heresy against 'One Day At A Time.' But that valuable principle really refers to our mental and emotional lives, and means chiefly that we are not foolishly to repine over the past nor wishfully daydream about the future." *Can I believe that "A day has a hundred pockets when one has much to put in them..."?*

Today I Pray

I pray that the bright colors of this day may not be blurred by muted vagaries of the future or dulled by storm-gray remnants from the past. I pray that my Higher Power will help me to choose my actions and concerns out of the wealth of busyness that each day offers.

Today I Will Remember

I will not lose for today,
If I choose for today.

Reflection for the Day

"As individuals and as a fellowship," Bill W. continued, "we shall surely suffer if we cast the whole idea of planning for tomorrow into a fatuous idea of providence. God's real providence has endowed us human beings with a considerable capability for foresight, and He evidently expects us to use it. Of course, we shall often miscalculate the future in whole or in part, but that is better than to refuse to think at all." *Have I begun to believe that I am only an actor in a play which the Manager directs?*

Today I Pray

May I make prudent use of the foresight and power of choice which God has given me, to plan wisely, one Step at a time, without becoming a slave to apprehension, regret, or anxiety. I pray that God's will be done through the exercising of my own will, which He, in His goodness, has given me.

Today I Will Remember

God wills my will to be.

Reflection for the Day

I'm beginning to see just how unnatural my old life actually was, and that it became increasingly unnatural as my illness progressed. The longer I'm in the Program, the more natural this new way of life seems. At first, it was impossible for me to extend my hand to a newcomer; such an act was wholly unnatural for me. But it is becoming increasingly easier for me to reach out to another person. Sharing my experience, strength, and hope is becoming a natural part of daily living. *Have I learned that I can't keep what I've gotten unless I "give it away"? Will I take the time to share today?*

Today I Pray

May I share my love, my joy, my happiness, my time, my hospitality, my knowledge of things on earth, and my faith in a Higher Power. Even though I may not see the results of my acts of sharing, my I take joy in the acts themselves. May sharing, according to God's plan, become as natural to me as speaking or breathing.

Today I Will Remember

Be never sparing in caring and sharing.

Reflection for the Day

Today is the day for which I asked and for which I have been given strength. That in itself is a miracle. In my old life, I constantly endangered myself as well as countless others. So the very fact that I am alive is the great miracle from which all other miracles will flow, providing I continue to do the things that have brought me this far in my new life. *Am I grateful that I have been given this day?*

Today I Pray

May God's goodness and mercy follow me all the days of my life. May I never cease to wonder at the greatest miracle in my life—that I am alive, here, on this green earth, and growing healthier with the life-preserving tools I have been given. Since God has chosen to give me life and to preserve my life, even through the dangers of addiction, may I always continue to listen for His plan for me. May I always believe in miracles.

Today I Will Remember

My life is a miracle.

Reflection for the Day

In the past, and sometimes even now, I automatically have thought, "Why *me*?", when I'm trying to learn that my first problem is to accept my present circumstances as they are, myself as I am, and the people around me as they are. Just as I finally accepted my powerlessness over my addiction, so must I accept my powerlessness over people, places, and things. *Am I learning to accept life on life's terms?*

Today I Pray

May I learn to control my urge to control, my compulsion to manage, neaten, organize, and label the lives of others. May I learn to accept situations and people as they are instead of as I would like them to be. Thus, may I do away with the ongoing frustrations that a controlling person, by nature, faces continually. May I be entirely ready to have God remove this defect of character.

Today I Will Remember

Control for the controller (me).

Reflection for the Day

Since I came to the Program, I've become increasingly aware of the Serenity Prayer. I see it on literature covers, the walls of meeting rooms, and in the homes of new-found friends. "God grant me the serenity to accept the things I cannot change, the courage to change the things I can, and the wisdom to know the difference." *Do I understand the Serenity Prayer? Do I believe in its power and repeat it often? Is it becoming easier for me to accept the things I cannot change?*

Today I Pray

God grant that the words of the Serenity Prayer never become mechanical for me or lose their meaning in the lulling rhythms of repetition. I pray that these words will continue to take on new depths of significance as I fit life's realities to them. I trust that I may find the solutions I need in this prayer, which, in its simplicity, encompasses all of life's situations.

Today I Will Remember

Share the prayer.

Reflection for the Day

The experiences of thousands upon thousands of people have proven that acceptance and faith are capable of producing freedom from dependence on chemicals. When we apply the same principles of acceptance and faith to our emotional problems, however, we discover that only relative results are possible. Obviously, for example, nobody can ever become completely free from fear, anger, or pride. None of us will ever achieve perfect love, harmony, or serenity. We'll have to settle for very gradual progress, punctuated occasionally by very heavy setbacks. *Have I begun to abandon my old attitude of "all or nothing"?*

Today I Pray

May God grant me the patience to apply those same principles of faith and acceptance which are keys to my recovery to the whole of my emotional being. May I learn to recognize the festering of my own human anger, my hurt, my frustration, my sadness. With the help of God, may I find appropriate ways to deal with these feelings without doing harm to myself or others.

Today I Will Remember

Feelings are facts.

Reflection for the Day

When I sit quietly and compare my life today with the way it used to be, the difference is almost beyond belief. But things aren't always rosy; some days are a lot better than others. I tend to accept the bad days more easily on an intellectual level than I do emotionally, or at gut-level. There are no pat answers, but part of the solution surely lies in a constant effort to practice all of the Twelve Steps. *Do I accept the fact that my Higher Power will never give me more than I can handle—one day at a time?*

Today I Pray

That I may receive strength in the knowledge that God never gives us more than we can bear, that I can always, somehow, endure present pain, whereas the trials of a lifetime, condensed into one disasterous moment, would surely overcome me. Thanks be to God for giving us only those tribulations which are in proportior to our strength, never destroying us in our frailty. May I remember that fortitude grows out of suffering.

Today I Will Remember

Present pain is endurable.

Reflection for the Day

The Program and my friends in the fellowship have provided me with a whole new set of tools for living. Even the slogans that once seemed so trite and corny are now becoming an important part of my daily life: Easy Does It; First Things First; This, Too, Will Pass. If I use all of my tools regularly and well, they'll also help rid me of such negative feelings as guilt, anxiety, rebellion, and pride. *When I'm feeling depressed, do I use the tools that have been proven effective? Or do I grit my teeth and suffer in painful silence?*

Today I Pray

I praise my wonder-working Higher Power for giving me the tools for recovery, once I admitted I was powerless over my addiction and gave myself over to the will of God as I understand Him. I give thanks for the Twelve Steps, and for the fellowship of the group, which can help me see myself honestly. I give thanks for those words and phrases which become, as we understand them more completely, banners in our celebration of sobriety.

Today I Will Remember

Pass on the passwords to recovery.

Reflection for the Day

I admitted that I couldn't win the booze and chemical battle on my own. So I finally began to accept the critically important fact that dependence on a Higher Power could help me achieve what had always seemed impossible. I stopped running. I stopped fighting. For the first time, I began accepting. And for the first time, I began to be really free. *Do I realize that it doesn't matter what kind of shoes I'm wearing when I'm running away?*

Today I Pray

May I know the freedom that comes with surrender to a Higher Power—that most important kind of surrender that means neither "giving in" nor "giving up" but "giving over" my will to the will of God. Like a weary fugitive from spiritual order, may I stop hiding, dodging, running. May I find peace in surrender, in the knowledge that God wills that I be whole and healthy and He will show me the way.

Today I Will Remember

First surrender, then serenity.

Reflection for the Day

I must never forget who and what I am and where I come from. I have to remember the nature of my illness and what it was like before I came to the Program. I'll try to keep the memory green, yet not spend my time dwelling morbidly on the past. I won't be afraid to enjoy what is beautiful, and to believe that as I give to others, so others will give to me. *Can I ever afford to forget what it used to be like, even for one minute?*

Today I Pray

May I never forget the painful days of my addiction. May I never forget that the same misery awaits me if I should slip back into the old patterns. At the same time, may such backwards glances serve only to bolster my own present strength and the strength of others like me. Please, God, do not let me dredge up these recollections in order to outdo or "out-drunk" my fellow members. Like others who are chemically dependent, I must be wary of my desire to be center stage in the spotlight.

Today I Will Remember

I do more when I don't "outdo."

Reflection for the Day

When we first came to the Program, whether for ourselves or under pressure from others, some of us were all but sickened by the concept of "surrender." To admit to defeat flew in the face of our life-long beliefs. And so we secretly vowed, at first, that the very idea of surrender was unthinkable. *Have I truly come to believe that only through utter defeat am I able to take the first step toward liberation and strength? Or do I still harbor reservations about the principle of "letting go and letting God..."?*

Today I Pray

May I really believe that the complete surrender of my whole being to a Higher Power is the way to serenity. For I can be whole only in Him, who has the power to make me whole. May I do away with any feelings of wanting to "hold out" and never admit defeat. May I unlearn the old adage which tells me that I must "never give up" and realize that such pridefulness could keep me from recovery.

Today I Will Remember

From wholly His to whole.

Reflection for the Day

I have been told over and over that I must constantly work to give up my old ideas. "That's
easy for you to say," I've sometimes thought.
All my life, I have been programmed, computer-
style; specific inputs brought forth predictable
responses. My mind still tends to react as a
computer reacts, but I am learning to destroy
the old tapes and literally reprogram myself.
*Am I fully willing to abandon my old ideas? Am I
being fearless and thorough on a daily basis?*

Today I Pray

Help me to take inventory each day of my stock
of my new, healthy thoughts, throwing out the
old ones as I happen upon them without regret
or nostalgia. For I have outgrown those old
ideas, which are as scuffed and run-over as an
old pair of shoes. Now, in the light, I can see
that they are filled with holes.

Today I Will Remember

The Program reprograms.

Reflection for the Day

If we are determined to stop drinking or using other chemicals, there must be no reservations whatsoever, nor any lurking notion that our allergy of the body and obsession of the mind will someday reverse themselves. Our regeneration comes through the splendid paradox of the Twelve Steps: Strength arises from complete defeat, and the loss of one's old life is a condition for finding a new one. *Am I convinced that in powerlessness, power comes? Am I certain that by releasing my life and will I am released?*

Today I Pray

May I know power through powerlessness, victory through surrender, triumph through defeat. May I learn to relinquish any trace of secret pride that I can "do it by myself." Let my will be absorbed and steered by the omnipotent will of God.

Today I Will Remember

Let go and let God.

Reflection for the Day

It was far easier for me to accept my powerlessness over my addiction than it was for me to accept the notion that some sort of Higher Power could accomplish that which I had been unable to accomplish myself. Simply by seeking help and accepting the fellowship of others similarly afflicted, the craving left me. And I realized that if I was doing what I was powerless alone to do, then surely I was doing so by some Power outside my own and obviously greater. *Have I surrendered my life into the hands of God?*

Today I Pray

May God erase in me the arrogant pride which keeps me from listening to Him. May my unhealthy dependence on chemicals and my clinging dependence on those nearby be transformed into reliance on God. Only in this kind of dependency/reliance on a Higher Power will I find my own transformation.

Today I Will Remember

I am God-dependent.

Reflection for the Day

The first psychiatrist to recognize the work of Alcoholics Anonymous, Dr. Harry Tiebout, used many concepts of the Program in his own practice. Over many years, the doctor's study of the "conversion experience" led him to see, first, that it is the act of surrender which initiates the switch from negative to positive; second, that the positive phase is really a *state* of surrender which follows the act of surrender; and third, that the state of surrender, if maintained, supplies an emotional tone to all thinking and feeling that ensures healthy adjustment. *Am I living in a constant state of surrender?*

Today I Pray

May I understand that I do not have to "unlearn" my respect for "self-reliance," that trait of character which I heard praised so often from the time I was a tiny child. Only my understanding of the word must change. For as I come to know that "self" is part of God, that I am nothing except in His Being, there is no quarrel between self-reliance and God-reliance. May I rely upon that self which is God's.

Today I Will Remember

Not part-god, but part of God.

Reflection of the Day

Every person, no matter what his or her balance for good or evil, is a part of the Divine economy. We are all children of God, and it is unlikely that He intends to favor one over another. So it is necessary for all of us to accept whatever positive gifts we receive with a deep humility, always bearing in mind that our negative attitudes were first necessary as a means of reducing us to such a state that we would be ready for a gift of the positive ones via the conversation experience. *Do I accept the fact that my addiction and the bottom I finally reached are the bedrock upon which my spiritual foundation rests?*

Today I Pray

May I know that from the first moment I admitted my powerlessness, God-given power was mine. Every step taken from that moment of defeat has been a step in the right direction. The First Step is a giant step. Through it is often taken in despair, may I realize that I must be drained of hope before I can be refilled with fresh hope, sapped of wilfulness before I can feel the will of God.

Today I Will Remember

Power through powerlessness.

Reflection for the Day

In a very real sense, we are imprisoned by our inability or unwillingness to reach out for help to a Power greater than ourselves. But in time, we pray to be relieved of the bondage of self, so that we can better do God's will. In the words of Ramakrishna, "The sun and moon are not mirrored in cloudy waters, thus the Almighty cannot be mirrored in a heart that is obsessed by the idea of 'me and mine.'" *Have I set myself free from the prison of self-will and pride which I myself have built? Have I accepted freedom?*

Today I Pray

May the word freedom take on new meanings for me, not just "freedom *from*" my addiction, but "freedom *to*" overcome it. Not just freedom *from* the slavery of self-will, but freedom *to* hear and carry out the will of God.

Today I Will Remember

Freedom *from* means freedom *to*.

Reflection for the Day

We must never be blinded by the futile philosophy that we are just the hapless victims of our inheritance, of our life experience, and of our surroundings—that these are the sole forces that make our decisions for us. This is not the road to freedom. We have to believe that we can really choose. As addictive persons, we lost our ability to choose whether we would pursue our addictions. Yet we finally did make choices that brought about our recovery. *Do I believe that in "becoming willing" I have made the best of all choices?*

Today I Pray

May I shed the idea that I am the world's victim, an unfortunate creature caught in a web of circumstance, inferring that others ought to "make it up to me" because I have been given a bad deal on this earth. We are always given choices. May God help me to choose wisely.

Today I Will Remember

God is not a puppeteer.

Reflection for the Day

Among the many gifts that we are offered in the Program is the gift of freedom. Paradoxically, however, the gift of freedom is not without a price tag; freedom can only be achieved by paying the price called *acceptance*. Similarly, if we can surrender to God's guidance, it will cost us our self-will, that "commodity" so precious to those of us who have always thought we could and should run the show. *Is my freedom today worth the price tag of acceptance?*

Today I Pray

May God teach me acceptance—the ability to accept the things I cannot change. God also grant me courage to change those things I can. God help me to accept the illness of my addiction and give me the courage to change my addictive behavior.

Today I Will Remember

Accept the addiction.
Change the behavior.

Reflection for the Day

Even with a growing understanding of the Program and its Twelve Steps, we sometimes might find it difficult to believe that our new way of life leads to personal freedom. Suppose, for example, I feel imprisoned in an uncomfortable job or troublesome personal relationship. What am I doing about it? In the past, my reflex reaction was to try to manipulate the things and people around me into being more acceptable to me. Today, I realize that happiness can't be won that way. *Am I learning that freedom from despair and frustration can come only from changing, in myself, the attitudes that are perpetuating the conditions that cause me grief?*

Today I Pray

May I be given clear eyes to see—and then to stop myself—when I am manipulating the lives of those around me, my daily associates, friends, family. May I always be aware that change must begin within myself.

Today I Will Remember

Change from the inside out.

Reflection for the Day

Personal freedom is mine for the taking. No matter how close are the ties of love and concern that bind me to my family and friends, I must always remember that I am an individual, free to be myself and live my own life in serenity and joy. The key word in this realization is *personal*. For I *can* free myself from many involvements that *seem* necessary. Through the Program, I am learning to develop my own personality. *Am I reinforcing personal freedom by leaving others free to control their actions and destinies?*

Today I Pray

May I find personal freedom, by reevaluating associations, establishing new priorities, gaining respect for my own personhood. May I give others equal room to find their own kinds of personal freedoms.

Today I Will Remember

Take the liberty; it's yours.

Reflection for the Day

I can attain real dignity, importance, and individuality only by a dependence on a Power which is great and good, beyond anything I can imagine or understand. I will try my utmost to use this power in making all my decisions. Even though my human mind cannot forecast what the outcome will be, I will try to be confident that whatever comes will be for my ultimate good. *Just for today, will I try to live this day only, and not tackle my whole life problem at once?*

Today I Pray

May I make no decision, engineer no change in the course of my lifestream, without calling upon my Higher Power. May I have faith that God's plan for me is better than any scheme I could devise for myself.

Today I Will Remember

God is the architect. I am the builder.

Reflection for the Day

Now that I am in the Program, I am no longer enslaved by alcohol and other drugs. Free, free at last from the morning-after tremors, the dry heaves, the three-day beard, the misplaced eyelashes. Free, free at last from working out the alibis and hoping they won't unravel; free from blackouts; free from watching the clock so that I can somehow get that desperately-needed "first one." *Do I treasure my freedom from chemical enslavement?*

Today I Pray

Praise God that I am free of chemicals. This is my first freedom, from which other freedoms will develop—freedom to appraise my behavior sanely and constructively, freedom to grow as a person, freedom to maintain relationships with others on a sound basis. I will never cease to thank my Higher Power for leading me away from my enslavement.

Today I Will Remember

Praise God for my freedom.

Reflection for the Day

I used to imagine my life as a grotesque abstract painting: a montage of crises framed by end-upon-end catastrophes. My days all were grey and my thoughts greyer still. I was haunted by dread and nameless fears. I was filled with self-loathing. I had no idea who I was, what I was, or why I was. I miss none of those feelings. Today, step by step, I am discovering myself and learning that I can be free to be me. *Am I grateful for my new life? Have I taken the time to thank God today for the fact that I am clean and sober—and alive?*

Today I Pray

May calm come to me after the turmoil and nightmares of the past. As my fears and self-hatred dissipate, may the things of the spirit replace them. For in the spiritual world, as in the material world, there is no empty space. May I be filled with the spirit of my Higher Power.

Today I Will Remember

Morning scatters nightmares.

Reflection for the Day

Have I gained freedom simply because one day I was weak and the next day I became suddenly strong? Have I changed from the helpless and hopeless person I once seemed to be simply by resolving, "from now on, things will be different..."? Is the fact that I am more comfortable today than ever before the result of my own will power? Can I take credit for pulling myself up by my own bootstraps? I know better, for I sought refuge in a Power greater than myself—a Power which is still beyond my ability to visualize. *Do I consider the change in my life a miracle far beyond the working of any human power?*

Today I Pray

As the days of sobriety lengthen, and the moment of decision becomes farther behind me, may I never lose sight of the Power that changed my life. May I remember that my sobriety is an ongoing miracle, not just a once-in-a-lifetime transformation.

Today I Will Remember

Life is an ongoing miracle.

Reflection for the Day

One of the most constructive things I can do is to learn to listen to myself and get in touch with my true feelings. For years, I tuned myself out, going along, instead, with what others felt and said. Even today, it sometimes seems that *they* have it all together, while I'm still stumbling about. Thankfully, I'm beginning to understand that people-pleasing takes many forms. Slowly but steadily, I've also begun to realize that it's possible for me to change my old patterns. *Will I encourage myself to tune in to the real me? Will I listen carefully to my own inner voice with the expectation that I'll hear some wonderful things?*

Today I Pray

I pray that I may respect myself enough to listen to my real feelings, those emotions which for so long I refused to hear or name or own, which festered in me like a poison. May I know that I need to stop often, look at my feelings, listen to the inner me.

Today I Will Remember

I will own my feelings.

Reflection for the Day

The longer I'm in the Program, the more clearly I see why it's important for me to understand *why* I do what I do, and say what I say. In the process, I'm coming to realize what kind of person I really am. I see now, for example, that it's far easier to be honest with other people than with myself. I'm learning, also, that we're all hampered by our need to justify our actions and words. *Have I taken an inventory of myself as suggested in the Twelve Steps? Have I admitted my faults to myself, to God, and to another human being?*

Today I Pray

May I not be stalled in my recovery process by the enormity of the Program's Fourth Step, taking a moral inventory of myself, or by admitting these shortcomings to myself, to God, and to another human being. May I know that honesty to myself about myself is all-important.

Today I Will Remember

I cannot mend if I bend the truth.

Reflection for the Day

Looking back, I realize just how much of my life has been spent in dwelling upon the faults of others. It provided much self-satisfaction, to be sure, but I see now just how subtle and actually perverse the process became. After all was said and done, the net effect of dwelling on the so-called faults of others was self-granted permission to remain comfortably unaware of my *own* defects. *Do I still point my finger at others and thus self-deceptively overlook my own shortcomings?*

Today I Pray

May I see that my preoccupation with the faults of others is really a smokescreen to keep me from taking a hard look at my own, as well as a way to bolster my own failing ego. May I check out the "why's" of my blaming.

Today I Will Remember

Blame-saying
Is game-playing.

Reflection for the Day

The Program enables us to discover two road-blocks that keep us from seeing the value and comfort of the spiritual approach: self-justification and self-righteousness. The first grimly assures me that I'm always right. The second mistakenly comforts me with the delusion that I'm better than other people—"holier than thou." *Just for today, will I pause abruptly while rationalizing and ask myself, "Why am I doing this? Is this self-justification really honest?"*

Today I Pray

May I overcome the need to be "always right" and know the cleansing feeling of release that comes with admitting, openly, a mistake. May I be wary of setting myself up as an example of self-control and fortitude, and give credit where it is due—to a Higher Power.

Today I Will Remember

To err is human, but I need to admit it.

FEBRUARY 4

Reflection for the Day

Rare is the recovering alcoholic who will now dispute the fact that *denial* is a primary symptom of the illness. The Program teaches us that alcoholism is the only illness which actually tells the afflicted person that he or she *really isn't sick at all*. Not surprisingly, then, our lives as practicing alcoholics were characterized by endless rationalization, countless alibis and, in short, a steadfast unwillingness to accept the fact that we were, without question, bodily and mentally different from our fellows. *Have I conceded to my innermost self that I am truly powerless over alcohol?*

Today I Pray

May the Program's First Step be not half-hearted for me, but a total admission of powerlessness over my addiction. May I rid myself of that first symptom—denial—which refuses to recognize any other symptom of my disease.

Today I Will Remember

Deny denial.

Reflection for the Day

If I am troubled, worried, exasperated, or frustrated, do I tend to rationalize the situation and lay the blame on someone else? When I am in such a state, is my conversation punctuated with, *"He* did...", *"She* said...", *"They* did..."? Or can I honestly admit that perhaps I'm at fault. My peace of mind depends on overcoming my negative attitudes and tendency toward rationalization. *Will I try, day by day, to be rigorously honest with myself?*

Today I Pray

May I catch myself as I talk in the third person, "He did..." or "They promised..." or "She said she would..." and listen for the blaming that has become such a pattern for me and preserves delusion. May I do a turnabout and face myself instead.

Today I Will Remember

Honesty is the only policy.

Reflection for the Day

I used to be an expert at unrealistic self-appraisal. At certain times, I would look only at that part of my life which seemed good. Then I would magnify whatever real or imagined virtues I had attained. Next, I would pat myself on the back for the fantastic job I was doing in the Program. Naturally, this generated a craving for still more "accomplishments" and still greater approval. Wasn't that the pattern of my days during active addiction? The difference now, though, is that I can use the best alibi known—the spiritual alibi. *Do I sometimes rationalize willful actions and nonsensical behavior in the name of "spiritual objectives"?*

Today I Pray

God help me to know if I still crave attention and approval to the point of inflating my own virtues and magnifying my accomplishments in the Program or anywhere. May I keep a realistic perspective about my good points, even as I learn to respect myself.

Today I Will Remember

Learn to control inflation.

Reflection for the Day

Why do I do what I do? Why did I say what I said? Why on earth did I put off an important responsibility? Questions like these, best asked of myself in a quiet time of meditation, demand honest answers. I may have to think deeply for those answers, going beyond the tempting rationalizations that lack the luster of truth. *Have I accepted the fact that self-deception can only damage me, providing a clouded and unrealistic picture of the person I really am?*

Today I Pray

May God allow me to push aside my curtain of fibs, alibis, rationalizations, justifications, distortions, and downright lies and let in the light on the real truths about myself. May I meet the person I really am and take comfort in the person I can become.

Today I Will Remember

Hello, Me. Meet the real Me.

Reflection for the Day

When we first stopped drinking, using, overeating, or gambling, it was an enormous relief to find that the people we met in the Program seemed quite different than those apparently hostile masses we know as "They." We were met not with criticism and suspicion, but with understanding and concern. However, we still encounter people who get on our nerves, both within the Program and outside it. Obviously, we must begin to accept the fact that there *are* people who'll sometimes say things with which we disagree, or do things we don't like. *Am I beginning to see that learning to live with differences is essential to my comfort and, in turn, to my continuing recovery?*

Today I Pray

May I recognize that people's differences make our world go around and tolerate people who "rub me the wrong way." May I understand that I must give them room, that some of my hostile attitudes toward others may be leftovers from the unhealthy days when I tended to view others as mobilized against me.

Today I Will Remember

Learn to live with differences.

Reflection for the Day

The slogan "Live and Let Live" can be extremely helpful when we are having trouble tolerating other people's behavior. We know for certain that nobody's behavior—no matter how offensive, distasteful, or vicious—is worth the price of a relapse. Our own recovery is primary, and while we must be unafraid of walking away from people or situations that cause us discomfort, we must also make a special effort to try to understand other people—especially those who rub us the wrong way. *Can I accept the fact, in my recovery, that it is more important to understand than to be understood?*

Today I Pray

When I run headlong into someone's unpleasant behavior, may I first try my best to understand. Then, if my own sobriety seems threatened, may I have the courage to remove myself from the situation.

Today I Will Remember

Live and let live.

Reflection for the Day

Until now, we may have equated the idea of beginning again with a previous record of failure. This isn't necessarily so. Like students who finish grade school and begin again in high school, or workers who find new ways to use their abilities, our beginnings must not be tinged with a sense of failure. In a sense, every day is a time of beginning again. We need never look back with regret. Life is not necessarily like a blackboard that must be erased because we didn't solve problems correctly, but rather a blackboard that must be cleaned to make way for the new. *Am I grateful for all that has prepared me for this moment of beginning?*

Today I Pray

May I understand that past failures need not hamper my new courage or give a murky cast to my new beginnings. May I know, from the examples of others in the Program, that former failings, once faced and rectified, can be a more solid foundation for a new life than easy-come successes.

Today I Will Remember

Failings can be footings for recovery.

Reflection for the Day

I can always take strength and comfort from knowing I belong to a worldwide fellowship. Hundreds and hundreds of thousands, just like me are working together for the same purpose. None of us needs ever to be alone again, because each of us in our own way works for the good of others. We are bound together by a common problem that can be solved by love and understanding and mutual service. The Program—like the little wheel in the old hymn—runs by the grace of God. *Have I thanked God today for helping me to find the Program, which is showing me the way to a new life?*

Today I Pray

May my thanks be lifted to God each day for dispelling my self-inflicted loneliness, for warming my stoicism, for leading me to the boundless fund of friendship in the Program.

Today I Will Remember

I have a world of friends.

Reflection for the Day

I am grateful for my friends in the Program. Right now I am aware of the blessings of friendship—the blessings of meeting, of sharing, of smiling, of listening, and of being available when needed. Right now I know that if I want a friend, I must be a friend. *Will I vow, this day, to be a better friend to more people? Will I strive, this day—in my thoughts, words, and actions—to disclose the kind of friend I am?*

Today I Pray

May I restore in kind to the fellowship of the Program the friendship I have so hungrily taken from it. After years of glossing my lonely existence with superficial acquaintanceships, may I learn again the reciprocal joys of caring and sharing.

Today I Will Remember

Be a friend.

Reflection for the Day

We sometimes hear someone say, "He is standing in his own light." A mental picture then clearly reveals that many of us tend to shadow our own happiness by mistaken thinking. Let us learn to stand aside so the light can shine on us and all we do. For only then can we see ourselves and our circumstances with true clarity. With the Program and the Twelve Steps, we no longer need to stand in our own light and try alone to solve our problems in darkness. *When I am faced with a seemingly insoluble problem, will I ask myself if I am standing in my own light?*

Today I Pray

May I not get in my own way, obscure my own clarity of thought, stumble over my own feet, block my own doorway to recovery. If I find that I am standing in my own light, may I ask my Higher Power and my friends in the group to show me a new vantage point.

Today I Will Remember

If all I can see is my shadow, I'm in my own light.

Reflection for the Day

Today I will take the time to list the positive aspects of my new life and the blessings that accompany the miracles of my recovery. I will be grateful for the seemingly simple ability to eat normally, to fall asleep with a feeling of contentment, to awaken with a gladness to be alive. I will be grateful for the ability to face life on life's terms—with peace of mind, self-respect, and full possession of all my faculties. *On a daily basis, do I count my blessings? Do I seek through prayer and meditation to improve my conscious contact with God as I understand Him?*

Today I Pray

On this day of love-giving, may I count all the good things in my life and give thanks for them. May I take no blessing for granted, including the beating of my own heart and the fresh feel of new air as I breathe.

Today I Will Remember

To count—and consider—my blessings.

Reflection for the Day

When I become angry, can I admit to it and state it as a fact without allowing it to build up and burst out in inappropriate ways? Pent-up anger, I've finally begun to learn, quickly shatters the peace of mind that's so critical to my ongoing recovery. When I become enraged and lose control, I unwittingly hand over control to the person, place, or thing with which I am enraged. *When I'm angry will I try to remember that I am endangering myself? Will I "count to ten" by calling a friend in the Program and say the Serenity Prayer aloud?*

Today I Pray

May I recognize angry feelings and let them out a little at a time, stating my anger as a fact, instead of allowing it to fester into rage and explode uncontrollably.

Today I Will Remember

Anger is. Rage need not be.

Reflection for the Day

What about "justifiable anger"? If somebody cheats us or acts toward us in an outrageous manner, don't we have the *right* to be furious? The hard-learned experiences of countless others in the Program tell us that adventures in rage are usually extremely dangerous. So, while we must recognize anger enough to say "I am angry," we must not allow the build-up of rage, however justifiable. *Can I accept the fact that if I am to live, I have to be free of anger?*

Today I Pray

Even though I go out of the way to skirt them, may I be aware that there always will be certain situations or certain people who will make me angry. When my anger doesn't seem justifiable—with arguable reason behind it—I may deny it, even to myself. May I recognize my anger, whether it is reasonable or not, before I bury it alive.

Today I Will Remember

It is all right to feel anger.

Reflection for the Day

If I become angry today, I'll pause and *think* before I say anything, remembering that my anger can turn back upon me and worsen my difficulties. I'll try to remember, too, that well-timed silence can give me command of a stressful situation as angry reproaches *never* can. In such moments of stress, I'll remember that my power over others is nonexistent, and that only God is all-powerful. *Have I learned that I alone can destroy my own peace of mind?*

Today I Pray

May I learn that I can choose how to handle my anger—in silence or as a tantrum, a rage, a fist fight, a pillow fight, a tirade, an elaborate plan to "get back at" whoever caused it, an icy glare, a cool pronouncement of hate—or a simple statement of fact, "I am angry at you because" (in 25 words or less). Or may I, if need be, turn my anger into energy and shovel the walk, bowl, or play a game of tennis, or clean the house. I pray that God will show me appropriate ways to deal with my anger.

Today I Will Remember

"I am angry because..."

Reflection for the Day

We learn in the Program that we cannot punish anyone without punishing ourselves. The release of my tensions, even justified, in a punishing way leaves behind the dregs of bitterness and pain. This was the monotonous story of my life before I came to the Program. So in my new life, "I'd do well to consider the long-range benefits of simply owning my emotions, naming them and thus releasing them. *Does the voice of God have a chance to be heard over my reproachful shouting?*

Today I Pray

May I avoid name-calling, ego-crushing exchanges. If I am angry, may I try to assign my anger to what someone did instead of what someone is. May I refrain from downgrading, lashing out at character flaws, or mindless abuse. May I count on my Higher Power to show me the way.

Today I Will Remember

To deal with anger appropriately.

Reflection for the Day

When a person says something rash or ugly, we sometimes say they are "forgetting themselves," meaning they're forgetting their best selves in a sudden outburst of uncontrolled fury. If I remember the kind of person I want to be, hopefully I won't "forget myself" and yield to a fit of temper. I'll believe that the positive always defeats the negative: courage overcomes fear; patience overcomes anger and irritability; love overcomes hatred. *Am I always striving for improvement?*

Today I Pray

Today I ask that God, to Whom all things are possible, help me turn negatives into positives—anger into super-energy, fear into a chance to be courageous, hatred into love. May I take time out to remember examples of such positive-from-negative transformations from the whole of my lifetime. Uppermost is God's miracle: my freedom from the slavery of addiction.

Today I Will Remember

Turn negatives into positives.

Reflection for the Day

We are often told in the Program that "more will be revealed." As we are restored to health and become increasingly able to live comfortably in the real world without using chemicals, we begin to see many things in a new light. Many of us have come to realize, for example, that our arch-enemy, anger, comes disguised in many shapes and colors: intolerance, contempt, snobbishness, rigidity, tension, sarcasm, distrust, anxiety, envy, hatred, cynicism, discontent, self-pity, malice, suspicion, jealousy. *Do I let my feelings get the best of me?*

Today I Pray

May I recognize that my anger, like a dancer at a masquerade, wears many forms and many faces. May I strip off its several masks and know it for what it is.

Today I Will Remember

Anger wears a thousand masks.

Reflection for the Day

Do I waste my time and energy wrestling with situations that aren't actually worth a second thought? Like Don Quixote, the bemused hero of Spanish literature, do I imagine windmills as menacing giants, battling them until I am ready to drop from exhaustion? Today, I'll not allow my imagination to build small troubles into big ones. I'll try to see each situation clearly, giving it only the value and attention it deserves. *Have I come to believe, as the second of the Twelve Steps suggests, that a Power greater than myself can restore me to sanity?*

Today I Pray

God, keep my perspective sane. Help me to avoid aggrandizing petty problems, tying too much significance to casual conversations, making a Vesuvius out of an anthill. Keep my fears from swelling out of scale, like shadows on a wall. Restore my values, which became distorted during the days of my chemical involvement.

Today I Will Remember

Sanity is perspective.

Reflection for the Day

When I came to the Program, I found people who knew exactly what I meant when I spoke finally of my fears. They had been where I had been; they *understood*. I've since learned that many of my fears have to do with projection. It's normal, for example, to have a tiny "back-burner" fear that the person I love will leave me. But when the fear takes the precedence over my present and very real relationship with the person I'm afraid of losing, then I'm in trouble. My responsibility to myself includes this: I must not fear things which do not exist. *Am I changing from a fearful person into a fearless person?*

Today I Pray

I ask God's help in waving away my fears—those figments, fantasies, monstrous thoughts, projections of disaster which have no bearing on the present. May I narrow the focus of my imagination and concentrate on the here-and-now, for I tend to see the future through a magnifying glass.

Today I Will Remember

Projected fears, like shadows, are larger than life.

Reflection for the Day

The Twelve Steps teach us that, as faith grows, so does security. The terrifying fear of nothingness begins to subside. As we work the Program, we find that the basic antidote for fear is a spiritual awakening. We lose the fear of making decisions, for we realize that if our choice proves wrong, we can learn from the experience. And should our decision be the right one, we can thank God for giving us the courage and the grace that caused us so to act. *Am I grateful for the courage and grace I receive from my Higher Power?*

Today I Pray

I ask that I be given the power to act, knowing that I have at least a half-chance to make the right decision and that I can learn from a wrong one. For so long, decision-making seemed beyond my capabilities. Now, I can find joy in being able to make choices. Thank you, God, for courage.

Today I Will Remember

Freedom is choosing.

Reflection for the Day

I can banish fear by realizing the truth. Am I afraid to be alone? This fear can be banished by the realization that I am never alone, that God is always with me wherever I am and whatever I do. Am I afraid that I won't have enough money to meet my needs? This fear can be banished by the realization that God is my inexhaustible, unfailing resource, now and always. Today I have the power to change fear into faith. *Can I say with confidence, "I will trust, and will not be afraid..."?*

Today I Pray

That I may fear no evil, for God is with me. That I may learn to turn to my Higher Power when I am afraid. I pray diligently that my faith in God and trust in what He has in store for me is strong enough to banish the fears that undermine my courage.

Today I will Remember

Turn fear into faith.

Reflection for the Day

Before we came to the Program, fear ruled our lives. Tyrannized by our addictions and obsessions, we feared everything and everybody. We feared ourselves and, perhaps most of all, feared fear itself. These days, when I am able to accept the help of my Higher Power, it makes me feel capable of doing anything I am called upon to do. I am overcoming my fears and acquiring a comfortable new confidence. *Can I believe that "courage is fear that has said its prayers..."?*

Today I Pray

God grant that through faith in Him I may overcome my obsessive fears. I have been running scared for so long it has become a habit. God help me to see that I may be purposely clinging to my fears to avoid making decisions, perhaps even to shirk the responsibility of success.

Today I Will Remember

Fear keeps me safe from risk-taking.

Reflection for the Day

"What if..." How often we hear these words from newcomers to the Program. How often, in fact, we tend to say them ourselves. *"What if* I lose my job?" *"What if* my car breaks down?" *"What if* I get sick and can't work?" *"What if* my child gets hooked on drugs?" What if—anything our desperate imaginings can project. Only two small words, yet how heavy-laden they are with dread, fear, and anxiety. The answer to "What if..." is, plainly and simply, "Don't panic." We can only live with our problems as they arise, living one day at a time. *Am I keeping my thoughts positive?*

Today I Pray

May I grow spiritually, without being held back by anxieties. May projected fears not hobble my pursuits or keep me from making the most of today. May I turn out fear by faith. If I will only make a place for God within me, He will remove my fears.

Today I Will Remember

I can only borrow trouble at high interest rates.

Reflection for the Day

If I live just one day at a time, I won't so quickly entertain fears of what *might* happen tomorrow. As long as I'm concentrating on today's activities, there won't be room in my mind for worrying. I'll try to fill every minute of this day with something good—seen, heard, accomplished. Then, when the day is ended, I'll be able to look back on it with satisfaction, serenity, and gratitude. *Do I sometimes cherish bad feelings so that I can feel sorry for myself?*

Today I Pray

That I will get out of the self-pity act and live for today. May I notice the good things from dawn to nightfall, learn to talk about them and thank God for them. May I catch myself if I seem to be relishing my moans and complaints more often than appreciating the goodness of my life.

Today I Will Remember

Today is good.

Reflection for the Day

We're taught in the Program and the Twelve Steps that the chief activator of our defects has been self-centered fear—mainly fear that we would lose something we already possessed or that we would fail to get something we demanded. Living on the basis of unsatisfied demands, we obviously were in a state of continual disturbance and frustration. Therefore, we are taught, no peace will be ours unless we find a means of producing these demands. *Have I become entirely ready to have God remove all my defects of character?*

Today I Pray

May I make no unrealistic demands on life, which, because of their grandiosity, cannot be met. May I place no excessive demands on others which, when they are not fulfilled, leave me disappointed and let down.

Today I Will Remember

The set-up for a let-down.

Reflection for the Day

Just for today, I'll not be afraid of anything. If my mind is clouded with nameless fears, I'll track them down and expose their unreality. I'll remind myself that God is in charge of me and my life, and that all I have to do is accept His protection and guidance. What happened yesterday need not trouble me today. *Do I accept the fact that it's in my power to make today a good one just by the way I think about it and what I do about it?*

Today I Pray

May I make today a good day. May I know that it is up to me to assign to it qualities of goodness, through a positive attitude toward what the present is providing. May I be untroubled by vestiges of yesterday. Please, God, remain close to me all through this day.

Today I Will Remember

To make it good.

Reflection for the Day

Now that we're free and no longer chemically dependent, we have so much more control over our thinking. More than anything, we're able to alter our attitudes. Some members of Alcoholics Anonymous, in fact, choose to think of the letters AA as an abbreviation for "Altered Attitudes." In the bad old days, I almost always responded to any optimistic or positive statement with "Yes, but..." Today, in contrast, I'm learning to eliminate that negative phrase from my vocabulary. *Am I working to change my attitude? Am I determined to "accentuate the positive..."?*

Today I Pray

May I find that healing and strength which God provides to those who stay near Him. May I keep to the spiritual guidelines of the Program, considering the Steps, taking the Steps—one by one—then practicing them again and again. In this is my salvation.

Today I Will Remember

To practice at least one Step.

Reflection for the Day

Why don't I spend part of today thinking about my assets, rather than my liabilities? Why not think about victories, instead of defeats—about the ways in which I am gentle and kind? It's always been my tendency to fall into a sort of cynical self-hypnosis, putting derogatory labels on practically everything I've done, said, or felt. Just for today, I'll spend a quiet half hour trying to gain a more positive perspective on my life. *Do I have the courage to change the things I can?*

Today I Pray

Through quietness and a reassessment of myself, may I develop a more positive attitude. If I am a child of God, created in God's image, there must be goodness in me. I will think about that goodness, and the ways it manifests itself. I will stop putting myself down, even in my secret thoughts. I will respect what is God's. I will respect myself.

Today I Will Remember

Self-respect is respect for God.

Reflection for the Day

I've begun to understand myself better since I've come to the Program. One of the most important things I've learned is that *opinions* aren't *facts.* Just because I feel that a thing is so doesn't necessarily *make* it so. "Men are not worried by things," wrote the Greek philosopher Epictetus, "but by their ideas about things. When we meet with difficulties, become anxious or troubled, let us not blame others, but rather ourselves. That is: our ideas about things." *Do I believe that I can never entirely lose what I have learned during my recovery?*

Today I Pray

May I learn to sort out realities from my ideas about those realities. May I understand that situations, things—even people—take on the colors and dimensions of my attitudes about them.

Today I Will Remember

To sort the real from the unreal.

Reflection for the Day

We may not know any specifics about the activities of today; we may not know whether we'll be alone or with others. We may feel the day contains too much time—or not enough. We may be facing tasks we're eager to complete, or tasks we've been resisting. Though the details of each person's day differ, each person's day does hold one similarity: each of us has the opportunity to choose to think positive thoughts. The choice depends less on our outside activities than on our inner commitment. *Can I accept that I alone have the power to control my attitude?*

Today I Pray

May I keep the fire of inner commitment alive through this whole, glorious day, whether my activities are a succession of workaday tasks or free-form and creative. May I choose to make this a good day for me, and for those around me.

Today I Will Remember

Keep the commitment.

Reflection for the Day

Before I became sober in the Program, I blamed all my problems on other people, or on places and things. Now I'm learning to look squarely at each difficulty, not seeking whom to "blame," but to discover how my attitude helped create my problem or aggravate it. I must also learn to face the consequences of my own actions and words, and to correct myself when I'm wrong. *Do I practice the Tenth Step by continuing to take personal inventory? When I am wrong, do I promptly admit it?*

Today I Pray

May I know the blessed relief and unburdening that come when I admit I have done something wrong. May I learn—perhaps for the first time in my entire life—to take responsibility for my own actions and to face the consequences. May I learn again how to match actions with consequences.

Today I Will Remember

To take responsibility for my own actions.

Reflection for the Day

There is no advantage, no profits, and certainly no growth when I deceive myself merely to escape the consequences of my own mistakes. When I realize this, I know I'll be making progress. "We must be true inside, true to ourselves, before we can know a truth that is outside us," wrote Thomas Merton in *No Man Is an Island*. "But we make ourselves true inside by manifesting the truth as we see it." *Am I true to myself?*

Today I Pray

May I count on my Higher Power to help me carry out the truth as I see it. May I never duck a consequence again. Consequence-ducking became a parlor game for chemically addictive persons like me, until we lost all sense of relationship between action and outcome. Now that I am healing, please God, restore my balance.

Today I Will Remember

Match the act with the consequence.

Reflection for the Day

It's time for me to realize that my attitude—toward the life I'm living and the people in it—can have a tangible, measurable, and profound effect on what happens to me day by day. If I expect good, then good will surely come to me. And if I try each day to base my attitude and point of view on a sound spiritual foundation, I know it will change all the circumstances of my life for the better, too. *Do I accept the fact that I have been given only a daily reprieve that is contingent on the maintenance of my spiritual condition?*

Today I Pray

Since my illness was spiritual—as well as physical and emotional—may I mend spiritually through daily communion with God. May I find a corner of quiet within me where I can spend a few moments with God. May God's will be known to me. May I worship God from that inner temple that is in myself.

Today I Will Remember

To spend a quiet moment with God.

Reflection for the Day

Merely to change my behavior, and what I say and do, doesn't prove there's been a change in my actual inner attitude. I'm deceiving myself if I believe I can somehow completely disguise my true feelings. They'll somehow come through, prolonging the difficulties in my relationships with others. I have to avoid half-measures in getting rid of the troublesome emotions I've been trying to hide. *Have I taken an honest inventory of myself?*

Today I Pray

May I know that feelings will come out somehow—sometimes barely disguised as behavior that I cannot always understand. But that perhaps is more acceptable to me than the root emotion that caused it. May I be completely and vigilantly honest with myself. May I be given the insight that comes through depending upon a Higher Power.

Today I Will Remember

Feelings can come out "sideways."

Reflection for the Day

We learn in the Program and its Twelve Steps that, as we grow spiritually, we find that our old attitudes toward our instinctual drives need to undergo drastic revisions. Our demands for emotional security and wealth, for personal prestige and power, all have to be tempered and redirected. We learn that the full satisfaction of these demands cannot be the sole end and aim of our lives. But when we're willing to place spiritual growth first—then and only then do we have a real chance to grow in healthy awareness and mature love. *Am I willing to place spiritual growth first?*

Today I Pray

May my development as a spiritual person temper my habitual hankerings for material security. May I understand that the only real security in life is spiritual. If I have faith in my Higher Power, these revisions in my attitudes will follow. May I grow first in spiritual awareness.

Today I Will Remember

Value the life of the spirit.

Reflection for the Day

In a letter to a friend, AA's co-founder Bill W. once wrote: "Nothing can be more demoralizing than a clinging and abject dependence upon another human being. This often amounts to the demand for a degree of protection and love that no one could possibly satisfy. So our hoped-for protectors finally flee, and once more we are left alone—either to grow up or to disintegrate." We discover, in the Program, that the best possible source of emotional stability is our Higher Power. We find that dependence upon His perfect justice, forgiveness, and love is healthy, and that it works where nothing else will. *Do I depend on my Higher Power?*

Today I Pray

May I realize that I am a dependent person. I have depended upon chemicals to alter my moods and attitudes. I have also developed parasitic attachments for others. May I stop making unrealistic emotional demands on others, which only serve to choke off mature human relationships and to leave me bewildered and let down. Only God can provide the kind of whole-hearted love which I, as a dependent person, seem to need. May I depend first upon God.

Today I Will Remember

God offers perfect love.

Reflection for the Day

Since I came to the Program, I've begun to recognize my previous inability to form a true partnership with another person. It seems that my egomania created two disasterous pitfalls. Either I insisted upon dominating the people I knew, or I depended on them far too much. My friends in the Program have taught me that my dependence meant demand—a demand for the possession and control of the people and the conditions surrounding me. *Do I still try to find emotional security either by dominating or being dependent on others?*

Today I Pray

May I turn first to God to satisfy my love-hunger, knowing that all He asks from me is my faith in Him. May I no longer cast emotional nets over those I love, either by dominating them or being excessively dependent upon them—which is just another form of domination. May I give others the room they need to be themselves. May God show me the way to mature human relationships.

Today I Will Remember

To have faith in God's love.

Reflection for the Day

If we examine every disturbance we have, great or small, we'll find at the root of it some unhealthy dependency and its consequent unhealthy demand. So let us, with God's help, continually surrender these crippling liabilities. Then we can be set free to live and love. We may then be able to Twelfth Step ourselves, as well as others, into emotional sobriety. *Do I try to carry the message of the Program?*

Today I Pray

May I first get my emotional and spiritual house in order before I seek to carry out serious commitments in human relationships. May I look long and thoroughly at "dependency"—upon alcohol or other drugs or upon other human beings—and recognize it as the source of my unrest. May I transfer my dependency to God, as I understand Him.

Today I Will Remember

I am God-dependent.

Reflection for the Day

All my life, I looked to others for comfort, security, and all the other things that add up to what I now call serenity. But I've come to realize that I was always looking in the wrong place. The source of serenity is not outside, but within myself. The kingdom is within me, and I already have the key. All I have to do is to be willing to use it. *Am I using the tools of the Program on a daily basis? Am I willing?*

Today I Pray

God gave me the courage to seek out the kingdom inside myself, to find that well-spring within me which has its source in the never-ending, life-giving receiver of God. May my soul be restored there. May I find the serenity I seek.

Today I Will Remember

To seek the inner kingdom.

Reflection for the Day

One thing that keeps me on the right track today is a feeling of loyalty to other members of the Program, no matter where they may be. We depend on each other. I know, for example, that I'd be letting them down if I ever took a drink. When I came into the Program, I found a group of people who were not only helping each other to stay sober, but who were loyal to each other by staying sober themselves. *Am I loyal to my group and to my friends in the Program?*

Today I Pray

I thank God for the loyalty and fellowship of the group and for the mutuality of commitment that binds us together. May I give to the group in the same proportion that I take from it. Having been a taker during so many of my years, my giving used to be no more than a commodity, for which I expected to be paid in approval or love or favors. May I learn the joy of pure giving, with no strings attached, no expectation of reward.

Today I Will Remember

A perfect gift asks nothing in return.

Reflection for the Day

There have been days during my recovery when just about everything seemed bleak and even hopeless. I allowed myself to become depressed and angry. I see now that it doesn't matter what I think, and it doesn't matter how I feel. It's what I do that counts. So when I become anxious or upset, I try to get into action by going to meetings, participating, and working with others in the Program. *If God seems far away, who moved?*

Today I Pray

May I not be immobilized by sadness or anger to the point of despair. May I look for the roots of despair in my tangle of emotions, sort out the tangle, pull out the culprit feelings, acknowledge that they belong to me. Only then can I get into gear, take action, begin to accomplish. May I learn to make use of the energy generated by anger to strengthen my will and achieve my goals.

Today I Will Remember

To sort out my feelings.

Reflection for the Day

The Program teaches us that we are bodily and mentally different from our fellows. We are reminded that the great obsession of every abnormal drinker—and every one of us who is otherwise addictive—is to prove that somehow, someday, we will be able to control our drinking, eating, or gambling. The persistence of this illusion is astonishing, we are told, and many pursue it to the gates of insanity or death. *Have I conceded to my innermost self that, for me, "One is too many and a thousand not enough..."?*

Today I Pray

May I have no illusions about someday becoming a moderate drinker or drug-user after being an obsessive one. May I muffle any small voice of destructive pride which lies to me, telling me that I can now go back to my former use and control it. This is a Program of no return, and I thank God for it.

Today I Will Remember

My goal must be lifelong abstinence—a day at a time.

Reflection for the Day

"Lead us not into temptation," we pray, for we know with certainty that temptation lurks around the corner. Temptation is cunning, baffling, powerful—and patient; we never know when it will catch us with our guard down. Temptation could come in the siren song of a four-color advertisement, the fragment of a help-remembered song or, more obviously, in the direct urgings of another person. We must remain forever vigilant, remembering that the first drink gets us drunk, that the first obsessive bite will likely trigger an overeating orgy, that the first roll of the dice could well destroy our lives. *Am I aware of my number one priority?*

Today I Pray

God, lead me out of temptation—whether it is the jolly-alcoholic abandon of my peers at a special-occasion celebration, the pressure from my friends to "get in the spirit" of a party, the familiar aura of an apartment where joints are passed around, the sound of rattling dice, the smell of a bakery. May I know the limits of my resistance and stay well within them. May my surrender to the will of God give a whole new meaning to that old phrase, "Get in the spirit."

Today I Will Remember

Get in the spirit.

Reflection for the Day

In the old days, we often had such devastating experiences that we fervently swore, "Never again." We were absolutely sincere in those moments of desperation. Yet, despite our intentions, the outcome was inevitably the same. Eventually, the memory of our suffering faded, as did the memory of our "pledge." So we did it again, ending up in even worse shape than when we had last "sworn off." Forever turned out to be only a week, or a day, or less. In the Program, we learn that we need only be concerned about today, this particular 24-hour period. *Do I live my life just 24 hours at a time?*

Today I Pray

May the long-term requirements of such phrases as "never again," "not on your life," "forever," "I'll never take another..." not weaken my resolve. "Forever," when it is broken down into single days—or even just parts of days—does not seem so impossibly long. May I awake each day with my goal set realistically at just 24 hours.

Today I Will Remember

Twenty-four hours at a time.

Reflection for the Day

I know today that "stopping in for a drink" will never again be—for me—simply killing a few minutes and leaving a buck on a bar. In exchange for the first drink, what I'd pluck down now would be my bank account, my family, our home, our car, my job, my sanity, and probably my life. It's too big a price, and too great a risk. *Do you remember your last drunk?*

Today I Pray

May I be strong in the knowledge that God's spirit is with me at all times. May I learn to feel that spiritual presence. May I know that nothing is hidden from God. Unlike the world, which approves or disapproves of my outward behavior, God sees all that I do, think, or feel. If I seek to do God's will, I can always count on reward for me—peace of mind.

Today I Will Remember

God knows all.

Reflection for the Day

The longer I'm in the Program, the more important becomes the slogan "First Things First." I used to believe that my family came first, that my home life came first, that my job came first. But I know today, in the depths of my heart, that if I can't stay sober, I'll have nothing. "First Things First," to me, means that everything in my life depends on my sobriety. *Am I grateful to be sober today?*

Today I Pray

May my first priority, the topmost item on my list of concerns, be my sobriety—maintaining it, learning to live comfortably with it, sharing the tools by which I maintain it. When other things crowd into my life and I am caught up in the busyness of living, may I still preserve that first-of-all goal—remaining free of chemicals.

Today I Will Remember

First Things First.

Reflection for the Day

The Program teaches us that we have an incurable illness. We always get worse, never better. But we're fortunate in that our incurable illness can be arrested, so long as we don't take the first drink, one day at a time. High-toned academic research and ivory-tower studies to the contrary, we know from experience that we can no more control our drinking than we can control the ocean tides. *Do I have any doubt that I am powerless over alcohol?*

Today I Pray

May I never fall prey to any short-term research results which tell me that alcoholism can be cured, that I would be safe to begin drinking again, supposedly, in a responsible manner. My experience—and the experience of those in the Program—will outshout such theories. May I know that my disease is arrestable, but not curable. May I know that if I took up my active addiction again, I would begin where I left off—closer than ever to possible death or insanity.

Today I Will Remember

Be wary of new theories.

Reflection for the Day

Once in a great while, I find myself thinking that perhaps things weren't quite so bad as they seemed to be. At such moments, I force myself to realize that my *illness* is talking to me, trying to tempt me into denying that I am, in fact, afflicted with an illness. One of the key action steps of the Program is that we give our illness to God as we understand Him, accepting our powerlessness in the face of His greater Power. *Do I believe that the grace of God can do for me what I could never do for myself?*

Today I Pray

May I know that much of our lives depends on faith. For we cannot know the limits of space and time—or explain the mysteries of life and death. But when we see God working through us—and through others who have found new life in the Program—it is all the evidence we need to know that God exists.

Today I Will Remember

The Big Wheel runs by faith.

Reflection for the Day

The Program teaches us, through the experience, strength, and hope of its fellowship, that the worst situation imaginable does not warrant a return to our addiction. No matter how bad a particular situation or set of circumstances, the return to our old ways for even a minute will assuredly make it worse. *Am I grateful for the sharing and caring of the Program?*

Today I Pray

May I insist that no stone can be heavy enough to drag me back down into the pool of my addiction. No burden, no disappointment, no blow to pride or loss of human love is worth the price of returning to my old way of life. When I harbor thoughts that life is "too much" for me, that no one should be expected to "take so much and still remain sane" or that I am "the fall guy," let me listen for the tone of my complaints and remember that I have heard that whine before—before I concluded that I was powerless over the chemical and gave my will over to the Will of God. Such wailing sets me up for getting high again. May God keep my ears alert to the tone of my own complaining.

Today I Will Remember

Hear my own complaints.

Reflection for the Day

All of us are faced with the troubles and problems of daily living, whether we've been in the Program two days or twenty years. We'd sometimes like to believe we could take care of all our problems *right now,* but it rarely works that way. If we remember the slogan "Easy Does It" when we are ready to panic, we may come to know that the very best way to handle all things is "Easy." We put one foot in front of the other, doing the best we are capable of doing. We say "Easy Does It," and we *do* it. *Are the Program's slogans growing with me as I grow with the Program?*

Today I Pray

May even the words "Easy Does It" serve to slow me down in my headlong rush to accomplish too much too fast. May just that word "Easy" be enough to make me ease up on the accelerator which plunges me into new situations without enough forethought, ease off on the number of hours spent in material pursuits. May I hark to the adage that Rome wasn't built in a single day. Neither can I build solutions to my problems all at once.

Today I Will Remember

Easy Does It.

Reflection for the Day

If a chemically dependent person wants to live successfully in society, he or she must replace the power of chemicals over his/her life with the power of something else—preferably positive, at least neutral, but not negative. That is why we say to the agnostic newcomer: If you can't believe in God, find a positive power that is as great as the power of your addiction, and give it the power and dependence you gave to your addiction. In the Program, the agnostic is left free to find his or her Higher Power, and can use the principles of the Program and the therapy of the meetings to aid in rebuilding his/her life. *Do I go out of my way to work with newcomers?*

Today I Pray

May the Power of the Program work its miracles equally for those who believe in the personal God or in a Universal spirit or in the strength of the group itself, or for those who define their Higher Power in their own terms, religious or not. If newcomers are disturbed by the religiosity of the Program, may I welcome them on their own spiritual terms. May I recognize that we are all spiritual beings.

Today I Will Remember

To each his own spirituality.

Reflection for the Day

I know today that getting active means trying to live the suggested Steps of the Program to the best of my ability. It means striving for some degree of honesty, first with myself, then with others. It means activity directed inward, to enable me to see myself and my relationship with my Higher Power more clearly. As I get active, outside and inside myself, so shall I grow in the Program. *Do I let others do all the work at meetings? Do I carry my share?*

Today I Pray

May I realize that "letting go and letting God" does not mean that I do not have to put any effort into the Program. It is up to me to work the Twelve Steps, to learn what may be an entirely new thing with me—honesty. May I differentiate between activity for activity's sake—busy-work to keep me from thinking—and the thoughtful activity which helps me to grow.

Today I Will Remember

"Letting God" means letting God show us how.

Reflection for the Day

Storing up grievances is not only a waste of time, but a waste of life that could be lived to greater satisfaction. If I keep a ledger of "oppressions and indignities," I'm only restoring them to painful reality.

"'The horror of that moment,' the King said, 'I shall never, never forget.'

"'You will though, if you don't make a memorandum of it.'"

(Lewis Carroll, *Through The Looking Glass*)

Am I keeping a secret storehouse for the wreckage of my past?

Today I Pray

God keep me from harboring the sludge for the past—grievances, annoyances, grudges, oppressions, wrongs, injustices, put-downs, slights, hurts. They will nag at me and consume my time in rehashing what I "might have said" or done until I face each one, name the emotion it produces in me, settle it as best I can—and forget it. May I empty my storehouse of old grievances.

Today I Will Remember

Don't rattle old bones.

Reflection for the Day

We must think deeply of all those sick persons still to come to the Program. As they try to make their return to faith and to life, we want them to find everything in the Program that we have found, yet more, if that be possible. No care, no vigilance, no effort to preserve the Program's constant effectiveness and spiritual strength will ever be too great to hold us in full readiness for the day of their homecoming. *How well do I respect the Traditions of the Program?*

Today I Pray

God, help me to carry out my part in making the group a lifeline for those who are still suffering from addictions, in maintaining the Steps and the Traditions which have made it work for me for those who are still to come. May the Program be a "homecoming" for those of us who share the disease of addiction. May we find common solutions to the common problems which that disease breeds.

Today I Will Remember

To do my part.

Reflection for the Day

What is the definition of humility? "Absolute humility," said AA co-founder Bill W., "would consist of a state of complete freedom from myself, freedom from all the claims that my defects of character now lay so heavily upon me. Perfect humility would be a full willingness, in all times and places, to find and to do the will of God." *Am I striving for humility?*

Today I Pray

May God expand my interpretation of humility beyond abject subservience or awe at the greatness of others. May humility also mean freedom from myself, a freedom which can come only through turning my being over to God's will. May I sense the omnipotence of God, which is simultaneously humbling and exhilarating. May I be willing to carry out God's will.

Today I Will Remember

Humility is freedom.

Reflection for the Day

"When I meditate upon such a vision," Bill W. continued, "I need not be dismayed because I shall never attain it, nor need I swell with presumption that one of these days its virtues shall all be mine. I only need to dwell on the vision itself, letting it grow and ever more fill my heart...Then I get a sane and healthy idea of where I stand on the highway to humility. I see that my journey towards God has scarcely begun. As I thus get down to my right size and stature, my self-concern and importance become amusing." *Do I take myself too seriously?*

Today I Pray

May the grandiosity which is a symptom of my chemical addiction be brought back into proportion by the simple comparison of my powerlessness with the power of God. May I think of the meaning of Higher Power as it relates to my human frailty. May it bring my ego back down to scale and help me shed my defenses of pomp or bluster or secret ideas of self-importance.

Today I Will Remember

God is great. I am small.

Reflection for the Day

My illness is unlike most other illnesses in that *denial* that I am sick is a primary symptom that I am sick. Like such other incurable illnesses as diabetes and arthritis, however, my illness is characterized by relapses. In the Program, we call such relapses "slips." The one thing I know for certain is that I alone can cause myself to slip. *Will I remember at all times that the thought precedes the action? Will I try to avoid "stinking thinking"?*

Today I Pray

May God give me the power to resist temptations. May the responsibility for giving in, for having a "slip," be on my shoulders and mine only. May I see *beforehand* if I am setting myself up for a slip by blame-shifting, shirking my responsibility to myself, becoming the world's poor puppet once again. My return to those old attitudes can be as much of a slip as the act of losing my sobriety.

Today I Will Remember

Nobody's slip-proof.

Reflection for the Day

If we don't want to slip, we'll avoid slippery places. For the alcoholic, that means avoiding old drinking haunts; for the overeater, that means by-passing a once-favorite pastry shop; for the gambler, that means shunning poker parties and racetracks. For me, certain emotional situations can also be slippery places; so can indulgence of old ideas such as a well-nourished resentment that is allowed to build to explosive proportions. *Do I carry the principles of the Program with me wherever I go?*

Today I Pray

May I learn not to test myself too harshly by "asking for it," by stopping in at the bar or the bakery or the track. Such "testing" can be dangerous, especially if I am egged on, not only by a thirst or an appetite or a craving for the old object of my addictions, but by others still caught in addiction whose moral responsibility has been reduced to zero.

Today I Will Remember

Avoid slippery places.

Reflection for the Day

What causes slips? What happens to a person who apparently seems to understand and live the way of the Program, yet decides to go out again? What can I do to keep this from happening to me? Is there any consistency among those who slip, any common denominators that seem to apply? We can each draw our own conclusions, but we learn in the Program that certain inactions will all but guarantee an eventual slip. *When a person who has slipped is fortunate enough to return to the Program, do I listen carefully to what he or she says about the slip?*

Today I Pray

May my Higher Power—if I listen—show me if I am setting myself up to get high again. May I glean from the experiences of others that the reasons for such a lapse of resolve or such an accident of will most often stem from what I have not done rather than from what I have done. May I "keep coming back" to meetings.

Today I Will Remember

Keep coming back.

Reflection for the Day

In almost every instance, the returned slipper says, "I stopped going to meetings," or "I got fed up with the same old stories and the same old faces," or "My outside commitments were such that I had to cut down on meetings," or "I felt I'd received the optimum benefits from the meetings, so I sought further help from more meaningful activities." In short, they simply stopped going to meetings. A saying I've heard in the Program hits the nail on the head: "Them which stops going to meetings are not present at meetings to hear about what happens to them that stops going to meetings." *Am I going to enough meetings for me?*

Today I Pray

God keep me on the track of the Program. May I never be too tired, too busy, too complacent, too bored to go to meetings. Almost always those complaints are reversed at a meeting if I will just get myself there. My weariness dissipates in serenity. My busyness is reduced to its rightful proportion. My complacency gives way to vigilance again. And how can I be bored in a place where there is so much fellowship and joy?

Today I Will Remember

Attend the meetings.

Reflection for the Day

Another common denominator among those who slip is failure to use the tools of the Program—the Twelve Steps. The comments heard most often are, "I never did work the Steps," "I never got past the First Step," "I worked the steps too slow," or "too fast" or "too soon." What it boils down to, is that these people considered the Steps, but didn't conscientiously and sincerely apply the Steps to their lives. *Am I learning how to protect myself and help others?*

Today I Pray

May I be a doer of the Steps and not a hearer only. May I see some of the common mis-Steps which lead to a fall: being too proud to admit Step One; being too tied to everyday earth to feel the presence of a Higher Power; being overwhelmed by the thought of preparing Step Four, a complete moral inventory; being too reticent to share that inventory. Please God, guide me as I work the Twelve Steps.

Today I Will Remember

To watch my Steps.

Reflection for the Day

Still another common thread we invariably see among slippers is that many of them felt dissatisfaction with today. "I forgot we live one day at a time," or "I began to anticipate the future," or "I began to plan *results*, not just plan." They seemed to forget that all we have is Now. Life continued to get better for them and, as many of us do, they forgot how bad it had been. They began to think, instead, of how dissatisfying it was compared to what it *could be*. *Do I compare today with yesterday, realizing, by that contrast, what great benefits and blessings I have today?*

Today I Pray

If I am discouraged with today, may I remember the sorrows and hassles of yesterday. If I am impatient for the future, let me appreciate today and how much better it is than the life I left behind. May I never forget the principle of "one day at a time..."

Today I Will Remember

The craziness of yesterday.

Reflection for the Day

What do we say to a person who has slipped, or one who calls for help? We can carry the message, if they're willing to listen; we can share our experience, strength, and hope. Perhaps the most important thing we can do, however, is to tell the person that we love him or her, that we're truly happy he or she is back, and that we want to help all we can. And we must mean it. *Can I still "go to school" and continue to learn from the mistakes and adversities of others?*

Today I Pray

May I always have enough love to welcome back to the group someone who has slipped. May I listen to that person's story-of-woe, humbly. For there, but for my Higher Power, go I. May I learn from others' mistakes and pray that I will not re-enact them.

Today I Will Remember

Sobriety is never fail-safe.

Reflection for the Day

Our spiritual and emotional growth in the Program doesn't depend so deeply upon success as it does upon our failures and setbacks. If we bear this in mind, a relapse can have the effect of kicking us upstairs, instead of down. We in the Program have had no better teacher than Old Man Adversity, except in those cases where we refuse to let him teach us. *Do I try to remain always teachable?*

Today I Pray

May I respect the total Program, with its unending possibilities for spiritual and emotional growth, so that I can view a relapse as a learning experience, not "the end of the world." May relapse for any one of our fellowship serve to teach not only the person who has slipped, but all of us. May it strengthen our shared resolve.

Today I Will Remember

If you slip, get up.

Reflection for the Day

Time after time, we learn in the Program, new-comers try to keep to themselves "shoddy facts" about their lives. Trying to avoid the humbling experience of the Fifth Step, they turn to a seemingly easier and softer way. Almost invariably, they slip. Having persevered with the rest of the Program, they then wonder why they fell. The probable reason is that they never completed their housecleaning. They took inventory all right, but hung on to some of the worst items in stock. *Have I admitted to God, to myself, and to another human being the exact nature of my wrongs?*

Today I Pray

That I may include all of the sleaziness of my past, my cruelties and my dishonesties, in a complete moral inventory of myself. May I hold back nothing out of shame or pride, for the "exact nature" of my wrongs means just that—a thorough and exact recounting of past mistakes and character flaws. We have been provided with an appropriate "dumping-ground." May I use it as it was intended. May all my throw-aways, the trash and outgrown costumes of the past, be foundation "fill" on which to build a new life.

Today I Will Remember

Trash can be a foundation for treasures.

Reflection for the Day

Faith is more than our greatest gift; sharing it with others is our greatest responsibility. May we of the Program continually seek the wisdom and the willingness by which we may well fulfill the immense trust which the Giver of all perfect gifts has placed in our hands. *If you pray, why worry? If you worry, why pray?*

Today I Pray

Our God is a mighty fortress, a bulwark who never fails us. May we give praise for our deliverance and for our protection. God gives us the gift of faith to share. May we pass it along to others as best we know how and in the loving spirit in which it was given to us.

Today I Will Remember

God will not fail us.

Reflection for the Day

Change is the characteristic of all growth. From drinking to sobriety, from dishonesty to honesty, from conflict to serenity, from childish dependence to adult responsibility—all this and infinitely more represent change for the better. Only God is unchanging; only He has all the truth there is. *Do I accept the belief that lack of power was my dilemma? Have I found a power by which I can live—a Power greater than myself?*

Today I Pray

I pray that the Program will be, for me, an outline for change—for changing me. These days of transition from active addiction to sobriety, from powerlessness to power through God, may be rocky, as change can be. May my restlessness be stilled by the unchanging nature of God, in whom I place my trust. Only God is whole and perfect and predictable.

Today I Will Remember

I can count on my Higher Power.

Reflection for the Day

I came; I came to; I came to believe. The Program has enabled me to learn that deep down in every man, woman, and child is the fundamental idea of a God. It may be obscured by pomp, by calamity, by worship of other things, but in some form or other it is there. For faith in a Power greater than ourselves and miraculous demonstrations of the Power in human lives are facts as old as man himself. *How well do I share my free gifts?*

Today I Pray

I pray that I may continue to look for—and find—the Godliness that is in me and in every other person, no matter how it is obscured. May I be aware that the consciousness of a Higher Power has been present in man since he was first given the power to reason, no matter what name he gave to it or how he sought to reach it. May my own faith in a Higher Power be reinforced by the experience of all mankind—and by the working of God's gracious miracles in my own life.

Today I Will Remember

God is in us all.

Reflection for the Day

If we attempt to understand rather than to be understood, we can more quickly assure a new-comer that we have no desire to convince anyone that there is only one way by which faith can be acquired. All of us, whatever our race, creed, color, or ethnic heritage, are the children of a living Creator, with whom we may form a relationship upon simple and understandable terms—as soon as we are willing and honest enough to try. *Do I know the difference between sympathy and empathy? Can I put myself in the newcomer's shoes?*

Today I Pray

May I try to love all humanity as children of a living God. May I respect the different ways through which they find and worship Him. May I never be so rigid as to discount another's path to God or so insensitive that I use the fellowship of the group as a preaching ground to extol my religious beliefs as the only way. I can only know what works for me.

Today I Will Remember

We are all children of God.

Reflection for the Day

Any number of addicted people are bedeviled by the dire conviction that if they ever go near the Program—whether by attending meetings or talking one-to-one with a member—they'll be pressured to conform to some particular brand of faith or religion. They don't realize that faith is never an imperative for membership in the Program; that freedom from addiction can be achieved with an easily acceptable minimum of it; and that our concepts of a Higher Power and God—as we understand him—afford everyone a nearly unlimited choice of spiritual belief and action. *Am I receiving strength by sharing with newcomers?*

Today I Pray

May I never frighten newcomers or keep away those who are considering coming to the Program by imposing on them my particular, personal ideas about a Higher Power. May each discover his or her own spiritual identity. May all find within themselves a link with some great universal Being or Spirit whose power is greater than theirs individually. May I grow, both in tolerance and in spirituality, every day.

Today I Will Remember

I will reach, not preach.

Reflection for the Day

Every man and woman who has joined the Program and intends to stick around has, without realizing it, made a beginning on Step Three. Isn't it true that, in all matters related to their addictions, each of them has decided to turn his or her life over to the care, protection, and guidance of the Program? So already a willingness has been achieved to cast out one's own will and one's own ideas about the addiction in favor of those suggested by the Program. If this isn't turning one's will and life over to a newfound "Providence," then what is it? *Have I had a spiritual awakening as the result of the Steps?*

Today I Pray

For myself, I pray for a God-centered life. I thank God often for the spiritual awakening I have felt since I turned my life over to Him. May the words "spiritual awakening" be a clue to others that there is a free fund of spiritual power within each person. It must only be discovered.

Today I Will Remember

I will try to be God-centered.

Reflection for the Day

Rare are the practicing alcoholics who have any idea how irrational they are, or, seeing their irrationality, can bear to face it. One reason is that they are abetted in their blindness by a world which doesn't yet understand the difference between sane drinking and alcoholism. The dictionary defines sanity as "soundness of mind." Yet no alcoholic, soberly analyzing his or her destructive behavior, can truly claim soundness of mind. *Have I come to believe, as the Second Step suggests, that a Power greater than myself can restore me to sanity?*

Today I Pray

May I see that my own behavior as a practicing alcoholic, a drug-user, or a compulsive overeater, could be described as "insane." For those still actively addicted, admitting to "insane" behavior is well-nigh impossible. I pray that I may continue to abhor the *insanities* and *inanities* of my addictive days. May others like me recognize their problems of addiction, find help in treatment and in the Program, and come to believe that a Higher Power can restore them to sanity.

Today I Will Remember

He restoreth my soul.

Reflection for the Day

I once heard it said that "the mind is the slayer of the real." Looking back at the insanity of those days when I was actively addicted, I know precisely what that phrase means. One of the Program's important fringe benefits for me today is an increasing awareness of the world around me, so I can see and enjoy reality. This alone helps diminish the difficulties I so often magnify, creating my own misery in the process. *Am I acquiring the sense of reality which is absolutely essential to serenity?*

Today I Pray

May I be revived by a sharpened sense of reality, excited to see—for the first time since the blur of my worst moments—the wonders and opportunities in my world. Emerging from the don't-care haze of addiction, I see objects and faces coming into focus again, colors brightening. May I take delight in this new-found brightness.

Today I Will Remember

To focus on my realities.

Reflection for the Day

The Program teaches me to remain on guard against impatience, lapses into self-pity, and resentments of the words and deeds of others. Though I must mever forget what it used to be like, neither should I permit myself to take tormenting excursions into the past—merely for the sake of self-indulgent morbidity. Now that I'm alert to the danger signals, I know I'm improving day by day. *If a crisis arises, or any problem baffles me, do I hold it up to the light of the Serenity Prayer?*

Today I Pray

I pray for perspective as I review the past. May I curb my impulse to upstage and outdo the members of my group by regaling them with the horrors of my addiction. May I no longer use the past to document my self-pity or submerge myself in guilt. May memories of those miserable earlier days serve me only as sentinels, guarding against hazardous situations or unhealthy sets of mind.

Today I Will Remember

I cannot change the past.

Reflection for the Day

We in the Program know full well the futility of trying to overcome our addictions by will power alone. At the same time, we do know that it takes great willingness to adopt the Program's Twelve Steps as a way of life that can restore us to sanity. No matter how severe our addictions, we discover with relief that choices can still be made. For example, we can choose to admit that we're personally powerless over chemical dependency; that dependence upon a Higher Power is a necessity, even if this be simply dependence upon our group in the Program. *Have I chosen to try for a life of honesty and humility, of selfless service to my fellows and to God as I understand Him?*

Today I Pray

God grant me the wisdom to know the difference between "will power" (which has failed me before) and "willingness" to seek help for my dependency, through God and through others who are also recovering. May I know that there are choices open to me as there are to my fellow sufferers in the foggiest stages of addiction. May I choose the kind of life God wants for me.

Today I Will Remember

Willingness, more than will power, is the key to recovery.

Reflection for the Day

As we continue to make these vital choices and so move toward these high aspirations, our sanity returns and the compulsion of our former addictions vanishes. We learn, in the words of Plutarch, that, "A pleasant and happy life does not come from external things. Man draws from within himself, as from a spring, pleasure and joy." *Am I learning to "travel first class" inside?*

Today I Pray

The grace of God has showed me how to be happy again. May the wisdom of God teach me that the source of that happiness is within me, in my new values, my new sense of self-worth, my new and open communication with my Higher Power.

Today I Will Remember

Happiness comes from within.

Reflection for the Day

"If a person continues to see only giants," wrote Anais Nin, "it means he is still looking at the world through the eyes of a child." During this 24-hour period, I won't allow myself to be burdened by thoughts of giants and monsters—of things that are past. I won't concern myself about tomorrow until it becomes my today. The better I use today, the more likely it is that tomorrow will be bright. *Have I extended the hand of caring to another person today?*

Today I Pray

God, may I please grow up. May I no longer see monsters and giants on my walls, those projections of a child's imagination. May I bury my hobgoblins and realize that those epic dream-monsters are distortions of my present fears. May they vanish with my fearfulness, in the daylight of my new serenity.

Today I Will Remember

I will put away childish fears.

Reflection for the Day

Can I be wholeheartedly grateful for today? If so, I'm opening doors to more and more abundant good. What if I can't be thankful for the "rain" that has fallen in my life—for the so-called bad times? What then? I can begin by giving thanks for all the sunshine I can remember, and for every blessing that has come my way. Perhaps then I'll be able to look back over the rainy periods of my life with new vision, seeing them as necessary; perhaps then, hidden blessings I've overlooked will come to my attention. *Am I grateful for all of life—both the sunshine and the rain?*

Today I Pray

May I be grateful for all that has happened to me, good and bad. Bad helps to define good. Sorrow intensifies joy. Humility brings spirituality. Disease turns health into a paradise. Loneliness makes love, both human and Divine, the greatest gift of all. I thank God for the contrasts which have made me know God better.

Today I Will Remember

I am grateful for the whole of life.

Reflection for the Day

As I attend meetings of the Program, may eyes open wider and wider. Other people's problems make mine look small, yet they are facing them with courage and confidence. Others are trapped in situations as bad as mine, but they bear their troubles with more fortitude. By going to meetings, I find many reasons to be grateful. My load has begun to lighten. *Do I expect easy solutions to my problems? Or do I ask only to be guided to a better way?*

Today I Pray

Make the Program my way of life. Its goals are my goals. Its members are my truest friends. May I pass along the skills for coping I have learned there. May my turnabout and the resulting transformation in my life inspire others, as others have inspired me.

Today I Will Remember

May I be grateful.

Reflection for the Day

No matter what it is that seems to be our need or problem, we can find something to rejoice in, something for which to give thanks. It is not God who needs to be thanked, but we who need to be thankful. Thankfulness opens new doors to good in our life. Thankfulness creates a new heart and a new spirit in us. *Do I keep myself aware of the many blessings that come to me each day and remember to be thankful for them?*

Today I Pray

May God fill me with a spirit of thankfulness. When I express my thanks, however fumbling, to God or to another human being, I am not only being gracious to God or that other person for helping me, but I am also giving myself the greatest reward of all—a thankful heart. May I not forget either the transitive "to thank," directed at someone else, or the intransitive "giving thanks," which fills my own great need.

Today I Will Remember

Thank and give thanks.

Reflection for the Day

We come to know in the Program that there is no deeper satisfaction and no greater joy than in a Twelfth Step well done. To watch the eyes of men and women open with wonder as they move from darkness to light, to see their lives quickly fill with new purpose and meaning, and above all to watch them awaken to the presence of a loving God in their lives—these things are the substance of what we receive as we carry the message of the Program. *Am I learning through Twelfth Step experiences that gratitude should go forward, rather than backward?*

Today I Pray

May my Twelfth Step be as wholehearted and as convincing and as constructive as others' Twelfth-Stepping has been to me. May I realize that the might of the Program and its effectiveness for all of us come through "passing it on." When I guide someone else to sobriety, my own sobriety is underlined and reinforced. I humbly ask God's guidance before each Twelfth Step.

Today I Will Remember

To pass it on.

Reflection for the Day

I have much more to be grateful for than I realize. Too often, I don't remember to give thought to all the things in my life that I could enjoy and appreciate. Perhaps I don't take time for this important meditation because I'm too preoccupied with my own so-called woes. I allow my mind to overflow with grievances; the more I think about them, the more monumental they seem. Instead of surrendering to God and God's goodness, I let myself be controlled by the negative thinking into which my thoughts are apt to stray unless I guide them firmly into brighter paths. *Do I try to cultivate an "attitude of gratitude"?*

Today I Pray

May God lead me away from my pile-up of negative thoughts, which make for detours in my path of personal growth. May I break the old poor-me habits of remembering the worst and expecting the most dire. May I turn my thoughts ahead to a whole new world out there. May I allow myself to envision the glory of God.

Today I Will Remember

Keep an attitude of gratitude.

Reflection for the Day

When I first came to the Program, I was stunned by the constant sound of laughter. I realize today that cheerfulness and merriment are useful. As the "Big Book" says, "Outsiders are sometimes shocked when we burst into laughter over a seemingly tragic experience out of the past. But why shouldn't we laugh? We have recovered, and have been given the power to help others." What greater cause could there be for rejoicing than this? *Have I begun to regain my sense of humor?*

Today I Pray

May God restore my sense of humor. May I appreciate the honest laughter that is the background music of our mutual rejoicing in our sobriety. May I laugh a lot, not the defensive ego-laugh which mocks another's weakness, not the wry laugh of the self-put-down, but the healthy laugh that keeps situations in perspective. May I never regard this kind of laughter as irreverent. I have learned, instead, that it is irreverent to take myself too seriously.

Today I Will Remember

A sense of humor is a sign of health.

Reflection for the Day

Am I so sure I'm doing everything possible to make my new life a success? Am I using my capabilities well? Do I recognize and appreciate all I have to be grateful for? The Program and its Twelve Steps teach me that I am the possessor of unlimited resources. The more I do with them, the more they will grow—to overshadow and cancel out the difficult and painful feelings that now get so much of my attention. *Am I less sensitive today than when I first came to the Program?*

Today I Pray

May I make the most of myself in all ways. May I begin to look outward to people and opportunities and wonderful resources around me. As I become less ingrown and understand myself better in relation to others, may I be less touchy and thin-skinned. May I shrug off my old "the-world-is-out-to-get-me" feeling and see that same world as my treasure-house, God-given and boundless.

Today I Will Remember

My resources are unlimited.

Reflection for the Day

I will resolve to observe with new interest even the commonplace things that happen today. If I learn to see everything with a fresh eye, perhaps I'll find I have countless reasons for contentment and gratitude. When I find myself trapped in the quicksand of my negative thoughts I'll turn away from them—and grab for the lifesaving strength of sharing with others in the Program. *Do I carry my weight as an all-important link in the worldwide chain of the Program?*

Today I Pray

I pray that God will open my eyes to the smallest everyday wonders, that I may notice and list among my blessings things like just feeling good, being able to think clearly. Even when I make a simple, unimportant choice, like whether to order coffee or tea or a soft drink, may I be reminded that the power of choice is a gift from God.

Today I Will Remember

I am blessed with the freedom of choice.

Reflection for the Day

As I grow in the Program—sharing, caring, and becoming more and more active—I find that it's becoming easier to live in the Now. Even my vocabulary is changing. No longer is every other sentence salted with such well-used phrases as *"could've," "should've," "would've," "might've."* What's done is done and what will be will be. The only time that really matters is Now. *Am I gaining real pleasure and serenity and peace in the Program?*

Today I Pray

That I may collect all my scattered memories from the past and high-flown schemes and overblown fears for the future and compact them into the neater confines of Today. Only by living in the Now may I keep my balance, without bending backwards to the past or tipping forward into the future. May I stop trying to get my arms around my whole unwieldy lifetime and carry it around in a gunny sack with me wherever I go.

Today I Will Remember

Make room for today.

Reflection for the Day

We're taught in the Program that "faith without works is dead." How true this is for the addicted person. For if addicted persons fail to perfect or enlarge their spiritual lives through work and self-sacrifice for others, they can't survive the certain trials and low spots ahead. If they don't practice the Programs they'll surely return to their addiction; and if they return to addiction, they'll likely die. Then faith will be dead indeed. *Do I believe, through my faith, that I can be uniquely useful to those who still suffer?*

Today I Pray

May my faith in my Higher Power and in the influence of the Program be multiplied within me as I pass it along to others who are overcoming similar addictions. May I be certain that my helping others is not simply repaying my debts, but it is the only way I know to continue my spiritual growth and maintain my own sobriety.

Today I Will Remember

The more faith I can give, the more I will have.

Reflection for the Day

For those of us who have lost our faith, or who have always had to struggle along without it, it's often helpful just to accept—blindly and with no reservations. It's not necessary for us to believe at first; we need not be convinced. If we can only *accept*, we find ourselves becoming gradually aware of a force for good that's always there to help us. *Have I taken the way of faith?*

Today I Pray

May I abandon my need to know the why's and wherefore's of my trust in a Higher Power. May I not intellectualize about faith, since by its nature it precludes analysis. May I know that "head-tripping" was a symptom of my disease, as I strung together—cleverly, I thought—alibi upon excuse upon rationale. May I learn acceptance, and faith will follow.

Today I Will Remember

Faith follows acceptance.

Reflection for the Day

When I was drinking, I was certain that my intelligence, backed by will power, could properly control my inner life and guarantee me success in the world around me. This brave and grandiose philosophy, by which I played God, sounded good in the saying, but it still had to meet the acid test: how well did it actually work? One good look in the mirror was answer enough. *Have I begun to ask God each day for strength?*

Today I Pray

May I stop counting on my old standbys, my "superior intelligence" and my "will power," to control my life. I used to think, with those two fabulous attributes, that I was all-powerful. May I not forget, as my self-image is restored, that only through surrender to a Higher Power will I be given the power that can make me whole.

Today I Will Remember

Check for "head-tripping."

Reflection for the Day

"To stand on one leg and prove God's existence is a very different thing," wrote Soren Kierkegaard, "from going down on one's knees and thanking Him." It is my confidence in a Higher Power, working in me, which today releases and activates my ability to make my life a more joyous, satisfying experience. I can't bring this about by relying on myself and my own limited ideas. *Have I begun to thank God every night?*

Today I Pray

May I remember constantly that it is my belief in my Higher Power that flips the switch to release the power in me. Whenever I falter in my faith, that power is shut off. I pray for undiminished faith, so that this power—given by God and regenerated by my own belief in it—may always be available to me as the source of my strength.

Today I Will Remember

Faith regenerates God-given power.

Reflection for the Day

Many people pray as though to overcome the will of a reluctant God, instead of taking hold of the willingness of a loving God. In the late stages of our addiction, the will to resist has fled. Yet when we admit complete defeat, and when we become entirely ready to try the principles of the Program, our obsession leaves us and we enter a new dimension—freedom under God as we understand Him. *Is my growth in the Program convincing me that God alone can remove obsessions?*

Today I Pray

May I pray not as a complaining child to a stern father, as though "praying" must always mean "pleading," usually in moments of helpless desperation. May I pray, instead, for my own willingness to reach out to Him, since He is ready at all times to reach out to me. May I regard my Higher Power as a willing God.

Today I Will Remember

God is willing.

Reflection for the Day

I knew I had to have a new beginning, and the beginning had to be here. I couldn't start anywhere else. I had to let go of the past and forget the future. As long as I held on to the past with one hand and grabbed at the future with the other hand, I had nothing with which to grasp today. So I had to begin here, now. *Do I practice the Eleventh Step, praying only for knowledge of God's will for me, and the Power to carry that out?*

Today I Pray

May I not worry about verbalizing my wants and needs in my prayers to a Higher Power. May I not fret over the language of my prayers, for God needs no language, and communication with Him is beyond speech. May the Eleventh Step guide me in my prayers at all times.

Today I Will Remember

God's will be done.

Reflection for the Day

So many of us suffer from despair. Yet we don't realize that despair is purely the absence of faith. As long as we're willing to turn to God for help in our difficulties, we cannot despair. When we're troubled and can't see a way out, it's only because we imagine that all solutions depend on *us*. The Program teaches us to *let go* of overwhelming problems and *let God* handle them for us. *When I consciously surrender my will to God's will, do I see faith at work in my life?*

Today I Pray

May I, as a recovering person, be free of despair and depression, those two "down D's" that are the result of feelings of helplessness. May I know that I am never without the help of God, that I am never helpless when God is with me. If I have faith, I need never be "helpless and hopeless."

Today I Will Remember

Despair is the absence of faith.

Reflection for the Day

If I believe that it's hopeless to expect any improvement in my life, I'm doubting the power of God. If I believe I have reason for despair, I'm confessing personal failure, for I *do* have the power to change myself; nothing can prevent it but my own unwillingness. I can learn in the Program to avail myself of the immense, inexhaustible power of God—if I'm willing to be *continually* aware of God's nearness. *Do I still imagine that my satisfaction with life depends on what someone else may do?*

Today I Pray

May I give over my life to the will of God, not to the whims and insensitivities of others. When I counted solely on what other people did and thought and felt for my own happiness, I became nothing more than a cheap mirror reflecting others' lives. May I remain close to God in all things. I value myself because God values me. May I be dependent only upon my Higher Power.

Today I Will Remember

Stay close to God.

Reflection for the Day

I've learned in the Program that I need not apologize to anyone for depending upon God as I understand Him. In fact, I now have good reason to disbelieve those who think spirituality is the way of weakness. For me, it is the way of strength. The verdict of the ages is that men and women of faith seldom lack courage. They trust their God. So I never apologize for my belief in Him, but, instead, I try to let Him demonstrate, through me and those around me, what He can do. *Do I walk as I talk?*

Today I Pray

May my faith be confirmed as I see how God has worked through others since the beginning of time. May I see that the brave ones, the miracle-workers, the happy people are those who have professed their spirituality. May I see, even now as I look around, how God works through those who believe in Him.

Today I Will Remember

To watch God at work.

Reflection for the Day

"Perfect courage," wrote La Rochefoucauld, "means doing unwitnessed what we would be capable of with the world looking on." As we grow in the Program, we recognize persistent fear for what it is, and we become able to handle it. We begin to see each adversity as a God-given opportunity to develop the kind of courage which is born of humility, rather than of bravado. *Do I realize that whistling to keep up my courage is merely good practice for whistling?*

Today I Pray

May I find courage in my Higher Power. Since all things are possible through God, I must be able to overcome the insidious fears that haunt me—so often fears of losing someone or something that has become important in my life. I pray for my own willingness to let go of those fears.

Today I Will Remember

Praying is more than whistling in the dark.

Reflection for the Day

As the doubter tries the process of prayer, he would do well to add up the results. If he persists, he'll almost surely find more serenity, more tolerance, less fear, and less anger. He'll acquire a quiet courage—the kind that isn't tension-ridden. He'll be able to look at "failure" and "success" for what they really are. Problems and calamity will begin to mean his instruction, instead of his destruction. He'll feel freer and saner. *Have wonderful and unaccountable things begun to happen to me in my new life?*

Today I Pray

Through prayer, communion with a Higher Power, may I begin to see my life sort itself out. May I become less tense, more sane, more open, more courageous, more loving, less tangled in problems, less afraid of losing, less afraid of living. May I know that God, too, wants these things for me. May God's will be done.

Today I Will Remember

Be still and know your God.

Reflection for the Day

Now that I know I can't use bottled courage, I seek and pray for 24-hour courage to change the things I can. Obviously, this isn't the kind of courage that will make me a strong and brave person for life, able to handle any and all situations courageously. Rather, what I need is a persistent and intelligent courage, continuing each day into the next one—but doing today only what can be done today and avoiding all fear and worry with regard to the final result. *What does courage mean to me today?*

Today I Pray

May I tackle only those things which I have a chance of changing. And change must start with me, a day at a time. May I know that acceptance often is a form of courage. I pray not for super-bravery, but just for persistence to meet what life brings to me without being overcome by it.

Today I Will Remember

Courage is meeting a day at a time.

Reflection for the Day

My courage must come each day, as does my desire to avoid a single drink, a single tranquilizer, a single addictive act. It must be a continuing courage, without deviations and procrastination, without rashness, and without fear of obstacles. This would seem like a large order indeed, were it not for the fact that it is confined to this one day, and that within this day much power is given to me. *Do I extend the Serenity Prayer to my entire life?*

Today I Pray

May each new morning offer me a supply of courage to last me during the day. If my courage is renewed each day and I know that I need just a day's worth, that courage will always be fresh and the supply will not run out. May I realize, as days pass, that what I feared during the earliest days of my recovery I no longer fear, that my daily courage is now helping me cope with bigger problems.

Today I Will Remember

God give me courage—just for today.

MAY 13

Reflection for the Day

When a person wakes up each morning and rises through sweaty nausea to face frightening reality with bones rattling and nerves screaming; when a person stumbles through the day in a pit of despair, wishing to die, but refusing to die; when a person gets up the next day and does it all over again—well, that takes guts. That takes a kind of real, basic survival courage, a courage that can be put to good use if that person ever finds his or her way to the Program. That person has learned courage the hard way, and when that person comes to the Program, he or she will find new and beautiful ways to use it. *Have I the courage to keep trying, one day at a time?*

Today I Pray

May I put the "guts-to-survive" kind of courage left over from my drinking days into good use in the Program. If I was able to "hang on" enough to live through the miseries of my addiction, may I translate that same will to survive into my recovery program. May I use my courage in new, constructive ways.

Today I Will Remember

God preserved me to help carry out His purpose.

Reflection for the Day

"A very popular error—having the courage of one's convictions; rather it is a matter of having the courage for an attack upon one's convictions," wrote Nietzsche. The Program is helping me to get rid of my old ideas by sharing with others and working the Twelve Steps. Having made a searching and fearless moral inventory of myself; having admitted to God, to myself, and to another human being the exact nature of my wrongs; and having become entirely ready to have God remove all my defects of character—I will humbly ask Him to remove my shortcomings. *Am I trying to follow the Program just as it is?*

Today I Pray

I pray that I may continue to practice the Twelve Steps, over and over again, if need be. The Program has worked for hundreds and hundreds of recovering chemically dependent people the world over. It can work for me. May I pause regularly and check to see if I am really practicing the Program, as it is set forth.

Today I Will Remember

Step by Step. Day by Day.

Reflection for the Day

Looking back at those last desperate days before I came to the Program, I remember more than anything the feelings of loneliness and isolation. Even when I was surrounded by people, including my own family, the sense of "aloneness" was overwhelming. Even when I tried to act sociable and wore the mask of cheerfulness, I usually felt a terrible anger of not belonging. *Will I ever forget the misery of "being alone in a crowd"?*

Today I Pray

I thank God for the greatest single joy that has come to me outside of my sobriety—the feeling that I am no longer alone. May I not assume that loneliness will vanish overnight. May I know that there will be a lonely time during recovery, especially since I must pull away from my former junkie friends or drinking buddies. I pray that I may find new friends who are recovering. I thank God for the fellowship of the Program.

Today I Will Remember

I am not alone.

Reflection for the Day

Many of us in the Program share the memory that we originally drank or used other chemicals to "belong," to "fit in," or to "be a part of the crowd." Others of us fueled our addictions to "get in"—to feel, at least for a short time, that we fitted in with the rest of the human race. Sometimes, the chemicals had the desired effect, temporarily assuaging our feelings of apartness. But when the chemicals' effects wore off, we were left feeling more alone, more left out, more "different" than ever. *Do I still sometimes feel that "my case is different"?*

Today I Pray

God, may I get over my feeling of being "different" or in some way unique, of not belonging. Perhaps it was this feeling that led me to my chemical use in the first place. It also kept me from seeing the seriousness of my addiction, since I thought "*I* am different. *I* can handle it." May I now be aware that I *do* belong, to a vast fellowship of people like me. With every shared experience, my "uniqueness" is disappearing.

Today I Will Remember

I am not unique.

Reflection for the Day

If we felt guilty, degraded, or ashamed of either our addiction itself or the things we did while "under the influence," that served to magnify our feelings of being outcasts. On occasion, we secretly feared or actually believed that we *deserved* every painful feeling; we thought, at times, that we truly *were* outsiders. The dark tunnel of our lives seemed formidable and unending. We couldn't even voice our feelings and could hardly bear to think about them. So we soon drank or used again. *Do I remember well what it used to be like?*

Today I Pray

May I remember how often, during my days of active addiction, I felt alone with my shame and guilt. The phony jollity of a drinking party or the shallow relationships struck up at a bar could not keep me from feeling like an outsider. May I appreciate the chance to make new friends through the fellowship of the group. May I know that my relationships now will be saner, less dependent, more mature.

Today I Will Remember

Thank God for new friends.

Reflection for the Day

I considered myself a "loner" in the days when I was actively addicted. Although I was often with other people—saw them, heard them, touched them—most of my important dialogues were with my inner self. I was certain that nobody else would ever understand. Considering my former opinion of myself, it's likely that I didn't *want* anybody to understand. I smiled through gritted teeth even as I was dying on the inside. *Have my insides begun to match my outside since I've been in the Program?*

Today I Pray

May my physical, emotional, intellectual, and spiritual selves become one, a whole person again. I thank my Higher Power for showing me how to match my outside to my inside, to laugh when I feel like laughing, to cry when I feel sad, to recognize my own anger or fear or guilt. I pray for wholeness.

Today I Will Remember

I am becoming whole.

Reflection for the Day

"When I was driven to my knees by alcohol, I was made ready to ask for the gift of faith," wrote AA co-founder Bill W. "And all was changed. Never again, my pains and problems notwithstanding, would I experience my former desolation. I saw the universe to be lighted by God's love; I was alone no more." *Am I convinced that my new life is real and that it will last so long as I continue doing what the Program and Twelve Steps suggest that I do?*

Today I Pray

May God be the ever-present third party in my relationships with others, whether they are casual or involve a deep emotional commitment. May I be aware that if there is real friendship or love between human beings, God's spirit is always present. May I feel God's spirit in all my human relationships.

Today I Will Remember

God is the Divine Third.

Reflection for the Day

Alcoholism is called the "lonely disease"; almost without exception, alcoholics are literally tortured by loneliness. Even before the end of our drinking—before people began to shun us and we were "eighty-sixes" from bars, restaurants, or people's homes—nearly all of us felt that we didn't quite belong. We were either shy, and dared not draw near others, or we were noisy good fellows craving attention and approval, but rarely getting it. There was always that mysterious barrier we could neither surmount nor understand. Finally, even Bacchus betrayed us; we were struck down and left in terrified isolation. *Have I begun to achieve an inner calm?*

Today I Pray

May I know the tenderness of an intimate relationship with God and the calm I feel when I touch God's spirit. May I translate this tenderness and calm to my relationships with others. May God deliver me from my lifelong feeling of loneliness and show me how to be a friend.

Today I Will Remember

God can teach me to be a friend.

Reflection for the Day

"The language of friendship is not words, but meanings," wrote Thoreau. Life indeed takes on new meanings, as well as new *meaning* in the Program. To watch people recover, to see them help others, to watch loneliness vanish, to see a fellowship grow up about you, to have a host of friends—this is an experience not to be missed. *Can I recall my initial reactions when I came to the Program? Do I believe that I've finally come home?*

Today I Pray

As the Program has given life new meanings for me, may I pass along to others that same chance to re-evaluate their lives in the light of sobriety, common purpose, friendships, and spiritual expansion. Praise God for my new vision of human life. Praise God for restoring for me the value and purpose of living.

Today I Will Remember

I value my life

Reflection for the Day

When I first listened to people in the Program talking freely and honestly about themselves, I was stunned. Their stories of their own addictive escapades, of their own secret fears, and of their own gnawing loneliness were literally mind-blowing for me. I discovered—and hardly dared believe it at first—that *I'm not alone.* I'm not all that different from everybody else and, in fact, *we're all very much the same.* I began to sense that I do belong somewhere, and my loneliness began to leave me. *Do I try to give to others what has been given freely to me?*

Today I Pray

May I begin to see, as the life stories of my friends in the Program unfold for me, that our similarities are far more startling than our differences. As I listen to their accounts of addiction and recovery, may I experience often that small shock of recognition, a "hey-that's-me!" feeling that is quick to chase away my separateness. May I become a wholehearted member of the group, giving and taking in equal parts.

Today I Will Remember

Sameness, not differences.

Reflection for the Day

When newcomers to the Program experience the first startling feeling that they're truly among *friends*, they also wonder—with almost a sense of terror—if the feeling is real. Will it last? Those of us who've been in the Program a few years can assure any newcomer at a meeting that it is very real indeed, and that it does last. It's not just another false start, nor just a temporary burst of gladness to be followed, inevitably, by shattering disappointment. *Am I convinced that I can have a genuine and enduring recovery from the loneliness of my addiction?*

Today I Pray

Please, God, let me not be held back by my fear of recurring loneliness. May I know that the openness which warms me in this group will not suddenly close up and leave me out. May I be patient with my fear, which is swollen with past disappointments and losses. May I know that the fellowship of the group will, in time, convince me that loneliness is never incurable.

Today I Will Remember

Loneliness is curable.

Reflection for the Day

Getting over years of suspicion and other self-protective mechanisms can hardly be an overnight process. We've become thoroughly conditioned to feeling and acting misunderstood and unloved—whether we really were or not. Some of us may need time and practice to break out of our shell and the seemingly comfortable familiarity of solitude. Even though we begin to believe and know we're no longer alone, we tend to sometimes feel and act in the old ways. *Am I taking it easy? Am I learning to wear the Program and life like a loose garment?*

Today I Pray

May I expect no sudden, total reversal of all my old traits. My sobriety is just a beginning. May I realize that the symptoms of my disease will wear off gradually. If I slip back, now and then, into my old self-pity bag or my grandiosity, may I not be discouraged, but grateful. At last, I can face myself honestly and not let my delusions get the best of me.

Today I Will Remember

Easy does it.

Reflection for the Day

When we're new in the Program, we're novices at reaching out for friendship—or even accepting it when it's offered. Sometimes we're not quite sure how to do it or, indeed, whether it will actually work. Gradually, however, we become restored; we become teachable. We learn, for example, as Moliere wrote, "The more we love our friends, the less we flatter them." *Just for today, will I reach out if I need a friend?*

Today I Pray

May God help me to discover what true friendship is. In my new relationships, I pray that I may not be so eager for approval that I will let myself be dishonest—through flattery, half-truths, false cheeriness, protective white lies.

Today I Will Remember

A friend is honest.

Reflection for the Day

I know today that I no longer have to proceed on my own. I've learned that it's safer, more sensible, and surer to move forward with friends who are going in the same direction as I. None of us need feel shame at using help, since we all help each other. It's no more a sign of weakness to use help in recovering from my addiction than it is to use a crutch if I have a broken leg. To those who need it, and to those who see its usefulness, a crutch is a beautiful thing. *Do I sometimes still refuse to accept easily obtained assistance?*

Today I Pray

God make me see that it is not a sign of weakness to ask for help, that the comraderie of the group is what makes it work for each of us. Like a vaccine for diphtheria or polio, the Program and the strength of the group have proved themselves as preventives for slips and backsliding. Praise God for the tools of recovery.

Today I Will Remember

Help is as near as my telephone.

Reflection for the Day

When I have only myself to talk to, the conversation gets sort of one-sided. Trying to talk myself out of a drink or a pill or a "small wager" or just one chocolate eclair is sort of like trying self-hypnosis. It simply doesn't work; most of the time, it's about as effective as trying to talk myself out of a case of diarrhea. When my heart is heavy and my resistance low, I can always find some comfort in sharing with a true and understanding friend in the Program. *Do I know who my friends are?*

Today I Pray

May I be convinced that, as part of God's master plan, we were put here to help each other. May I be as open about asking for help as I am ready to give it, no matter how long I have been in the Program. May the experiences of countless others be enough to prove to me that "talking myself out of it" seldom works, that the mutual bolstering that comes from sharing with a friend usually does.

Today I Will Remember

When I ask for help, I am helping.

Reflection for the Day

We've all had times when we felt alienated, when it seemed we had nowhere to turn and no one to turn to. When we don't know which way to turn, when there seems to be no one to help us, even then we're not alone or without help; the presence of God is always with us. When we need strength or courage or comfort, God is there with us as the help we need. Even before we turn to God, His love reaches out to us; His loving Spirit in us hears our cry and answers us. *Do I truly believe that I no longer need be alone?*

Today I Pray

May I never be alone, even in a place by myself, if I take time to talk to my Higher Power. May God be my companion, my joy, my ever-present help in trouble. May the knowledge of that constant presence fill me with calm, so that I will not fear either the solitude of my own room or alienation in a roomful of people.

Today I Will Remember

Listen for the presence of God.

Reflection for the Day

When we first reached the Program and for the first time in our lives stood among people who seemed to understand, the sense of belonging was exhilarating. We felt that the problem of isolation had been solved. We soon discovered, however, that while we weren't alone anymore, in a social sense, we still suffered many of the old pangs of anxious apartness. Until we had talked with complete candor of our conflicts, and had listened to someone else do the same thing, we still didn't belong. Step Five was the answer. *Have I found through the Fifth Step the beginning of true kinship with my fellows and God?*

Today I Pray

May God help me learn to share myself, my attributes, and my failings, not just as I take the Fifth Step but in a continuing give-and-take process with my friends. May I cultivate an attitude of openness and honesty with others, now that I have begun to be honest with myself. May I remember who I used to be—the child in a game of hide-and-seek, who hid so well that nobody could find her/him and everyone gave up trying and went home.

Today I Will Remember

I will be open to friendship.

Reflection for the Day

Since I've been in the Program, I've learned to redefine love. I've come to understand, for example, that sometimes it's necessary to place love ahead of indiscriminate "factual honesty." No longer, under the guise of "perfect honesty," can I cruelly and unnecessarily hurt others. Today, I must always ask myself, "What's the best and most loving thing I can do?" *Have I begun to sow the seeds of love in my daily living?*

Today I Pray

May God's love show me how to be loving. May I first sense the feelings of love and caring within me and then find ways to show those feelings. May I remember how many times I cut myself off from relationships because I did not know how either to let myself feel love or to show what I did feel.

Today I Will Remember

When I feel love, I will be loving.

Reflection for the Day

Giving love is a fulfillment in itself. It must not matter whether love is returned or not. If I give love only to get a response on my terms, my love is canceled out by my motives. If I have the capacity to give love, then any return I get for it is a special bonus. It is through giving love, freely and without expectation of return, that we find ourselves and build ourselves spiritually. *Have I begun to believe, in the words of Goethe, that "Love does not dominate, it cultivates..."?*

Today I Pray

May I, the inveterate people-pleaser and approval-seeker, know that the only real love does not ask for love back. May God be patient as I try to practice this principle. May I rid myself of pride that throws itself in the way of love. May I discard my silly cat-and-mouse games that have no place in real love.

Today I Will Remember

I will not give love to get love.

Reflection for the Day

Slowly, but surely, I'm becoming able to accept other people's faults as well as their virtues. The Program is teaching me to "always love the best in others—and never fear their worst." This is hardly an easy transition from my old way of thinking, but I'm beginning to see that all people—including myself—are to some extent emotionally ill as well as frequently wrong. *Am I approaching true tolerance? Am I beginning to see what real love actually means?*

Today I Pray

May God give me tolerance for any shortcomings or sick symptoms or insensitivities of others, so that I can love the qualities that are good in them. May God instruct me in the truest meaning of love—which must also include patience. May I not overlook the faults of those I love, but may I try to understand them.

Today I Will Remember

Love is understanding.

Reflection for the Day

In the process of learning to love myself and, in turn, to love others freely with no strings attached, I've begun to understand these words of Saint Augustine: "Love slays what we have been, that we may be what we were not." More and more, I feel the enormous power of such love in the Program; for me, the words "we care" also mean "we love." *Just for today, will I try to be loving in every thought and action?*

Today I Pray

I pray that I may feel the enormity and the power of the love I find in the Program. May my own caring be added to that great energy of love which belongs to all of us. May I care with my whole heart that my fellow members maintain their sobriety and are learning to live with it comfortably and creatively. May I never doubt that they care the same way about me.

Today I Will Remember

Caring makes it happen.

Reflection for the Day

"The beginning of love is to let those we love be perfectly themselves, and not to twist them to fit our own image," wrote Thomas Merton. "Otherwise, we love only the reflection of ourselves we find in them." As I replace my self-destructive addictions with a healthy dependence on the Program and its Twelve Steps, I'm finding that the barriers of silence and hatred are melting away. By accepting each other as we are, we have learned again to love. *Do I care enough about others in the Program to continue working with them as long as necessary?*

Today I Pray

May I be selfless enough to love people as they are, not as I want them to be, as they mirror my image or feed my ego. May I slow down in my eagerness to love—now that I am capable of feeling love again—and ask myself if I really love someone or only that someone's idea of me. May I remove the "self" from my loving.

Today I Will Remember

Love is unconditional.

Reflection for the Day

"It seems to me," wrote AA co-founder Bill W., "that the primary object of any human being is to grow, as God intended, that being the nature of all growing things. Our search must be for what reality we can find, which includes the best definition and feeling of love that we can acquire. If the capability of loving is in the human being, then it must surely be in his Creator." *Will I pray today not so much to be loved, as to love?*

Today I Pray

God grant me the patience of a lifetime in my search for the best answer to the question, "What is love?" May I know that the definition will come to me in parts as I live life's several roles—as child, lover, parent, teacher, friend, spiritual being. May I be grateful for my experience as an addictive person, which adds a special dimension to the meaning of love.

Today I Will Remember

All love reflects God's love.

Reflection for the Day

The Program teaches me that not too many people can truthfully assert that they love everybody. Most of us have to admit that we've loved only a few, and that we've been quite indifferent to many. As for the rest, well, we've really disliked or hated them. We in the Program find we need something much better than this in order to keep our balance. The idea that we can be possessively loving of a few, can ignore the many, and can continue to fear or hate anyone at all, has to be abandoned—if only a little at a time. *At meetings, do I concentrate on the message rather than the messenger?*

Today I Pray

May I understand that there is no place in my recovery—or in my entire life as a chemically dependent person—for toxic hatred or lackadaisical indifference. One of the most important positive ideas that I must carry with me is that all humans, as the children of God, make up a loving brother- and sisterhood. May I find it hard to hate a brother.

Today I Will Remember

Hear the message. Don't judge the messenger.

Reflection for the Day

Adjusting myself to things as they are, and being able to love without trying to interfere with or control anyone else, however close to me—that's one of the important things I search for and can find in the Program. The learning is sometimes painful; however, the reward is life itself—full and serene. *Is the Program helping restore me to a sane and reasonable way of thinking, so I can handle my interpersonal relationships with love and understanding?*

Today I Pray

May I respect those that I love enough to set them free—to stop controlling, manipulating, scheming, bailing them out of trouble. May I love them enough to let them make their own mistakes and take responsibility for them May I learn to let go.

Today I Will Remember

Loving is letting go.

Reflection for the Day

Few of us are entirely free from a sense of guilt. We may feel guilty because of our words or actions, or for things left undone. We may even feel guilty because of irrational or false accusations by others. When I'm troubled by a gnawing feeling of guilt, obviously I can't put into my day all I'm capable of. So I must rid myself of guilt—not by pushing it aside, or ignoring it, but by identifying it and correcting the cause. *Have I finally begun to learn to "keep it simple..."?*

Today I Pray

May I learn not to let myself be "guilted," made to feel guilty when I don't consider that I am. Since I doubtless have the dregs of guilt left over from my behavior, I do not need the extra burden of unreasonable blame laid on me. I count on God to help me sort out and get rid of these twinges and pangs of guilt, which whether justified or not, need to be recognized and unloaded.

Today I Will Remember

The verdict of guilty is not for life.

Reflection for the Day

A friend in the Program taught me to look at excessive guilt in an entirely new way, suggesting that guilt was nothing but a sort of reverse pride. A decent regret for what has happened is fine, he said. But guilt, no. I've since learned that condemning ourselves for mistakes we've made is just as bad as condemning others for theirs. We're not really equipped to make judgments, not even of ourselves. *Do I still sometimes "beat myself to death" when I appear to be failing?*

Today I Pray

May I be wary of keeping my guilty role alive long after I should have left it behind. May I know the difference between regret and guilt. May I recognize that long-term guilt may imply an exaggerated idea of my own importance, as well as present self-righteousness. May God alone be my judge.

Today I Will Remember

Guilt may be pride in reverse.

Reflection for the Day

Some of us, new in the Program, couldn't resist telling anyone who would listen just how "terrible" we were. Just as we often exaggerated our modest accomplishments by pride, so we exaggerated our defects through guilt. Racing about and "confessing all," we somehow considered the widespread exposure of our sins to be true humility, considering it a great spiritual asset. Only as we grew in the Program did we realize that our theatrics and storytelling were merely forms of exhibitionism. And with that realization came the beginning of a certain amount of humility. *Am I starting to become aware that I'm not so important after all?*

Today I Pray

May I learn that there is a chasm of difference between real humility and the dramatic self-put-down. May I be confronted if I unconsciously demand center-stage to out-do and "out-drunk" others with my "adventure" stories. May I be cautious that the accounts of my addictive misdeeds do not take on the epic grandeur of heroic exploits.

Today I Will Remember

I will not star in my own drunkologue (or junkologue).

Reflection for the Day

When I least expect it, my keen addictive mind will try to divert me back toward my old ideas and old ways. My mind is expert, in fact, at planting and nourishing negative feelings within me—feelings such as envy, fear, anxiety, or guilt. The minute I spot any of these poisonous feelings rising up, I have to deal with them. If not, the more I think about them, the stronger they'll get; the stronger they get, the more I'll think about them—to the point of obsession. *When negative feelings arise, do I "name them, claim them, and dump them..."?*

Today I Pray

I should know—and may I never forget—that a sure way to let my feelings get the best of me is to pretend they aren't there. Like spoiled offspring, they act up when they are ignored. But also like offspring, they are here, they are mine, and I am responsible for them. May I learn to pay attention to my feelings, even if sometimes I would rather make believe they didn't belong to me.

Today I Will Remember

Name them, claim them, dump them.

Reflection for the Day

Guilt is a cunning weapon in the armory of the addictive person which continues to lurk patiently inside each of us. We can use the weapon against ourselves in many subtle ways; it can be deftly wielded, for example, in an attempt to convince us that the Program doesn't really work. I have to protect myself constantly against guilt and self-accusations concerning my past. If necessary, I must constantly "re-forgive" myself, accepting myself as a mixture of good as well as bad. *Am I striving for spiritual progress? Or will I settle for nothing less than the human impossibility of spiritual perfection?*

Today I Pray

May I look inside myself now and then for any slow-burning, leftover guilt which can, when I'm unwary, damage my purpose. May I stop kicking myself and pointing out my own imperfections—all those lesser qualities which detract from the ideal and "perfect" me. May I no longer try to be unreachably, inhumanly perfect, but just spiritually whole.

Today I Will Remember

I am human—part good, part not-so-good.

Reflection for the Day

Many of us have had difficulty ridding our-selves of the ravages of guilt. In my own case, during the early days in the Program, I either misunderstood certain of the Steps, or tried to apply them too quickly and too eagerly. The result was that I increased my feelings of guilt and worthlessness, rather than freeing myself as the Steps intend. Soon, though, I became at least willing to forgive myself, and I made a new beginning. I undertook all the soul-search-ing and cleansing Steps in our Program as they were intended to be taken, and not from a below-ground position of crippling hate and guilt. *Have I made amends to myself?*

Today I Pray

May I forgive myself, as God has forgiven me. May I know that if I am hanging on to an old satchel full of guilt, then I am not following the example God has shown me. If my Higher Power, who has demonstrated forgiveness by leading me to this healing place, can forgive me, then so can I. May I not begrudge myself what God has so generously offered.

Today I Will Remember

God forgives; so must I.

Reflection for the Day

I don't believe that the Program and Twelve Steps work because I read it in a book, or because I hear other people say so. I believe it because I see other people recovering and because I know that I, too, am recovering. No longer do I believe that I am "helpless and hopeless." When I see the change in other people and in myself, I *know* that the Program works. When a television reporter once asked the philosopher Jung if he believed in God, Jung replied slowly, "I don't believe, I know." *Do I know that the Program works?*

Today I Pray

Show me the happy endings, the mended lives, the reconstituted selves, the rebuilt bridges, so I will not have to accept on faith the fact that the Program works. May I see it working—for others and for me. May I be grateful for the documented reality of the Program's success. May this certainty help me find the faith I need to follow the Twelve Steps.

Today I Will Remember

The Program works.

Reflection for the Day

Somewhere along the line as we become more involved in the Program, we reach a sharp awareness of the growth-value of honesty and candor. When this happens, one of the first things we're able to admit is that our past behavior has been far from sane or even reasonable. As soon as we can make this admission—without shame or embarrassment—we find still another dimension of freedom. *In my gradual recovery, am I expectant that life will become ever richer and ever more serene?*

Today I Pray

May I know, even as I take that mighty First Step, which may be the first really honest move I have made in a long time, that honesty takes practice. My old, deluded, head-tripping self is as different from the honest self that I must become as night is from day. May I realize that it will take more than just one grey dawn to change me.

Today I Will Remember

Honesty takes practice.

Reflection for the Day

Learning how to live in peace, partnership, and brotherhood—with all men and women—is a fascinating and often very moving adventure. But each of us in the Program has found that we're not able to make much headway in our new adventure of living until we first take the time to make an accurate and unsparing survey of the human wreckage we've left in our wake. *Have I made a list of all persons I have harmed, as Step Eight suggests, and become willing to make amends to them all?*

Today I Pray

May God give me the honesty I need, not only to look inside myself and discover what is really there, but to see the ways that my sick and irresponsible behavior has affected those around me. May I understand that my addiction is not—as I used to think—a loner's disease, that, no matter how alone I felt, my lies and fabrications spread out around me in widening circles of hurt.

Today I Will Remember

Lies spread to infinity.

Reflection for the Day

The Ninth Step of the Program is: "Made direct amends to such people wherever possible, except when to do so would injure them or others." To make restitution for the wrongs we've done can be extremely difficult, to say the least; if nothing else, it deflates our egos and batters our pride. Yet that in itself is a reward, and such restitution can bring still greater rewards. When we go to a person and say we're sorry, the reaction is almost invariably positive. Courage is required, to be sure, but the results more than justify the action. *Have I done my best to make all the restitution possible?*

Today I Pray

May I count on my Higher Power to stop me if I start to crawl out from under my Ninth Step responsibility. May I feel that blessed, liberating wash of relief that goes with saying, out loud, to someone I have harmed, "I was wrong. I made mistakes. I am honestly sorry." May I not worry about cracking that brittle, cover-up crust of my ego, because the inside will be more mature.

Today I Will Remember

Restitution is blessed.

Reflection for the Day

Readiness to take the full consequences of our past acts, and to take responsibility for the well-being of others at the same time, is the very spirit of Step Nine. A casual apology, on the one hand, will rarely suffice in making amends to one we have harmed; a true change of attitude, in contrast, can do wonders to make up for past unkindnesses. If I've deprived anyone of any material thing, I'll acknowledge the debt and pay it as soon as I'm able. *Will I swallow my pride and make the first overtures toward reconciliation?*

Today I Pray

God, show me the best ways to make "direct amends." Sometimes simply admitting my mistakes may make it up to someone and unload my own simmering guilt. Other times restitution may take some creative thought. May I be wholly aware that I cannot take this Ninth Step unless I develop some caring, some real concern about how others feel, along with changes in my behavior.

Today I Will Remember

First I care, then I apologize.

Reflection for the Day

I believe today that I have a right to make spiritual progress. I have a right to be emotionally mature. I have a right to take pleasure in my own company, and that makes me more pleasant to be with. I also have a right to become willing—deeply willing, entirely willing—to make amends to all those I've harmed. Because I can now accept myself the way I am, I can accept other people the way they are—not entirely, but to a much greater degree than in the past. *Have I begun to make friends with God, and thus with myself?*

Today I Pray

May God show me that it's okay to like myself, even while trying to repair old wrongs and rebuild from splinters. May I keep telling myself that I am different, now, I have changed, I am a better and wiser and healthier person, I have made some good choices. As this "new person," may I find it easier to make atonements for what happened long ago and in another spiritual place. May those I have wronged also find it easier to accept my amends.

Today I Will Remember

It's okay to like myself.

Reflection for the Day

The Program teaches us that only one consideration should qualify our desire to completely disclose the damage we've done. And that's where a full revelation would seriously harm the one to whom we're making amends. Or, just as important, other people. We can hardly unload a detailed account of extramarital misadventures, for example, on the shoulders of an unsuspecting wife or husband. When we recklessly make the burdens of others heavier, such actions surely can't lighten our own burden. Sometimes, in that sense, "telling all" may be almost a self-indulgence for us. So in making amends, we should be tactful, sensible, considerate, and humble—without being servile. *As a child of God, do I stand on my feet and not crawl before anyone?*

Today I Pray

May God show me that self-hatred has no role in making amends to others. Neither has the play-acting of self-indulgence. I ask most humbly for my Higher Power's guidance as I strive to maintain a mature balance in interpersonal relations, even in the most casual or fragile ones.

Today I Will Remember

Making amends is mending.

Reflection for the Day

When we take the Ninth Step, we must be willing to be absolutely honest. Obviously, though, indiscriminate "absolute honesty" would blow the roof off many a house and entirely destroy some relationships. We must hold nothing back through deceit and pride; we may need to hold something back through discretion and consideration for others. Just when and how we tell the truth—or keep silent—can often reveal the difference between genuine integrity and none at all. *Am I grateful for the products of truth which, through the grace of Jesus, I have been privileged to receive?*

Today I Pray

May I have the wisdom to know the fine-line difference between tact and dishonesty. In my eagerness to make restitution, may I not be the charmer, the flatterer, or the crawler who insists, "You're so good, and I'm so bad." All are forms of dishonesty and hark back to the role-playing days of my active addiction. May I recognize them.

Today I Will Remember

Tact is honest selectivity.

Reflection for the Day

"Direct" is a key word in the Ninth Step. There are times, unfortunately, when many of us are hopeful that indirect amends will suffice, sparing us the pain and supposed humiliation of approaching people in person and telling them of our wrongs. This is evasion and will never give us a true sense of breaking with the wrongdoings of the past. It shows that we're still trying to defend something that isn't worth defending, hanging on to conduct that we ought to abandon. The usual reasons for sidestepping direct amends are pride and fear. *As I make amends to others, do I realize that the real, lasting benefits accrue to me?*

Today I Pray

May I be sure that the best reward for coming on straight as I try to repair my damages is, after all, my own. But may I avoid making amends purely for my own benefit—to be forgiven, to be reinstated, to flaunt the "new me." Ego-puffing and people-pleasing are not part of the real "new me." God save me from opportunism.

Today I Will Remember

No puffery or people-pleasing.

Reflection for the Day

The minute we think about a twisted or broken relationship with another person, our emotions go on the defensive. To avoid looking at the wrongs we've done another, we resentfully focus on the wrong he or she has done us. With a sense of triumph, we seize upon his or her slightest misbehavior as the perfect excuse for minimizing or forgetting our own. We have to remember that we're not the only ones plagued by sick emotions. Often, we're really dealing with fellow sufferers, including those whose woes we've increased. *If I'm about to ask forgiveness for myself, why shouldn't I start out by forgiving them?*

Today I Pray

When I blame or fault-find, may my Higher Power tell me to look under the rug for my own feeling of guilt, which I have neatly swept under it. May I recognize these behavior clues for what they really are.

Today I Will Remember

Resentment, inside-out, is guilt.

Reflection for the Day

Complacency is my enemy, easy to recognize in others, but difficult to identify and accept in myself. Complacency simply means being sure we're right—taking it for granted that we couldn't possibly be wrong. It means, moreover, judging others by what we think is right. It blocks out understanding and kindness, and seems to justify qualities in ourselves that we'd find wholly intolerable in others. *Do I tend to assume that my views are always correct?*

Today I Pray

God, please steer me past complacency, that state of being on dead center. When I am smug, I am no longer a seeker. If I assume I am always right, I am never on guard for my own mistakes, which can run away with me. Keep me teachable. Keep me growing, in heart, mind, and spirit.

Today I Will Remember

Complacency stunts growth.

Reflection for the Day

The primary purpose of the Program is freedom from addition; without that freedom we have nothing. But that doesn't mean I can say, for example, "Sobriety is my only concern. Except for my drinking, I'm really a super person, so give me sobriety, and I've got it made." If I delude myself with such specious nonsense, I'll make so little progress with my real life problems and responsibilities that I'll likely return to my addiction. That's why the Program's Twelfth Step urges us to "practice these principles in all our affairs." *Am I living just to be free of chemical dependence, or also to learn, to serve, and to love?*

Today I Pray

May I relish and be grateful for my sobriety, which is where all good things begin. But let me not stop at that and give up trying to understand myself, the nature of God and of humanity. Freedom from dependency is the first freedom. May I be certain that there are more to come—freedom from tight-mindedness, from the unrest of bottled-up feelings, from over-dependence on others, from a Godless existence. May the Program which answered my acute needs also answer my chronic ones.

Today I Will Remember

Sobriety is just a beginning.

Reflection for the Day

If ever I come to the complacent conclusion that I don't need the Program any longer, let me quickly remind myself that it can do far more than carry me through the anguish of living in the bondage of addiction. Let me further remind myself that I can make even greater strides in fulfilling myself, for the Program and the Twelve Steps is a philosophy—a way of life. *Will I ever outgrow my need for the Program?*

Today I Pray

May my Higher Power lead me through the Twelve Steps, not just once, but again and again, until they become the guiding principles of my existence. This is no quickie seminar on improving the quality of my life; this is my life, restored to me through Divine Power and the friendship of my fellow addicts, who, like me, are recovering in the best known way.

Today I Will Remember

Step by Step, from bondage to abundant life.

Reflection for the Day

How many of us would presume to announce, "Well, I'm sober and I'm happy. What more can I want, or do? I'm fine just the way I am." Experience has taught us that the price of such smug complacency—or, more politely, self-satisfaction—is an inevitable backslide, punctuated sooner or later by a very rude awakening. We have to grow, or else we deteriorate. For us, the status quo can only be for today, never for tomorrow. Change we must; we can't stand still. *Am I sometimes tempted to rest on my laurels?*

Today I Pray

May I look around me and see that all living things are either growing or deteriorating; nothing that is alive is static, life flows on. May I be carried along on that life-flow, unafraid of change, disengaging myself from the snags along the way which hold me back and interrupt my progress.

Today I Will Remember

Living is changing.

Reflection for the Day

Little by little, I'm getting over my tendency to procrastinate. I always used to put things off till tomorrow, and, of course, they never got done. Instead of "Do it now," my motto was "Tomorrow's another day." When I was loaded, I had grandiose plans; when I came down, I was too busy getting "well" to start anything. I've learned in the Program that it's far better to make a mistake once in a while than to never do anything at all. *Am I learning to do it now?*

Today I Pray

May God help me cure my habitual tardiness and "get me to the church on time." May I free myself of the self-imposed chaos of lifelong procrastination: library books overdue, appointments half-missed, assignments turned in late, schedules unmet, meals half-cooked. May I be sure if I, as an addict, led a disordered life, I, as a recovering addict, need order. May God give me the serenity I need to restore order and organization to my daily living.

Today I Will Remember

I will not be put off by my tendency to put off.

Reflection for the Day

Almost daily, I hear of seemingly mysterious coincidences in the lives of my friends in the Program. From time to time, I've experienced such "coincidences" myself: showing up at the right place at exactly the right time; phoning a friend who, unbeknownst to me, desperately needed that particular phone call at that precise moment; hearing "my story" at an unfamiliar meeting in a strange town. These days, I choose to believe that many of life's so-called "coincidences" are actually small miracles of God, who prefers to remain anonymous. *Am I continuingly grateful for the miracle of my recovery?*

Today I Pray

May my awareness of a Higher Power working in our lives grow in sensitivity as I learn, each day, of "coincidences" that defy statistics, illnesses that reverse their prognoses, hairbreadth escapes that defy death, chance meetings that change the course of a life. When the ununderstandable happens, may I perceive it as just another of God's frequent miracles. My own death-defying miracle is witness enough for me.

Today I Will Remember

My life is a miracle.

Reflection for the Day

Once we surrendered and came to the Program, many of us wondered what we would do with all that time on our hands. All the hours we'd previously spent planning, hiding, alibiing, getting loaded, coming down, getting "well," juggling our accounts—and all the rest—threatened to turn into empty chunks of time that somehow had to be filled. We needed new ways to use the energy previously absorbed by our addictions. We soon realized that substituting a new and different activity is far easier than just stopping the old activity and putting nothing in its place. *Am I redirecting my mind and energy?*

Today I Pray

I pray that, once free of the encumbrance of my addiction, I may turn to my Higher Power to discover for me how to fill my time constructively and creatively. May that same Power that makes human paths cross and links certain people to specific situations, lead me along good new roads into good new places.

Today I Will Remember

Happenstance may be more than chance.

Reflection for the Day

I've learned in the Program that the trick, for me, is not stopping drinking, but staying stopped and learning how not to *start* again. It was always relatively easy to stop, if only by sheer incapacity alone; God knows, I stopped literally thousands of times. To stay stopped, I've had to develop a positive program of action. I've had to learn to *live* sober, cultivating new habit patterns, new interests, and new attitudes. *Am I remaining flexible in my new life? Am I exercising my freedom to abandon limited objectives?*

Today I Pray

I pray that my new life will be filled with new patterns, new friends, new activities, new ways of looking at things. I need God's help to overhaul my lifestyle to include all the newness it must hold. I also need a few ideas of my own. May my independence from chemicals or compulsive behavior help me make my choices with an open mind and a clear, appraising eye.

Today I Will Remember

Stopping is starting.

Reflection for the Day

Fear may have originally brought some of us to the Program. In the beginning, fear alone may help some of us stay away from the first drink, pill, joint, or whatever. But a fearful state is hardly conducive to comfort and happiness— not for long. We have to find alternatives to fear to get us through those first empty hours, days, or even weeks. For most of us, the answer has been to become active in and around the Program. In no time, we feel that we truly belong; for the first time in a long time, we begin to feel a "part of" rather than "apart from." *Am I willing to take the initiative?*

Today I Pray

May God please help me find alternatives to fear—that watchdog of my earliest abstinence. I thank my Higher Power for directing me to a place where I can meet others who have experienced the same compulsions and fears. I am grateful for my feeling of belonging.

Today I Will Remember

I am "a part of," not "apart from."

Reflection for the Day

During our days of active addiction, many of us displayed almost dazzlingly fertile powers of imagination. In no time at all, we could dream up more reasons—or *excuses*—for pursuing our addictions than most people use for all other purposes in their entire lives. When we first come to the Program, our once-imaginative minds seem to become lethargic and even numb. "Now what do I do?" many of us wonder. Gradually, however, the lethargy disappears. We begin learning to live and become turned on to life in ways that we never dreamed possible. *Am I finding that I can now enjoy activities that I wouldn't even consider in the old days?*

Today I Pray

May God give me a new surge of energy directed toward "turning on to life" rather than making excuses for not handling my responsibilities. May my Higher Power allow my out-of-order imagination to be restored—not to the buzzing overactivity of my compulsive days, but to a healthy openness to life's boundless possibilities.

Today I Will Remember

Turn on to life.

Reflection for the Day

Change is a part of the flow of life. Sometimes we're frustrated because change seems slow in coming. Sometimes, too, we're resistant to a change that seems to have been thrust upon us. We must remember that change, in and of itself, neither binds us nor frees us. Only our attitude toward change binds or frees. As we learn to flow with the stream of life, praying for guidance about any change that presents itself—praying, also, for guidance if we want to make a change and none seems in view—we become willing. *Am I willing to let God take charge, directing me in the changes I should make and the actions I should take?*

Today I Pray

When change comes too fast—or not fast enough—for me, I pray I can adjust accordingly to make use of the freedom the Program offers to me. I pray for the guidance of my Higher Power when change presents itself—or when it doesn't and I wish it would. May I listen for direction from that Power.

Today I Will Remember

God is in charge.

Reflection for the Day

It's time for me to start being responsible for my own actions. It's time for me to be willing to take some chances. If my new life in the Program is valid and right, as I truly believe, then surely it can stand the test of exposure to real-life situations and problems. So I won't be afraid to be human and, if necessary, to some-times fall on my face in the process of living. Living is what the Program is all about. And living entails sharing, accepting, giving—inter-acting with other people. Now is the time for me to put my faith into action. *Have I begun to practice what I preach by putting my new thoughts and ideas into action?*

Today I Pray

May the Program, with God's help, give me a chance to live a steady, creative outreaching life, so that I may share with others what has been given to me. May I realize on this Declaration of Independence Day that I, too, have a celebration of freedom—freedom from my addiction.

Today I Will Remember

To celebrate my personal freedom.

Reflection for the Day

I am free to be, to do, to accept, to reject. I am free to be the wise, loving, kind, and patient person I want to be. I'm free to do that which I consider wise—that which will in no way harm or hinder another person. I'm free to do that which will lead me into paths of peace and satisfaction. I'm free to decide for or against, to say no and to say yes. I'm free to live life in a productive way and to contribute what I have to give to life. *Am I coming to believe that I'm free to be the best self I'm able to be?*

Today I Pray

Let the freedom I am now experiencing continue to flow through my life into productiveness, into the conviction of life's goodness I have always wanted to share. May I accept this freedom with God's blessing—and use it wisely.

Today I Will Remember

Let freedom ring true.

Reflection for the Day

Some people in the Program don't feel that they can do the things they want to do. They doubt their own ability. But actually, every person has untapped ability. We're children of God, which should give us a strong clue as to the *infinite* nature of our ability. As spiritual beings, we're unlimited. True, we may find it easier to accept this as true of some person who shines in a particular field. I may compare my own accomplishments with another's and feel discouraged. But the only comparison I need make or should make is with myself. *Am I a better, more productive person today?*

Today I Pray

May I realize that I am a child of God. And His loving-parent promise to give me what I need, not what I might want, is His way of teaching me to be what I am, not what I dreamed I should be. As a spiritual being, I can truly become a productive person, perhaps even do some of the things I once felt unable to do without the aid of props—drinks, pills, excesses of food, which lulled me into false confidence.

Today I Will Remember

To compare me with the old me.

Reflection for the Day

What wonderful things could happen in my life if I could get rid of my natural impulse to justify my actions. Is honesty so deeply repressed under layers of guilt that I can't release it to understand my motives? Being honest with ourselves isn't easy. It's difficult to search out why I had this or that impulse and, more importantly, why I acted upon it. Nothing makes us feel so vulnerable as to give up the crutch of "the alibi," yet my willingness to be vulnerable will go a long way toward helping me grow in the Program. *Am I becoming more aware that self-deception multiplies my problems?*

Today I Pray

May God remove my urge to make excuses. Help me to face up to the realities that surface when I am honest with myself. Help me to know, as certainly as day follows sunrise, that my difficulties will be lessened if I can only trust His will.

Today I Will Remember

I will be willing to do God's will.

Reflection for the Day

When we speak with a friend in the Program, we shouldn't hesitate to remind him or her of our need for privacy. Intimate communication is normally so free and easy among us that even a friend or sponsor may sometimes forget when we expect him to remain silent. Such "privileged communications" have important advantages. For one thing, we find in them the perfect opportunity to be as honest as we know how to be. For another, we don't have to worry about the possibility of injury to other people, nor the fear of ridicule or condemnation. At the same time, we have the best possible chance to spot self-deception. *Am I trustworthy to those who trust me?*

Today I Pray

I pray for God's assistance in making me a trusted confidant. I need to be a person others will be willing to share with. I need to be an open receiver, not just a transmitter. Today I pray for a large portion of tried-and-trueness, so that I may be a better and more receptive friend to those who choose to confide in me.

Today I Will Remember

Be a receiver.

Reflection for the Day

When we make only superficial changes in ourselves, and give only lip service to the Program, our progress is slow and the likelihood of relapse great. Our regeneration must take the form of a true spiritual rebirth. It must go very deep, with each character flaw replaced by a new and positive quality. *Am I being completely honest with myself in uncovering the faults which hamper my spiritual growth? Am I beginning to replace them with positive qualities?*

Today I Pray

May God's protective hand lead me out of the darkness of my deepest fear—that I could return to being what I do not want to be. Please, God, give me courage to make an honest appraisal of myself. Please help me cultivate my positive qualities and begin to be free of my fears.

Today I Will Remember

I must be reborn in the Spirit.

Reflection for the Day

The Program is a road, not a resting place. Before we came to the Program—and, for some of us, many times afterward—most of us looked for answers to our living problems in religion, philosophy, psychology, self-help groups, and so on. Invariably, these fields held forth the goals that were precisely what we wanted; they offered freedom, calm, confidence, and joy. But there was one major loophole: they never gave us a workable method of getting there. They never told us how to get from where we were to where we were supposed to be. *Do I truly believe that I can find everything that I need and really want through the Twelve Steps?*

Today I Pray

May I know that, once through the Twelve Steps, I am not on a plane surface. For life is not a flat field, but a slope upward. And those flights of steps must be taken over and over and remembered. May I be sure that, once I have made them totally familiar to me, they will take me anywhere I want to go.

Today I Will Remember

The Steps are a road, not a resting place.

Reflection for the Day

Someone once defined the ego as "the sum total of false ideas about myself." Persistent reworking of the Twelve Steps enables me gradually to strip away my false ideas about myself. This permits nearly imperceptible but steady growth in my understanding of the truth about myself. And this, in turn, leads to a growing understanding of God and other human beings. *Do I strive for self-honesty, promptly admitting when I'm wrong?*

Today I Pray

God, teach me understanding; teach me to know truth when I meet it; teach me the importance of self-honesty, so that I may be able to say, sincerely, "I was wrong," along with, "I am sorry." Teach me that there is such a thing as a "healthy ego" which does not require that feelings be medicated by mood-alterers. May I—slowly, on my tightrope—move toward the ideal of balance, so I can do away with the nets of falsehood and compulsion.

Today I Will Remember

To keep my balance.

Reflection for the Day

In many respects, the fellowship of the Program is like a reasonably happy cruise ship or, in time of trouble, like a convoy. But in the long run each of us must chart his or her own course through life. When the seas are smooth, we may become careless. By neglecting Step Ten, we may get out of the habit of checking our position. If we're mindful of Step Ten, however, then we rarely go so far wrong that we can't make a few corrections and get back on course again. *Do I realize that regular practice of Step Ten can help to bring me into a happier frame of mind and into serenity?*

Today I Pray

May Step Ten be the sextant by which I read my whereabouts at sea, so that I can correct my course, rechart it as I am heading for shallow places. May I keep in mind that, if it weren't for an all-knowing Captain and the vigilance of my fellow crew members, this ship could be adrift and I could easily panic.

Today I Will Remember

To steer by a steady star.

Reflection for the Day

These days, I go to meetings to listen for the similarities between myself and others in the Program—not the differences. And when I look for the similarities, it's amazing how many I find, particularly in the area of feelings. Today I go to meetings thinking that I'm here not because of anyone else's addictions, but because of mine and, most importantly, what my addiction did to my spirit and body. I'm here because there's no way I can stay free of my addiction by myself. I need the Program and my Higher Power. *Am I becoming less harsh in my judgment of others?*

Today I Pray

May I stay alert as I listen, just one more time, to Jack or Jill or Fred or Sam or Martha go through his or her tale of woe or wail. May I find, when I listen with the wholehearted attention I want to be able to give, that each has something to offer me to add to my own life-tale. May I be struck once again by our samenesses. May each sameness draw us nearer to each other's needs.

Today I Will Remember

In sameness, there is strength.

Reflection for the Day

Conditioned as we are by our old ideas and old ways of living, it's understandable that we tend to resist certain suggestions made to us when we first come to the Program. If that's the case, there's no need to *permanently* reject such suggestions; it's better, we've found, just temporarily to set them aside. The point is, there's no hard-and-fast "right" way or "wrong" way. Each of us uses what's best for himself or herself at a particular time, keeping an open mind about other kinds of help we may find valuable at another time. *Am I trying to remain open-minded?*

Today I Pray

May I be enlightened about the real meaning of an open mind, aware that my one-time definition of "open-minded" as "broad-minded" doesn't seem to fit here. May I constantly keep my mind open to the suggestions of the solid many who came into the Program before me. What has worked for them may work for me, no matter how far-fetched or how obvious it may be.

Today I Will Remember

Only an open mind can be healed.

Reflection for the Day

Faced with almost certain destruction by our addictions, we eventually had no choice but to become open-minded on spiritual matters. In that sense, the chemicals and drugs we used were potent persuaders; they finally whipped us into a state of reasonableness. We came to learn that when we stubbornly close the doors on our minds, we're locking out far more than we're locking in. *Do I immediately reject new ideas? Or do I patiently strive to change my old way of living?*

Today I Pray

May I keep an open mind especially on spiritual matters, remembering that "spiritual" is a bigger word than "religious." (I was born of the Spirit, but I was taught religion.) May I remember that a locked mind is a symptom of my addiction and an open mind is essential to my recovery.

Today I Will Remember

If I lock more out than I lock in, what am I protecting?

Reflection for the Day

Long experience has proven that the Program and Twelve Steps will work for any person who approaches them with an open mind. We have to remember that we can't expect miracles overnight; after all, it took years to create the situation in which we find ourselves today. I'll try to be less hasty in drawing judgmental conclusions. I'll hang on to the expectation that the Program can change my entire life as long as I give it a chance. *Have I begun to realize that my ultimate contentment doesn't depend on having things work out my way?*

Today I Pray

I pray for a more receptive attitude; for a little more patience; a little less haste and more humility in my judgments. May I always understand that change will come—it will all happen—if I will listen for God's will. God grant me perserverance, for sometimes I must wait a while for the Program's Steps to take effect.

Today I Will Remember

Patience.

Reflection for the Day

For my own good, I'll go to meetings and participate in discussions with an open mind that's ready to receive and accept new ideas. For my own peace of mind and comfort, I'll determinedly try to apply those new ideas to my own life. I'll remember that the Program offers me the instruction and support I can't find elsewhere. I'll seek out others who understand my problems, and I'll accept their guidance in matters which cause me discomfort and confusion. *Will I try to be willing to listen—and to share?*

Today I Pray

Thank you, God, for bringing the Program into my life, and with it a better understanding of Divine Power. Help me to remember that attendance and attentiveness at meetings are all-important to continuing in this happily discovered way of life. May I listen and share with honesty, open-mindedness, and willingness.

Today I Will Remember

Here's HOW: Honesty, Open-mindedness, Willingness.

Reflection for the Day

Very few of us know what we really want, and none of us knows what is best for us. That knowledge is in the hands of God. This is a fact I must ultimately accept, in spite of my rebelliousness and stubborn resistance. From this day forward, I'll limit my prayers to requests for guidance, an open mind to receive it, and the strength to act upon it. To the best of my capability, I'll defer all decisions until my contact with my Higher Power has made it seemingly apparent that the decisions are right for me. *Do I "bargain" with my Higher Power, assuming that I know what's best for me?*

Today I Pray

May I not try to make pacts with my Higher Power. Instead, may I be a vessel, open to whatever inspiration God wishes to pour into me. I pray that I will remember that God's decisions are better for me than my own fumbling plans, and that they will come to me at the times I need them.

Today I Will Remember

I will not bargain with God.

Reflection for the Day

Many of us come to the Program professing that we're agnostic or atheistic. As someone once put it, our will to *dis*believe is so strong that we prefer a date with the undertaker to an experimental and open-minded search for a Higher Power. Fortunately for those of us with closed minds, the constructive forces in the Program almost always overcome our obstinacy. Before long, we discover the bountiful world of faith and trust. It was there all along, but we lacked the willingness and open-mindedness to accept it. *Does obstinacy still sometimes blind me to the power for good that resides in faith?*

Today I Pray

I want to thank my Higher Power for this opportunity to open my mind; to learn again about faith and trust; to realize that my wanderings did not change God's place within me or God's loving concern for me. May I know that it was my own doing that I lost faith. Thank God for another chance to believe.

Today I Will Remember

Discard the will to disbelieve.

Reflection for the Day

"It is the privilege of wisdom to listen," Oliver Wendell Holmes once wrote. If I try as hard as I can to cultivate the art of listening—uncritically and without making premature judgments—chances are great that I'll progress more rapidly in my recovery. If I try as hard as I can to listen to the feelings and thoughts expressed—rather than to the "speaker"—I may be blessed with an unexpectedly helpful idea. The essential quality of good listening is humility, which reflects the fact that God's voice speaks to us even through the least and most inarticulate of His children. *Does a holier-than-thou attitude sometimes close my mind to the shared suggestions of others?*

Today I Pray

May my Higher Power keep me from being "holier-than-thou" with anyone whose manner or language or opposite point of view or apparent lack of knowledge turns me off to what they are saying. May I be listening always for the voice of God, which can be heard through the speech of any one of us.

Today I Will Remember

Hear the speech, not the speaker.

Reflection for the Day

When we're faced with some condition or situation not to our liking, how can we have faith that all things are working together for good? Perhaps we have to ask ourselves just what is faith. Faith has its foundation in truth and love. We can have faith, if we so choose, no matter what the situation. And, if we so choose, we can expect ultimate good to come forth. *Have I made my choice?*

Today I Pray

May I be grateful for my God-given ability to make a choice. Out of this gratitude and my sense of the nearness of God, I have chosen faith. May the faith, as my chosen way, become strong enough to move mountains, strong enough to keep me free of my compulsion, mighty enough to hold back the tide of temptations which threaten me, optimistic enough to look past my present pain to ultimate good.

Today I Will Remember

With faith, nothing is impossible.

Reflection for the Day

The Program has taught me that the essence of all growth for me is a willingness to change for the better. Following that, I must have further willingness to shoulder whatever responsibility this entails, and to take courageously every action that is required.

> "I am and know and will;
> I am knowing and willing;
> I know myself to be and to will;
> I will to be and to know."

> —Saint Augustine

Is willingness a key ingredient of my life and the way I work the Program?

Today I Pray

I pray for willingness to do what I can, willingness to be what I can be and—what is sometimes hardest—willingness to be what I am. I pray, too, for energies to carry out my willingness in all that I do, so that I may grow in the ways of God and practice the principles of the Program in all my affairs.

Today I will Remember

"I am and know and will."

Reflection for the Day

Today I'll try to settle for less than I wish were possible, and be willing to not only accept it but to appreciate it. Today, I'll not expect too much of anyone—especially myself. I'll try to remember that contentment comes from gratefully accepting the good that comes to us, and not from being furious at life because it's not "better." *Do I realize the difference between resignation and realistic acceptance?*

Today I Pray

May I not set my sights unrealistically high, expect too much. May I look backwards long enough to see that my self-set, impossible goals were the trappings of my addiction; too often I ended up halfway there, confronted by my own failure. Those "foiled-again," "I've-failed-again" feelings became monumental excuses to give in to my compulsion, which blanketed my miseries. May I avoid that sick old pattern. May I be realistic.

Today I Will Remember

Good is good enough.

Reflection for the Day

How, exactly, can a person turn his own will and his own life over to the care of a Power greater than himself? All that's needed is a beginning, no matter how small. The minute we put the key of willingness in the lock, the latch springs open. Then the door itself starts to open, perhaps ever so slightly; in time we find that we can always open it wider. Self-will may slam the door shut again, and it often does. But the door can always be reopened, time and time again if necessary, so long as we use our key of willingness. *Have I reaffirmed my decision to turn my will and my life over to the care of God as I understand Him?*

Today I Pray

May I reaffirm my decision to turn my will and my life over to a Higher Power. May my faith be staunch enough to keep me knowing that there is, indeed, a power greater than I am. May I avail myself of that Power simply by being willing to "Walk humble with my Lord."

Today I Will Remember

Self-will minus self equals will.

Reflection for the Day

The slogans of the Program are seemingly clear and simple. Yet they may still have different meanings for different people, according to their own experiences and reactions to the words and ideas. Take, for example, the slogan, *Let Go and Let God*. For some people, it may suggest that all we have to do is sidestep the challenges that confront us and, somehow, God will do all the work. We must remember that God gives us free will, intelligence, and good senses—it is clearly His intention that we use these gifts. If I'm receptive, God will make His will known to me step by step, but I must carry it out. *Do I sometimes act as if surrender to God's will is a passport to inertia?*

Today I Pray

May my "passport" be stamped with "action." May my travels be motivated by challenges I can readily recognize as things to do, not things to watch. I pray that I may make the most of my gifts from God, of talents that I am aware of and some I have yet to discover. May I not "let go" and give up but keep on learning, growing, doing, serving, praying, carrying out the will of God as I understand it.

Today I Will Remember

God meant me to make the most of myself.

Reflection for the Day

Now that I avail myself of the letters H-O-W suggested by friends in the Program—Honesty, Open-Mindedness, Willingness—I see things differently. In ways that I couldn't have predicted and surely never expected, I've come to see things quite differently from the person I was before coming to the Program. I feel good most days. I seldom feel bad, and never for long. Certainly never as bad as I used to feel all of the time. *Is my worst day now infinitely better than my best day previously?*

Today I Pray

May I remember today to say "thank you" to my Higher Power, to my friends in the group and to the whole, vast fellowship of recovering persons for making me know that things do get better. I give thanks, too, for those verbal boosters, the tags and slogans which have so often burst into my brain at exactly the moments when they were needed, redefining my purpose, restoring my patience, reminding me of my God.

Today I Will Remember

How it was.

Reflection for the Day

Over and over, I see that those who make the best and steadiest progress in the Program are those who readily accept the help of a Higher Power. Once they can do that, it's easier for them to get out of their own way. Their problems then seem to resolve themselves in a way that is beyond human understanding. *Do I realize that the effectiveness with which I use the consciousness of God in my daily life depends not on Him, but on me?*

Today I Pray

May I know that my recovery and growth depends on my being in touch with my Higher Power, not just once in a while, but always. It means turning to that Power several times a day to ask for strength and knowledge of His will. When I understand that my own life is part of a Higher Plan, I will be less apt to trip and fall, head off in the wrong direction, or just to sit tight and let life pass me by.

Today I Will Remember

To be God-conscious.

Reflection for the Day

We learn the value of meditation in the Program. As the beginning of the Eleventh Step suggests, we seek through prayer and meditation to improve our conscious contact with God as we understand Him. One of the great values of meditation is that it clears the mind. And as the mind becomes clearer, it becomes more capable and willing to acknowledge the truth. Less pain is required to force honest recognition of defects and their results. The real needs of the whole person are revealed. *Are prayer and meditation a regular part of my daily living?*

Today I Pray

May God's truths be revealed to me through meditation and these small prayers, through contact with my group which keeps me mindful of my need to clear my mind with daily meditation. For only an uncluttered mind can receive God; only a mind cleansed of self-interest can acknowledge the truth.

Today I Will Remember

Meditation is a mind-cleanser.

Reflection for the Day

The feeling of self-pity, which we've all suffered at one time or another, is one of the ugliest emotions we can experience. We don't even relish the thought of admitting to others that we're awash in self-pity. We hate being told that it shows; we quickly argue that we're feel-ing *another* emotion instead; we go so far as to "cleverly" hide from ourselves the fact that we're going through a siege of "poor-meism." By the same token, in a split-second we can eas-ily find several dozen "valid" reasons for feeling sorry for ourselves. *Do I sometimes enjoy rubbing salt into my own wounds?*

Today I Pray

May I recognize the emotions I am feeling for what they are. If I am unable to point them out to myself, may I count on others who know what it's like to be a feelings-stuffer. May I stay in touch with my feelings by staying in touch with my Higher Power and with the others in my group.

Today I will Remember

Stay in touch.

Reflection for the Day

When we first come to the Program, the most
common variety of self-pity begins: "Poor me!
Why can't I (*fill in your own addiction*) like everybody else? Why me?" Such bemoaning, if
allowed to persist, is a surefire invitation for a
long walk off a short pier—right back to the
mess we were in before we came to the
Program. When we stick around the Program
for a while, we discover that it's not just "me"
at all; we become involved with people, from all
walks of life, who are in exactly the same boat.
*Am I losing interest in my comfortably familiar
"pity pot"?*

Today I Pray

When self-pity has me droopy and inert, may I
look up, look around, and perk up. Self-pity,
God wills, vanishes in the light of other people's shared troubles. May I always wish for
friends honest enough to confront me if they
see me digging my way back down into my old
pity pit.

Today I Will Remember

Turn self-involvement into involvement.

Reflection for the Day

One of the most serious consequences of the me-me-me syndrome is that we lose touch with practically everyone around us—not to mention reality itself. The essence of self-pity is total self-absorption, and it feeds on itself. Rather than ignore such an emotional state—or deny that we're in it—we need to pull out of our self-absorption, stand back, and take a good honest look at ourselves. Once we recognize self-pity for what it is, we can begin to do something about it. *Am I living in the problem rather than the answer?*

Today I Pray

I pray that my preoccupation with self, which is wound up tight as a Maypole, may unwind itself and let its streamers fly again for others to catch and hold. May the thin, familiar wail of me-me-me become a chorus of us-us-us, as we in the fellowship pick apart our self-fulness and look at it together.

Today I Will Remember

Change me-me-me to us-us-us.

Reflection for the Day

Self-pity is one of the most miserable and con-
suming defects I know. Because of its inter-
minable demands for attention and sympathy,
my self-pity cuts off my communication with
others, especially communication with my
Higher Power. When I look at it that way, I
realize that self-pity limits my spiritual progress.
It's also a very real form of martyrdom, which is
a luxury I simply can't afford. The remedy, I've
been taught, is to have a hard look at myself
and a still harder one at the Program's Twelve
Steps to recovery. *Do I ask my Higher Power to
relieve me of the bondage of self?*

Today I Pray

May I know from observation that self-pitiers
get almost no pity from anyone else.
Nobody—not even God—can fill their outsized
demands for sympathy. May I recognize my
own unsavory feeling of self-pity when it creeps
in to rob me of my serenity. May God keep me
wary of its sneakiness.

Today I Will Remember

My captor is my self.

Reflection for the Day

When I begin to compare my life with the lives of others, I've begun to move toward the edge of the murky swamp of self-pity. On the other hand, if I feel that what I'm doing is right and good, I won't be so dependent on the admiration or approval of others. Applause is well and good, but it's not essential to my inner contentment. I'm in the Program to get rid of self-pity, not to increase its power to destroy me. *Am I learning how others have dealt with their problems so I can apply these lessons to my own life?*

Today I Pray

God, make me ever mindful of where I came from and the new goals I have been encouraged to set. May I stop playing to an audience for their approval, since I am fully capable of admiring or applauding myself if I feel I have earned it. Help me make myself attractive from the inside, so it will show through, rather than adorning the outside for effect. I am tired of stage make-up and costumes, God; help me be myself.

Today I Will Remember

Has anyone seen ME?

Reflection for the Day

The Twelve Steps were designed specifically for people like us—as a short cut to God. The Steps are very much like strong medicine which can heal us of the sickness of despair, frustration, and self-pity. Yet we're sometimes unwilling to use the Steps. Why? Perhaps because we have a deep-down desire for martyrdom. Consciously and intellectually, we think we want help; on a gut level, though, some hidden sense of guilt makes us crave punishment more than relief from our ills. *Can I try to be cheerful when everything seems to be leading me to despair? Do I realize that despair is very often a mask for self-pity?*

Today I Pray

May I pull out the secret guilt inside that makes me want to punish myself. May I probe my despair and discover whether it is really an importer—self-pity with a mask on. Now that I know that the Twelve Steps can bring relief, may I please use them instead of wallowing in my discomforts.

Today I Will Remember

The Twelve Steps are God's stairway.

Reflection for the Day

One of the best ways to get out of the self-pity trap is to do some "instant bookkeeping." For every entry of misery on the debit side of our ledger, we can surely find a blessing to mark on the credit side: the health we enjoy, the illnesses we *don't* have, the friends who love us and who allow us to love them, a clean and sober twenty-four hours, a good day's work. If we but try, we can easily list a whole string of credits that will far outweigh the debit entries which cause self-pity. *Is my emotional balance on the credit side today?*

Today I Pray

May I learn to sort out my debits and credits, and add it all up. May I list my several blessings on the credit side. May my ledger show me, when all is totaled, a fat fund of good things to draw on.

Today I Will Remember

I have blessings in my savings.

Reflection for the Day

Among the important things we learn in the
Program is to be good to ourselves. For so
many of us, though, this is a surprisingly difficult thing to do. Some of us relish our suffering
so much that we balloon each happening to
enormous proportions in the reliving and
telling. Self-pitiers are drawn to martyrdom as
if by a powerful magnet—until the joys of
serenity and contentment come to them
through the Program and Twelve Steps. *Am I
gradually learning to be good to myself?*

Today I Pray

May I learn to forgive myself. I have
asked—and received—forgiveness from God
and from others, so why is it so hard to forgive
myself? Why do I still magnify my suffering?
Why do I go on licking my emotional wounds?
May I follow God's forgiving example, get on
with the Program, and learn to be good to
myself.

Today I Will Remember

Martyrdom; martyr dumb.

Reflection for the Day

Sometimes through bitter experience and painful lessons, we learn in our fellowship with others in the Program that resentment is our number one enemy. It destroys more of us than anything else. From resentment stem all forms of spiritual disease, for we've been not only mentally and physically ill, but spiritually ill as well. As we recover and as our spiritual illness is remedied, we become well physically and mentally. *Am I aware that few things are more bitter than to feel bitter? Do I see that my venom is more poisonous to me than to my victim?*

Today I Pray

I ask for help in removing the pile of resentments I have collected. May I learn that resentments are play-actors, too; they may be fears—losing a job, a love, an opportunity; they may be hurts or guilty feelings. May I know that God is my healer. May I admit my need.

Today I Will Remember

Resentments are rubbish; haul them away.

Reflection for the Day

What can we do about our resentments? Fruitful experience has shown that the best thing to do is to write them down, listing people, institutions, or principles with which we're angry or resentful. When I write down my resentments and then ask myself why I'm resentful, I've discovered that in most cases my self-esteem, my finances, my ambitions, or my personal relationships have been hurt or threatened. *Will I ever learn that the worst thing about my resentments is my endless rehearsal of the acts of retribution?*

Today I Pray

May God help me find a way to get rid of my resentments. May I give up the hours spent making up little playlets, in which I star as the angry man or woman cleverly shouting down the person who has threatened me. Since these dramas are never produced, may I instead list my resentful feelings and look at the why's behind each one. May this be a way of shelving them.

Today I Will Remember

Resentments cause violence: resentments cause illness in non-violent people.

Reflection for the Day

As a recovering alcoholic, I have to remind myself that no amount of social acceptance of resentments will take the poison out of them. In a way, the problem of resentments is very much like the drinking problem. Alcohol is never safe for me, no matter who is offering it. I've attended cocktail receptions for worthy causes, often in a convivial atmosphere that makes drinking seem almost harmless. *Just as I politely but adamantly decline alcohol under any conditions, will I also refuse to accept resentments—no matter who is serving them?*

Today I Pray

When anger, hurt, fear, or guilt—to be socially acceptable—put on their polite, party manners, dress up as resentment, and come in the side door, may I not hobnob with them. These emotions, disguised as they are, can be as full of trickery as the chemicals themselves.

Today I Will Remember

Keep an eye on the side door.

Reflection for the Day

On numerous occasions, I've found that there's a strong connection between my fears and my resentments. I secretly fear that I'm inadequate; for example, I'll tend to resent deeply anybody whose actions or words expose my imagined inadequacy. But it's usually too painful to admit that my own fears and doubts about myself are the cause of my resentments. It's a lot easier to pin the blame on someone else's "bad behavior" or "selfish motives"—and use that as the justificaton for my resentments. *Do I realize that by resenting someone, I allow that person to live rent-free in my head?*

Today I Pray

May God help me overcome my feelings of inadequacy. May I know that when I consistently regard myself as a notch or two lower than the next person, I am not giving due credit to my Creator, who has given each of us a special and worthwhile blend of talents. I am, in fact, grumbling about God's Divine Plan. May I look behind my trash-pile of resentments for my own self-doubt.

Today I Will Remember

As I build myself up, I tear down my resentments.

Reflection for the Day

We've been our own worst enemies most of our lives, and we've often injured ourselves seriously as a result of a "justified" resentment over a slight wrong. Doubtless there are many causes for resentment in the world, most of them providing "justification." But we can never begin to settle all the world's grievances or even arrange things so as to please everybody. If we've been treated unjustly by others or simply by life itself, we can avoid compounding the difficulty by completely forgiving the persons involved and abandoning the destructive habit of reviewing our hurts and humiliations. *Can I believe that yesterday's hurt is today's understanding, rewoven into tomorrow's love?*

Today I Pray

Whether I am unjustly treated or just *think* I am, may I try not to be a resentful person, stewing over past injuries. Once I have identified the root emotion behind my resentment, may I be big enough to forgive the person involved and wise enough to forget the whole thing.

Today I Will Remember

Not all injustice can be fixed.

Reflection for the Day

When I dwell on piddling things that annoy me—and they sprout resentments that grow bigger and bigger like weeds—I forget how I could be stretching my world and broadening my outlook. For me, that's an ideal way to shrink troubles down to their real size. When somebody or something is causing me trouble, I should try to see the incident in relation to the rest of my life—especially the part that's good and for which I should be grateful. *Am I willing to waste my life worrying about trifles which drain my spiritual energy?*

Today I Pray

May God keep me from worrying unduly about small things. May He, instead, open my eyes to the grandeur of His universe and the ceaseless wonders of His earth. May He grant me the breadth of vision which can reduce any small, fretful concern of mine to the size of a fly on a cathedral window.

Today I Will Remember

Microscopic irritations can ruin my vision.

Reflection for the Day

"Quiet minds cannot be perplexed or frightened," wrote Robert Louis Stevenson, "but go on in fortune or misfortune at their own private pace, like a clock during a thunderstorm." In the Program we hear many warnings against harboring resentments, and rare is the person who doesn't occasionally yield to resentment when he feels wronged. We must remember that we have no room for resentment in our new way of life. Rather than exhausting myself by fighting resentment with grim determination, I can reason it out of existence by uncovering its cause with a quiet mind. *Will I try to believe that the best antidote for resentment is the continual expression of gratitude?*

Today I Pray

Praise God from whom all blessings flow. Praise God for our human sensitivity which, although it can feel the smallest, pin-prick hurts, can also feel the warmth of a smile. Praise God for our human insight which can peel the wraps from our resentments and expose them for what they are.

Today I Will Remember

I am grateful for feelings.

Reflection for the Day

The Program's Fourth Step suggests that we make a searching and fearless moral inventory of ourselves. For some of us, no challenge seems more formidable; there's nothing more difficult than facing ourselves as we really are. We flee from one wrong-doing after another as they catch up with us, forever making excuses, pleading always that our virtues in other areas far outweigh our flaws. Yet once we become willing to look squarely and self-searchingly at ourselves, we're then able to illuminate the dark and negative side of our natures with new vision, action, and grace. *Am I willing to open my eyes and step out into the sunlight?*

Today I Pray

May my Higher Power stop me in my tracks if I am running away from myself. For I will never overcome my misdeeds, or the flaws in my character which brought them about, by letting them chase me. May I slow down and turn to face them with the most trusty weapon I know—truth.

Today I Will Remember

I will not be a fugitive from myself.

Reflection for the Day

Step Four enables me to see myself as I really am—my characteristics, motives, attitudes, and actions. I'm taught in the Program to search out my mistakes resolutely. Where, for example, had I been selfish, dishonest, self-seeking, and frightened? I'm taught, also, that my deeply rooted habit of self-justification may tempt me to "explain away" each fault as I uncover it, blaming others for my own short-comings. *Will I believe that personal honesty can achieve what superior knowledge often cannot?*

Today I Pray

May I not make the Fourth Step a once-over-lightly, let's-get-it-over-with exercise in self-appraisal. May I know that, once I take this Step, I must review it again many times until it becomes, like the other eleven, a way of life for me. May I protect the value of my Fourth Step from my old habit of head-tripping and buck-passing my way out of responsibility.

Today I Will Remember

Personal honesty paves the way to recovery.

Reflection for the Day

It's often said that you can't tell a book by its cover. For many of us, our "covers" or surface records haven't looked all that bad; it seemed at first, that making an inventory would be "a breeze." As we proceeded, we were dismayed to discover that our "covers" were relatively blemish-free only because we'd deeply buried our defects beneath layers of self-deception. For that reason, self-searching can be a long-term process; it must go on for as long as we remain blind to the flaws that ambushed us into addiction and misery. *Will I try to face myself as I am, correcting whatever is keeping me from growing into the person I want to be?*

Today I Pray

May God aid me in my soul-searching, because I have hidden my faults neatly from friends, family, and especially myself. If I feel "more sinned against, than sinning," may I take it as a clue that I need to dig deeper for the real me.

Today I Will Remember

Taking stock of myself is buying stock in my future.

Reflection for the Day

Inventory-taking isn't always done in red ink. It's a rare day when we haven't done something right. As I uncover and face my shortcomings, my many good qualities will be revealed to me also, reminding me that they have the same reality as my faults. Even when we've tried hard and failed, for instance, we can chalk that up as one of the greatest credits of all. I'll try to appreciate my good qualities, because they not only offset the faults, but give me a foundation on which to grow. It's just as self-deceptive to discount what's good in us as to justify what is not. *Can I take comfort in my positive qualities, accepting myself as a friend?*

Today I Pray

If I find only defects when I look in that Fourth Step mirror, may I be sure that I am missing something—namely my good points. Although my ultra-modesty may be approved socially, may I learn that it is just as dishonest as rationalizing away my faults. Even an out-and-out failure, if examined from all sides, may turn up a plus along with the obvious minuses.

Today I Will Remember

To give myself, if not an A for effort, at least an average B minus.

Reflection for the Day

The Fourth Step suggests we make a searching and fearless *moral* inventory—not an *immoral* inventory of ourselves. The Steps are guidelines to recovery, not whipping posts for self-flagellation. Taking my inventory doesn't mean concentrating on my shortcomings until all the good is hidden from view. By the same token, recognizing the good need not be an act of pride or conceit. If I recognize my good qualities as God-given, I can take an inventory with true humility while experiencing satisfaction in what is pleasant, loving, and generous in me. *Will I try to believe, in Walt Whitman's works, that "I am larger, better than I thought; I did not know I held so much goodness..."?*

Today I Pray

When I find good things about myself, as I undertake this inner archaeological dig, may I give credit where it is due—to God, who is the giver of all good. May I appreciate whatever is good about me with humility, as a gift from God.

Today I Will Remember

Goodness is a gift from God.

Reflection for the Day

As addictive persons, self-delusion was intricately woven through almost all our thoughts and actions. We became experts at convincing ourselves, when necessary, that black was white, that wrong was right, or even that day was night. Now that we're in the Program, our need for self-delusion is fading. If I'm fooling myself these days, my sponsor can spot it quickly. And, as he skillfully steers me away from my fantasies, I find that I'm less and less likely to defend myself against reality and unpleasant truths about myself. Gradually, in the process, my pride, fear, and ignorance are losing their destructive power. *Do I firmly believe that a solitary self-appraisal wouldn't be nearly enough?*

Today I Pray

May I understand that not only must I look to my Higher Power, but that I need to trust my fellow members of the group in this Step of self-evaluation. For we mirror each other in all of our delusions and fantasies, and with these facing mirrors, we produce a depth of perspective that we could never come by alone.

Today I Will Remember

To see myself all around, I need a three-way mirror—with reflections from God, my friends, and me.

Reflection for the Day

"How does the Program work?" newcomers sometimes ask. The two answers I most often hear are "very well" and "slowly." I'm appreciative of both answers, facetious as they may first sound, because my self-analyzing tends to be faulty. Sometimes I've failed to share my defects with the right people; other times, I've confessed *their* defects, rather than my own; at still other times, my sharing of defects has been more in the nature of shrill complaints about problems. The fact is that none of us likes the self-searching, the leveling of our pride, and the confession of shortcomings which the Steps require. But we eventually see that the Program really works. *Have I picked up the simple kit of spiritual tools laid at my feet?*

Today I Pray

May God keep me from laying out my defects by comparing them to someone else's. We are, by nature, relativists and comparers, who think in terms of "worse than...", "not quite as bad as...", or "better than..." May I know that my faults are faults, whether or not they are "better than..." others'.

Today I Will Remember

Bad is bad, even when it is "better than."

Reflection for the Day

All of the Program's Twelve Steps ask us to go contrary to our natural inclinations and desires; they puncture, squeeze, and finally deflate our egos. When it comes to ego deflation, few Steps are harder to take than the Fifth, which suggests that we "admit to God, to ourselves, and to another human being the exact nature of our wrongs." Few Steps are harder to take, yes, but scarcely any Step is necessary to long-term freedom from addiction and peace of mind. *Have I quit living by myself with the tormenting ghosts of yesterday?*

Today I Pray

May God give me strength to face that great ego-pincher—Step Five. May I not hesitate to call a trusted hearer of Fifth Steps, set up a meeting and share it. By accepting responsibility for my behavior, and then sharing my account of it with God and one other, I am actually unburdening myself.

Today I Will Remember

My Fifth Step pain is also my liberation.

Reflection for the Day

After we take an inventory, determining and admitting the exact nature of our wrongs, we become "entirely ready," as the Sixth Step suggests, "to have God remove all these defects of character." Sure, it's easy to feel like that and be "entirely ready" on a morning-after, but we know in such desperate moments that our motive may be remorse rather than repentance, induced more by a throbbing head than a contrite heart. The further we get away from the last addictive binge, the better the wrong-doing looks—more innocent, possibly even more attractive. *Am I ready THEN to "have God remove all these defects of character..."?*

Today I Pray

May I be "entirely ready" for God to remove my defects of character. May those words "entirely ready" re-summon my determination in case it should fade with time and sobriety. May God be my strength, since I alone cannot erase my faults.

Today I Will Remember

I am "entirely ready."

Reflection for the Day

So often, in the past, we prayed for "things," or favoring circumstances, or a thousand requests that were really selfish in nature. I've learned in the Program that real prayer begins—not ends—in asking God to *change* me. In fact, that's exactly what the Seventh Step suggests: *Humbly asked Him to remove our shortcomings.* We ask God for help through His grace and the amazing thing is that such a prayer is answered if we truly want it to be. Our own wills are so much a required part of the result that it seems almost as if we had done it. But the help from God is even more necessary; without Him, we couldn't possibly have done it alone. *Have I asked God to help me change myself?*

Today I Pray

May I learn to pray broadly—that God's will be done, that God remove my shortcomings. No need to specify what these shortcomings are; God who knows all, knows. May I learn that details are not necessary in my praying. All that matters is my humility and my faith that God, does indeed, have the Power to change my life.

Today I Will Remember

I ask God to change me.

Reflection for the Day

I heard someone in the Program once read, "Burn the idea into the consciousness of every man that he can get well, regardless of anyone. The only condition is that he trust in God and clean house." That is what Step Seven means to me—that I'm going to clean house and will have all the help I need. *Do I realize, by taking the Seventh Step, that I'm not really giving a thing, but, instead, getting rid of whatever might lead me back to my addiction and away from peace of mind?*

Today I Pray

May I know that if I should give up that key word "humbly," which combines all in one my humility, my awe, my faith—I would once again be taking too much on my shoulders and assuming that the Power is my own. May God in His wisdom make His will mine, His strength mine, His goodness mine. As He fills me with these Divine gifts, there can be little space left in me for looming defects.

Today I Will Remember

Trust in God and clean house.

Reflection for the Day

Some of us, after we've taken the Fourth, Fifth, Sixth, and then the Seventh Step, sit back and simply *wait* for our Higher Power to remove our shortcomings. The Program's teachings remind us of the story of St. Francis working in a beautiful garden. A passerby said, "You must have prayed very hard to get such beautiful plants to grow." The good saint answered, "Yes, I did. But every time I started to pray, I reached for the hoe." As soon as our "wait" is changed to "dig," the promise of the Seventh Step begins to become reality. *Do I expect my Higher Power to do it all?*

Today I Pray

May I not just pray and wait—for my Higher Power to do everything. Instead may I pray as I reach for the tools the Program gives me. May I ask now for guidance on how I can best use these precious tools.

Today I Will Remember

Pray and act.

Reflection for the Day

Without freedom from addiction, we have nothing. Yet we can't be free of our addictive obsessions until we become willing to deal with the character defects which brought us to our knees. If we refuse to work on our glaring defects, we'll almost certainly return to our addiction. If we stay clean and sober with a minimum of self-improvement, perhaps we'll settle into a comfortable but dangerous sort of limbo for a while. Best of all, if we continuously work the Steps, striving for fineness of spirit and action, we'll assuredly find true and lasting freedom under God. *Am I walking with confidence that I'm at last on the right track?*

Today I Pray

May God show me that freedom from addiction is an insecure state unless I can be freed also of my compulsions. May God keep me from a half-hearted approach to the Program, and make me know that I cannot be spiritually whole if I am still torn apart by my own dishonesty and selfishness.

Today I Will Remember

Half-hearted, I cannot be whole.

Reflection for the Day

We all want to be rid of our most obvious and destructive flaws. No one wants to be so greedy that she or he is angry enough to kill, lustful enough to rape, gluttonous enough to become ill. No one wants to be agonized by envy or paralyzed by procrastination. Of course, few of us suffer these defects at such rock-bottom levels. Not that that's reason to congratulate ourselves; chances are, pure self-interest enabled us to escape such extremes. Not much spiritual effort is involved in avoiding excesses which will bring severe punishment. *When I face up to the less violent and less deadly aspects of the very same defects, where do I stand then?*

Today I Pray

May I give myself no back-pats for not committing murder or rape, beating up a rival, robbing a sweets shop, or stealing from a down-and-outer. In all humility, may I understand that these are only more violent manifestations of human flaws I harbor in myself. May God give me the perseverance to change these from inside, rather than just lessening the degree to which I act them out for the world to see.

Today I Will Remember

Change the inside first.

Reflection for the Day

Taking a long hard look at those defects I'm unwilling or reluctant to give up, I ought to rub out the rigid lines I've drawn. Perhaps, in some cases, I'll then be able to say, "Well, this one I can't give up *yet*..." The one thing I shouldn't say: "This one I'll *never* give up." The minute we say, "No, never," our minds close against the grace of God. Such rebelliousness, as we have seen in the experiences of others, may turn out to be fatal. Instead, we should abandon limited objectives and begin to move toward God's will for us. *Am I learning never to say "never..."?*

Today I Pray

May God remove any blocks of rebellion which make me balk at changing my undesirable qualities. Out of my delusion that I am "unique" and "special" and somehow safe from consequences, I confess to God that I have defied the natural laws of health and sanity, along with Divine laws of human kindness. May God drain away the defiance which is such a protected symptom of my addiction.

Today I Will Remember

Defiance is an offspring of delusion.

Reflection for the Day

"Prayer does not change God," wrote Soren Kierkegaard, "but it changes him who prays." Those of us in the Program who've learned to make regular use of prayer would no more do without it than we'd turn down sunshine, fresh air, or food—and for the same reason. Just as the body can wither and fail for lack of nourishment, so can the soul. We all need the light of God's reality, the nourishment of His strength, and the atmosphere of His grace. *Do I thank God for all that He has given me, for all that He has taken away from me, and for all He has left me?*

Today I Pray

Dear Higher Power: I want to thank you for spreading calm over my confusion, for making the jangled chords of my human relationships harmonize again, for putting together the shattered pieces of my Humpty Dumpty self, for giving me as a sobriety present a whole great expanded world of marvels and opportunities. May I remain truly Yours. Yours truly.

Today I Will Remember

Prayer, however simple, nourishes the soul.

Reflection for the Day

Prayer can have many rewards. One of the greatest rewards is the sense of belonging it brings to me. No longer do I live as a stranger in a strange land, alien in a completely hostile world. No longer am I lost, frightened, and purposeless. I belong. We find, in the Program, that the moment we catch a glimpse of God's will—the moment we begin to see truth, justice, and love as the real and eternal things in life—we're no longer so deeply upset by all the seeming evidence to the contrary surrounding us in purely human affairs. *Do I believe that God lovingly watches over me?*

Today I Pray

May I be grateful for the comfort and peace of belonging—to God the ultimately wise "parent" and to His family on earth. May I no longer need bumper stickers or boisterous gangs to give me my identity. Through prayer, I am God's.

Today I Will Remember

I find my identity through prayer.

Reflection for the Day

I'll begin today with prayer—prayer in my heart, prayer in my mind, and words of prayer on my lips. Through prayer, I'll stay tuned to God today, reaching forward to become that to which I aspire. Prayer will redirect my mind, helping me rise in consciousness to the point where I realize that there's no separation between God and me. As I let the power of God flow through me, all limitations will fall away. *Do I know that nothing can overcome the power of God?*

Today I Pray

Today may I offer to my Higher Power a constant power, not just a "once-in-the-morning-does-it" kind. May I think of my Higher Power at coffee breaks, lunch, tea time, during a quiet evening—and at all times in between. May my consciousness expand and erase the lines of separation, so that the Power is a part of me and I am a part of the Power.

Today I Will Remember

To live an all-day prayer.

Reflection for the Day

From time to time, I begin to think I know what God's will is for other people. I say to myself, "This person ought to be cured of his terminal illness," or "That one ought to be freed from the torment she's going through," and I begin to pray for those specific things. My heart is in the right place when I pray in such fashion, but those prayers are based on the supposition that I know God's will for the person for whom I pray. The Program teaches me, instead, that I ought to pray that God's will—whatever it is—be done for others as well as for myself. *Will I remember that God is ready to befriend me, but only to the degree that I trust Him?*

Today I Pray

I praise God for the chance to help others. I thank God also for making me want to help others, for taking me out of my tower of self so that I can meet and share with and care about people. Teach me to pray that "Thy will be done" in the spirit of love, which God inspires in me.

Today I Will Remember

I will put my trust in the will of God.

SEPTEMBER 1

Reflection for the Day

Based on their collective experience, the Program's founders suggested a prayer to be said when taking the Third Step—and making *a decision to turn our will and our lives over to the care of God as we understood Him.* "God, I offer myself to Thee, to build with me and to do with me as Thou wilt. Relieve me of the bondage of self, that I may better do Thy will. Take away my difficulties, that victory over them may bear witness to those I would help of Thy power, Thy love, and Thy way of life. May I do Thy will always!" *Have I abandoned myself to God as I understand Him?*

Today I Pray

I praise my Higher Power for my freedom to find my own understanding of God. May my life be God's, whether I think of Him as a Father whose hand and spirit I can touch with an upward reach of my own, or as a universal Spirit that I can merge with as the hard outlines of my "self" begin to melt, or as a core of Divine and absolute goodness inside myself. May I know Him well, whether I find Him within me, without me, or in all things everywhere.

Today I Will Remember

I thank God, as I understand Him, for my understanding of Him.

Reflection for the Day

When I wake up, I'll think quietly about the twenty-four hours ahead. I'll ask God to direct my thinking, especially asking that it be free from self-pity and from dishonest or self-seeking motives. If I have to determine which of several courses to take, I'll ask God for inspiration, for an intuitive thought, or a decision. Then I'll relax and take it easy, confident that all will be well. *Can I believe that when I give up my "rights" of expectations, I'll know freedom...?*

Today I Pray

I praise God for being able to praise God, to choose the times when I will seek Him, to find my own words when I talk to Him, to address Him in the way that seems most right to me. May I expect that He in turn must be free of my expectations, to affect my life as He sees fit.

Today I Will Remember

Who am I to try to tell God what to do?

Reflection for the Day

Sometimes, even when friends in and outside of the Program tell us how well we're doing, we know deep down that we're really not doing well enough. We still have trouble handling life and facing reality on reality's terms. We suspect, at those times, that there must be a serious flaw in our spiritual practice and development. Chances are strong that our trouble lies in either misunderstanding or neglect of Step Eleven—prayer, meditation, and the guidance of God. The other Steps can keep most of us clean and sober, free from other addictions, and functioning. But Step Eleven can keep us growing—so long as we try hard and work at it continuously. *Do I trust infinite God rather than my finite self?*

Today I Pray

I pray for a deepening of my spiritual awareness, for a stronger faith in the Unseen, for a closer communion with God. May I realize that my growth in the Program depends on my spiritual development. May I give over more of my trust to God's eternal wisdom.

Today I Will Remember

I will not give in or give up, but give over to the power of God.

Reflection for the Day

Though I have prayed at various times in my life, I realized after several months in the Program that I'd never really prayed properly. I'd always tried to make deals with God, much like a foxhole atheist; I'd always pleaded, "Grant me my wishes," instead of "Thy will—not mine—be done." The result was that I remained self-deceived and was thus incapable of receiving enough grace to restore me to sanity. *Do I see that in the past, when I prayed to God, I usually asked that two and two not make four?*

Today I Pray

May I look back and review how I have prayed before, for specific solutions that I from my earthly vantage felt were best. May I question, in the longer view of time, whether those solutions would have been right, had God chosen to do things my way. In retrospect, may I see that my pleas were not always so wise. May I be content to trust God.

Today I Will Remember

God may not do it my way.

Reflection for the Day

We're often told that alcoholics and addictive persons are perfectionists, impatient about any shortcomings—especially our own. We tend to set impossible goals for ourselves, struggling fiercely to reach our unattainable ideals. Then, of course—since no person could possibly meet the extremely high standards we demand of ourselves—we find ourselves falling short. Discouragement and depression set in; we angrily punish ourselves for being less than superhuman. The next time around, rather than setting more realistic goals, we set them even higher. And we fall farther, then punish ourselves more severely. *Isn't it about time I stopped setting unattainable goals for myself?*

Today I Pray

May God temper my own image of myself as a superperson. May I settle for less than perfection from myself, as well as from others. For only God is perfect, and I am limited by being human.

Today I Will Remember

I am not God; I am only human.

Reflection for the Day

"During acute depression," wrote AA co-founder Bill W., "avoid trying to set your whole life in order at once. If you take on assignments so heavy that you are sure to fail in them at the moment, then you are allowing yourself to be tricked by your unconscious. Thus you will continue to make sure of your failure, and when it comes you will have another alibi for still more retreat into depression. In short, the 'all or nothing' attitude is a most destructive one. It is best to begin with whatever the irreducible minimums of activity are. Then work for an enlargement of these—day by day." *When I'm discouraged by setbacks, am I willing to start over?*

Today I Pray

When I am immobilized by depression, may I set small, reasonable goals—as miniature perhaps as saying hello to a child, washing my own coffee cup, neatening my desk, offering a short prayer. May I scrap my own script for failure, which sets me up for deeper depression.

Today I Will Remember

Goals set too high set me back.

Reflection for the Day

"If you're not all right the way you are," it's been said, "it takes a lot of effort to get better. Realize you're all right the way you are, and you'll get better naturally." Sometimes we find ourselves in a situation so difficult that it seems insoluble. The more we think about it, the more we get on our own backs for our imagined inadequacy to overcome the situation—and we sink into depression. That's the moment to recall a single phrase, slogan, or bit of philosophy, saying it over and over until it replaces thoughts of the tormenting problem—which, in the final analysis will take care of itself. *Do I sometimes forget that the thorns have roses?*

Today I Pray

May I see that God gives us patterns so that we can take comfort in opposites—day follows night; silence follows din; love follows loneliness; release follows suffering. If I am ineffectual, may I realize it and try to do something constructive. If I am insensitive, may my friends confront me into greater sensitivity.

Today I Will Remember

Clouds have linings. Problems have endings.

Reflection for the Day

We are told in the Program that no situation is hopeless. At first, of course, we find this hard to believe. The opposites—hope and despair—are human emotional attitudes. It is we who are hopeless, not the condition of our lives. When we give up hope and become depressed, it's because we're unable, for now, to believe in the possibility of a change for the better. *Can I accept this: "Not everything that is faced can be changed; but nothing can be changed until it is faced..."?*

Today I Pray

May I remember that, because I am human and can make choices, I am never "hopeless." Only the situation I find myself in may seem hopeless, which may reduce me to a state of helpless depression as I see my choices being blocked off. May I remember, too, that even when I see no solution, I can choose to ask God's help.

Today I Will Remember

I can choose not to be hopeless.

Reflection for the Day

The longer I'm in the Program and the longer I try to practice its principles in all my affairs, the less frequently I become morose and depressed. Perhaps, too, there's something to that cynical old saying, "Blessed is he that expecteth nothing, for he *shall not* be disappointed, but instead will be delighted daily by new and fresh evidence of the love of God and the friendliness of men and women." *Does someone, somewhere, need me today? Will I look for that person and try to share what I've been given in the Program?*

Today I Pray

May I be utterly grateful to God for lifting my depression. May I know that my depression will always lighten if I do not expect too much. May I know that the warmth of friends can fill the cold hollow of despair. May I give my warmth to someone else.

Today I Will Remember

To look for someone to share with.

Reflection for the Day

Years ago, Dr. Alfred Adler prescribed this remedy for depression to a patient: "You can be healed if every day you begin the first thing in the morning to consider how you can bring a real joy to someone else. If you can stick to this for two weeks, you will no longer need therapy." Adler's "prescription," of course, is not much different from the suggestion that we work more intensively the Program's Twelve Steps to rid ourselves of depression. *When I am depressed, do I keep my feelings to myself? Or do I do what friends in the Program have suggested that I do?*

Today I Pray

May I turn myself inside out, air out the depression which has been closeted inside me, replace it with the comfortable feeling that I am cared about by real friends, then pass along that comfort to others caught in the same despair.

Today I Will Remember

The only real despair is loneliness.

Reflection for the Day

The one thing, more than anything else, that can relieve my occasional feeling of depression is love. I have to keep myself "lovable" in the sense of being able to love others, rather than being concerned with whether others love me. In somehow losing myself in others, emotionally or spiritually, I usually *find* myself. Today I understand what they meant at those first blurry meetings of the Program when they told me that I was the most important person in the room. *Do I say the same thing to other new members today, and mean it?*

Today I Pray

May I know that if I can love others, without expecting to be loved back, chances are that I will receive a share of love in return. It is only my expectation of approval which cancels out the value of my love.

Today I Will Remember

Love is not an investment, but a charitable contribution.

Reflection for the Day

"At certain moments," wrote Coleridge, "a single almost insignificant sorrow may, by association, bring together all the little relics of pain and discomfort, bodily and mental, that we have endured even from infancy." The Program doesn't teach us to pretend that hardships and sorrow are meaningless. Grief really hurts, and so do other kinds of pain. But now that we're free of our addictions, we have much greater control over our thinking. And the thoughts we choose to spend time on during any given day can strongly influence the complexion of our feelings for that day. *Am I finding different and better ways of using my mind?*

Today I Pray

May I thank God for the pain—however insignificant—that magnetizes my succession of old hurts into one large one that I can take out and look at, and then discard to make room for new and present concerns. May I thank God for restoring my sensitivity to pain after the numbness of addiction.

Today I Will Remember

I can thank God for restoring my feelings.

Reflection for the Day

We hear often in the Program that pain is the touchstone of spiritual progress. We eventually realize that just as the pains of alcoholism had to come before sobriety, emotional turmoil comes before serenity. We no longer commiserate with all people who suffer, but only with those who suffer in ignorance—those who don't understand the purpose and ultimate utility of pain. In Proust's words, "To goodness and wisdom we make only promises; pain we obey." *Do I believe that pain is God's way of trying to get my attention?*

Today I Pray

May I understand the value of pain in my life, especially if I am headed breakneck down a track of self-destruction. May I know that pain is God's way of flagging down the train I'm on before it gets to a bridge wash-out. May I be thankful that pain forced me to throw the switch in time.

Today I Will Remember

Pain saves lives.

Reflection for the Day

Until we came to the Program, our lives had been spent running from pain and problems. Escape by way of alcohol or other chemicals was always our temporary solution. Then we started going to meetings. We looked and listened, often with amazement. Everywhere around us, we saw failure and misery transformed by humility into priceless assets. To those who've made progress in the Program, humility is simply a clear recognition of what and who we really are—followed by a sincere attempt to become what we could be. *Is the Program showing me what I could be?*

Today I Pray

I pray for humility, which is another word for perspective, a level look at the real me and where I stand in relation to God and other people. May I be grateful to humility: it is the processing plant through which my raw hurts and ragged delusions are refined into new courage and sensitivities.

Today I Will Remember

Humility restores my "sight."

Reflection for the Day

No one welcomes pain with open arms, but it does have its uses. Just as physical pain serves as a warning that we may be suffering a bodily illness, so can emotional pain be a useful sign that something is wrong—as well as a warning that we need to make a change. When we can meet pain without panic, we can learn to deal with the cause of the hurt, rather than running away as we did when we were actively addicted. *Can I bear some emotional discomfort? Am I less fragile than I once believed?*

Today I Pray

I pray I may be better able to face hurt or pain, now that I am getting to know reality—good and bad. I sincerely pray that the supersensitivity of my addictive days will disappear, that people will not feel they must treat me like blown glass, which could shatter at a puff of criticism.

Today I Will Remember

Throw away my stamp: "Fragile—Handle with Care."

Reflection for the Day

We learn from others in the Program that the best way to deal with painful situations is to meet them head on, to deal with them honestly and realistically, and to try to learn from them and use them as springboards for growth. Through the Program and our contact with a Higher Power, we can find the courage to use pain for *triumphant* growth. *Will I believe that whatever pain I experience is a small price to pay for the joy of becoming the person I was always meant to be?*

Today I Pray

May my Higher Power give me the courage I need to stop running away from painful situations. The chemical was my escape hatch, the trap door I counted on to swallow me when life became too monstrous or villainous to bear. Now that I have locked that door, may I face pain and learn from it.

Today I Will Remember

My compulsion: a trap door—and a trap.

Reflection for the Day

In a letter to a friend, AA co-founder Bill W. wrote, "I don't think happiness or unhappiness is the point. How do we meet the problems we face? How do we best learn from them and transmit what we have learned to others, if they would receive the knowledge? In my view, we of this world are pupils in a great school of life. It is intended that we try to grow, and that we try to help our fellow travelers to grow in the kind of love that makes no demands...When pain comes, we are expected to learn from it willingly, and help others to learn. When happiness comes, we accept it as a gift, and thank God for it." *Can I accept both pain and happiness willingly?*

Today I Pray

God, please help me remember that everything that happens to me has its worth, including the misery of addiction. May I believe that even my dependence was part of God's Grand Scheme to bring me to Him.

Today I Will Remember

All that I am is all that has happened to me.

Reflection for the Day

In every story we hear from others in the Program, pain has been the price of admission into a new life. But our admission price purchased far more than we expected. It led us to a degree of humility, which we soon discovered to be a healer of pain. And, in time, we began to fear pain less, and desire humility more than ever. *Am I learning to "sit loosely in the saddle"—making the most of what comes and the least of what goes?*

Today I Pray

If God's plan for us is spiritual growth, a closer alliance with His principles of what is good and what is true, then may I believe that all my experiences have added up to a new and improved me. May I not fear the lessons of pain. May I know that I must continue to grow through pain, as well as joy.

Today I Will Remember

I hurt; therefore I am.

Reflection for the Day

It's still not exactly a "piece of cake" for me to accept today's occasional pain and anxiety with any great degree of serenity, but I'm increasingly able to be thankful for a certain amount of pain. In the Program, we find the willingness to do this by going over the lessons learned from past sufferings—lessons which have led to the blessings we now enjoy. We can remember how the agonies of addiction—and the pain of rebellion and bruised pride—have often led us to God's grace, and thus to new freedom. *Have I thanked my Higher Power for the miracle of my life this day?*

Today I Pray

When I was helpless, I asked God for help. When I was hopeless, I reached out for His hope. When I was powerless over my addiction, I asked to share His power. Now I can honestly thank God that I was helpless, hopeless, and powerless, because I have seen a miracle.

Today I Will Remember

From powerless highs to a Higher Power.

Reflection for the Day

"When a man has reached a condition in which he believed that a thing must happen when he does not wish it, and that which he wishes to happen can never be, this is really the state called desperation," wrote Schopenhauer. The very real pain of emotional difficulties is sometimes very hard to take while we're trying to maintain sobriety. Yet we learn, in time, that overcoming such problems is the real test of the Program's way of living. *Do I believe that adversity gives me more opportunity to grow than does comfort or success?*

Today I Pray

May I believe firmly that God, in His infinite wisdom, does not send me those occasional moments of emotional stress in order to tease my sobriety, but to challenge me to grow in my control and my conviction. May I learn not to be afraid of emotional summits and canyons, for the Program has outfitted me for all kinds of terrain.

Today I Will Remember

Strength through adversity.

Reflection for the Day

I've heard it said that when God closes a door, He opens a window. Since I started working the Twelve Steps, much of the fear and pain that haunted my life is gone. Some of my defects have been lifted from me, though I'm still wrestling with others. I believe that if I continue to work the Twelve Steps over and over again, my life will continue to improve—physically, mentally, and spiritually. *Am I more willing and better able to help others by working the Steps myself?*

Today I Pray

I give thanks to God for showing me that the Twelve Steps are a stairway to a saner life. As I re-work them conscientiously, my life does get better, healthier, and nearer to my Higher Power. As I continue to live them, may I feel the same gratitude and exaltation of spirit as those who are just now discovering them.

Today I Will Remember

Step by Step, day by day.

Reflection for the Day

For a considerable period of time after I reached the Program, I let things I couldn't do keep me from doing the things I could. If I was bothered by what a speaker or other people said, I retreated, sulking, into my shell. Now, instead of being annoyed or defensive when someone strikes a raw nerve, I try to welcome it—because it allows me to work on my attitudes and perceptions of God, self, other people, and my life situation. We may no longer have active addictions, but we all certainly have an active thinking problem. *Am I willing to grow—and grow up?*

Today I Pray

May God give me courage to test my new wings—even a feather at a time. May I not wait to be entirely whole before I re-enter the world of everyday opportunity, for recovery is ongoing and growth comes through challenges. May I no longer make desperate stabs at perfection, but keep my aims in sight and develop as I live—a day at a time.

Today I Will Remember

Things I can't do should not get in the way of things I can.

Reflection for the Day

On studying the Twelve Steps, many of the first members of the Program exclaimed, "What an order! I can't go through with it." "Do not be discouraged," we're told at meeting after meeting. "No one among us has been able to maintain anything like perfect adherence to these principles. We are not saints. The point is that we are willing to grow along spiritual lines. The principles we have set down are guides to progress. We claim spiritual progress rather than spiritual perfection." *Can I believe, in the words of Browning, that my business is not to remake myself, but to make the absolute best of what God made...?*

Today I Pray

Even if I am an old hand at the Program, may I not forget that the Twelve Steps do not represent an achievement that can be checked off my "things to do" list. Instead, they are a striving for an ideal, a guide to getting there. May I keep my mind open to deepening interpretations of these principles.

Today I Will Remember

Progress rather than perfection.

Reflection for the Day

"Everybody wants to *be* somebody; nobody wants to grow," wrote *Goethe*.

I ask myself sometimes, as we all do: "Who am I?" "Where Am I?" "Where am I going?" "What's it all about?" The learning and growing process is usually slow. But eventually our seeking always brings a finding. What seem like great mysteries often turn out to be enshrined in complete simplicity. *Have I accepted the fact that my willingness to grow is the essence of my spiritual development?*

Today I Pray

God give me patience and the perseverance to keep on hoeing the long row, even when the end of it is out of sight. The principles of the Program are my almanac for growing, even more than harvesting. The harvest will come, abundant enough to share, if I can stick to my garden tending.

Today I Will Remember

Getting there, not being there.

Reflection for the Day

At the suggestion of a long-timer in the Program, I began taking "recovery inventories" periodically. The results showed me—clearly and unmistakably—that the promises of the Program have been true for me. I am not the sick person I was in years past; I am no longer bankrupt in all areas; I have a new life and a path to follow, and I'm at peace with myself most of the time. And that's a far cry from the time in my life when I dreaded facing each new day. Perhaps we should all write recovery inventories from time to time, showing how the Program is working for each of us. *Just for today, will I try to sow faith where there is fear?*

Today I Pray

God, let me compare my new life with the old one—just to see how things have changed for me. May I make progress reports for myself now and then—and for those who are newer to the Program. May these reports be—hearteningly—about "what I am doing" rather than—smugly—about "what I have done."

Today I Will Remember

Has the Program kept its promise? Have I kept mine?

Reflection for the Day

Is freedom from addiction all that we're to expect from a spiritual awakening? Not at all. Freedom from addiction is only the bare beginning; it's only the first gift of our first awakening. Obviously, if more gifts are to come our way, our awakening has to continue. As it does continue, we find that slowly but surely we can scrap the old life—the one that didn't work—for a new life that can and does work under any and all conditions. *Am I willing to continue my awakening through the practice of the Twelve Steps?*

Today I Pray

May I remember how it was when my only goal in life was to be free of my addiction. All the words and phrases I used were stoppers—"giving it up, quitting, cutting myself off." Once I was free, I began to realize that my freedom had more to do with beginning than stopping. May I now continue to think in terms of starters—"expanding, awakening, growing, learning, becoming..."

Today I Will Remember

My stopping was a starting point.

Reflection for the Day

In times past, even as adults, many of us child-ishly insisted that people protect, defend, and care for us. We acted as if the world owed us a living. And then, when the people we most loved became fed up, pushing us aside or per-haps abandoning us completely, we were bewil-dered. We couldn't see that our overdepen-dence on people was unsuccessful because all human beings are fallible; even the best of them will sometimes let us down, especially when our demands are unreasonable. Today, in contrast, we rely upon God, counting on Him rather than on ourselves or other people. *Am I trying to do as I think God would have me do, trusting the outcome of His will for me?*

Today I Pray

May I know, from the dependencies of my past, that I am a dependent person. I depended on alcohol, mood-altering chemicals, food, or other addictive pursuits. I was inclined to hang on other people, depending on them for more than they could give. May I, at last, switch from these adolescent dependencies to a mature, healthy dependency on my Higher Power.

Today I Will Remember

I have more than one dependency.

Reflection for the Day

Now that we're free from our addictions, living life one day at a time, we can begin to stop making unreasonable demands upon those we love. We can show kindness where we had shown none; we can take the time and initiative to be thoughtful, considerate, and compassionate. Even with the people we dislike, we can at least try to be courteous, at times literally going out of our way to understand and help them. *Just for today, will I try to understand rather than be understood, being courteous and respectful to all people with whom I'm in contact?*

Today I Pray

May I never forget my old sponge-like self, who soaked up every drop of affection and attention my family or friends could give me, until they were sapped dry. May I learn to be a giver, rather than a constant taker. May I practice offering interest, kindness, consideration, and compassion until sensivity to others becomes second nature to me.

Today I Will Remember

Giving is part of being.

Reflection for the Day

In our first weeks or months in the Program, our shaky emotional condition sometimes affects our feelings toward old friends and family. For many of us, these relationships heal quickly in the initial stages of our recovery. For others, a time of "touchiness" seems to persist; now that we're no longer drinking or using other chemicals, we have to sort out our feelings about spouses, children, relatives, employers, fellow workers, and even neighbors. Experience in the Program over the years has taught me that we should avoid making important decisions early in our recovery—especially emotion-charged decisions about people. *Am I becoming better equipped to relate maturely to other people?*

Today I Pray

May God help me through the edginess, the confusion of re-feeling and re-thinking my relationships, the getting it all together stages of my recovery. May I not rush into new relationships or new situations that demand an investment of my emotions—not yet.

Today I Will Remember

No entangling alliances too soon.

Reflection for the Day

No matter what other people do or don't do, we have to remain sober and free from other addictions for ourselves. When our program of recovery becomes contingent on the actions or inactions of another person—especially someone with whom we're emotionally involved—the results are invariably disastrous. We also need to remember that intense dislike is as much an emotional involvement as newfound romantic love. In short, we have to cool *any* risky emotional involvements in the first few months of our recovery, trying to accept the fact that our feelings could change quickly and dramatically. Our watchword must be First Things First, concentrating on our number one problem before anything else. *Am I building a firm foundation while steering clear of slippery emotional areas?*

Today I Pray

May I always remember that healthy relationships with people are necessary for my recovery. But—that substituting an obsession with either a love or hate object is as dangerous to my well-being as any other addiction.

Today I Will Remember

A dependency is a dependency is a dependency.

Reflection for the Day

We can be surrounded by people and still feel lonely. We can be all by ourselves and still feel happy and content. What makes the difference? We feel lonely if we look to other people for something they really can't provide. No one else can give us peace of mind, an inner sense of acceptance, and serenity. And when we find ourselves alone, we needn't feel lonely. God is with us; His presence is like a warm shawl enfolding us. The more we're aware of ourselves as beloved by God, the more we're able to feel content and secure—whether we're with others or alone. *Am I experiencing a sense of God and His love at all times and in all places?*

Today I Pray

May I understand that we each have our own kind of loneliness—whether we are young and friendless, old and kept waiting by death, bereft, left, running away, or just feeling out of it in a crowd. May my loneliness be eased a bit by the fact that loneliness is, indeed, a universal feeling that everyone knows firsthand—even though some lives seem more empty than others. May I—and all the lonely people—take comfort in the companionship of God.

Today I Will Remember

Shared loneliness is less lonely.

Reflection for the Day

An entire philosophy of life is condensed in the slogan, *Live and Let Live.* First we're urged to live fully, richly, and happily—to fulfill our destiny with the joy that comes from doing well whatever we do. Then comes a more difficult challenge: *Let live.* This means accepting the right of every other person to live as he or she wishes, without criticism or judgment from us. The slogan rules out contempt for those who don't think as we do. It also warns against resentments, reminding us not to interpret other people's actions as intentional injuries to us. *Am I becoming less tempted to involve my mind with thoughts of how others act or live?*

Today I Pray

May I live my life to the fullest, understanding that pure pleasure-seeking is not pleasure-finding, but that God's goodness is here to be shared. May I partake of it. May I learn not to take over the responsibility for another's adult decisions; that is my old controlling self trying, just one more time, to be the executive director of other people's lives.

Today I Will Remember

Live and let live.

Reflection for the Day

I've learned in the Program that I'm wholly powerless over my addiction. At long last, I've conceded my powerlessness; as a result, my life has taken a 180-degree turn for the better. However, I *do* have a power, derived from God, to change my own life. I've learned that *acceptance* does not mean *submission* to an unpleasant or degrading situation. It means accepting the reality of the situation and then deciding what, if anything, I can and will do about it. *Have I stopped trying to control the uncontrollable? Am I gaining the courage to change the things I can?*

Today I Pray

I ask my Higher Power for direction as I learn to sort out the things I can change from the things I can't, for that sorting process does, indeed, require God-given wisdom. May "the things I cannot change" not give me an excuse for inaction. May "the things I can" not include managing other people's lives. May I start to understand my own reality.

Today I Will Remember

Acceptance is not inaction. Change is not domination.

Reflection for the Day

We are powerless over our addictions; that admission brought us to the Program, where we learn through unconditional surrender that there is victory in defeat. After a time, we learn in Twelfth Step work that we're not only powerless over our own addiction, but over the addictions of others. We cannot *will* another person to sobriety, for example, any more than we can hold back the sunset. We may minister to another person's physical needs; we may share with him, cry with him, and take him to meetings. But we cannot get inside his head and push some sort of magic button that will make him—or her—take the all-important First Step. *Do I still sometimes try to play God?*

Today I Pray

May I understand my all-too-human need to be the boss, have the upper hand, be the final authority—even in the humbling business of my own addiction. May I see how easy it would be to become a big-shot Twelfth Stepper. May I also see that, no matter how much I care and want to help, I have no control over another's addiction—any more than someone else has control over mine.

Today I Will Remember

I cannot engineer another's sobriety.

Reflection for the Day

Soon after I came to the Program, I found a Higher Power whom I choose to call God. I've come to believe that He has all power; if I stay close to Him and do His work well, He provides me not with what I think I want, but with what I *need*. Gradually, I'm becoming less interested in myself and my little schemes; at the same time, I'm becoming more interested in seeing what I can contribute to others and to life. *As I become more conscious of God's presence, am I beginning to lose my self-centered fears?*

Today I Pray

May I see that the single most evident change in myself—beyond my own inner sense of peace—is that I have come out from behind my phony castle walls, dropped the drawbridge that leads into my real village and crossed it. I am back among people again, interested in them, caring what happens to them. May I find my joy here in this peopled reality, now that I have left behind those old self-protective fears and illusions of my own uniqueness.

Today I Will Remember

What is life without people?

Reflection for the Day

As we "keep coming back" to meetings, we're able to recognize those people who have an abundance of serenity. We are drawn to such people. To our surprise, we sometimes find that those who seem most grateful for today's blessings are the very ones who have the most serious and continuing problems at home or at work. Yet they have the courage to turn away from such problems, actively seeking to learn and help others in the Program. How have they gotten this serenity? It must be because they depend less on themselves and their own limited resources—and more on a Power greater than themselves in whom they have confidence. *Am I acquiring the gift of serenity? Have my actions begun to reflect my inner faith?*

Today I Pray

May I never cease to be awed by the serenity I see in others in my group—a serenity which manifests their comfortable surrender to a Higher Power. May I learn from them that peace of mind is possible even in the thick of trouble. May I, too, learn that I need to pull back from my problems now and then and draw upon the God-provided pool of serenity within myself.

Today I Will Remember

Serenity is surrender to God's plan.

Reflection for the Day

When I first read the Serenity Prayer, the word "serenity" itself seemed like an impossibility. At the time, the word conjured up images of lethargy, apathy, resignation, or grim-faced endurance; it hardly seemed a desirable goal. But I've since found that serenity means none of those things. Serenity for me today is simply a clear-eyed and realistic way of seeing the world, accompanied by inner peace and strength. My favorite definition is, "Serenity is like a gyroscope that lets us keep our balance no matter what turbulence swirls around us." *Is that a state of mind worth aiming for?*

Today I Pray

May I notice that "serenity" comes first, ahead of "courage" and "wisdom," in the sequence of the Serenity Prayer. May I believe that "serenity" must also come first in my life. I must have the balance, realistic outlook, and acceptance that is part of this blessing of serenity before I can go on to the kind of action and decision-making that will bring order to my existence.

Today I Will Remember

Serenity comes first.

Reflection for the Day

Determination—our clenched-jaw resolve that we can *do something* about everything—is perhaps the greatest hindrance to achieving serenity. Our old tapes tell us, "The difficult can be done immediately; the impossible will take a little longer." So we tighten up and prepare ourselves for battle, even though we know from long experience that our own will dooms us in advance to failure. Over and over we are told in the Program that we must "Let Go and Let God." And we eventually do find serenity when we put aside our own will while accepting His will for us. *Am I learning to relax my stubborn grip? Do I allow the solutions to unfold by themselves?*

Today I Pray

May I loosen my tight jaw, my tight fists, my general uptightness—outward indications of the "do it myself" syndrome which has gotten me into trouble before. May I know from experience that this attitude—of "keep a grip on yourself" and on everybody else, too—is accompanied by impatience and followed by frustration. May I merge my own will with the greater will of God.

Today I Will Remember

Let up on the strangle hold.

Reflection for the Day

I remember once hearing someone in the Program say, "Life is a series of agreeings or disagreeings with the universe." There is much truth in that statement, for I'm only a small cog in the machinery of the universe. When I try to run things my way, I'll experience only frustration and a sense of failure. If, instead, I learn to let go, success will assuredly be mine. Then I'll have time to count my blessings, work on my shortcomings, and live fully and richly in the Now. *Do I believe that what I am meant to know will come to my knowledge if I practice the Eleventh Step—praying only for the knowledge of God's will for me and the power to carry that out?*

Today I Pray

May I take my direction from the Eleventh Step—and not fall into my usual habit of making itemized lists for God of all my pleas and entreaties and complaints. May I no longer second-guess God with my specific solutions, but pray only that His will be done. May I count my blessings instead of my beseechings.

Today I Will Remember

Stop list-making for God.

Reflection for the Day

When we allow our Higher Power to take charge, without reservations on our part, we stop being "anxious." When we're not anxious about some person or situation, that doesn't mean we're disinterested or have stopped caring. Just the opposite is true. We can be interested and caring *without* being anxious or fearful. The poised, calm, and faith-filled person brings something positive to every situation. He or she is able to do the things that are necessary and helpful. *Do I realize how much better prepared I am to do wise and loving things if I banish anxious thoughts and know that God is in charge?*

Today I Pray

I pray that I may be rid of the anxiety which I have equated in my mind with really caring about people. May I know that anxiety is not an item of outerwear that can be doffed like a cap. May I know that I must have serenity within myself and confidence that God can do a better job than I can—and then my anxiety will lessen.

Today I Will Remember

Anxiety never solved anything.

Reflection for the Day

When I say the Serenity Prayer, sometimes over and over, I occasionally lose sight of the prayer's meaning even as I repeat its words. So I try to think of the meaning of each phrase as I say it, whether aloud or silently. As I concentrate on the meaning, my understanding grows, along with my capability to realize the difference between what I can change, and what I cannot. *Do I see that most improvements in my life will come from changing my own attitudes and actions?*

Today I Pray

May my Higher Power show me new and deeper meanings in the Serenity Prayer each time I say it. As I apply it to my life's situations and relationships, may its truth be underlined for me again and again. May I realize that serenity, courage, and wisdom are all that I need to cope with value unless they grow out of my trust in a Higher Power.

Today I Will Remember

God's formula for living: serenity, courage, and wisdom.

Reflection for the Day

Many people we meet in the Program radiate a kind of special glow—a joy in living that shows in their faces and bearing. They've put aside alcohol and other mood-altering chemicals and have progressed to the point where they're "high" on life itself. Their confidence and enthusiasm are contagious—especially to those who are new in the Program. The astonishing thing to newcomers is that those same joyous people also were once heavily burdened. The miracle of their before-and-after stories and new outlook is living proof that the Program works. *Does my progress in the Program serve to carry the message to others?*

Today I Pray

I pray that my own transformation through the Program—from burdened to unburdened, beaten down to upbeat, careless to caring, tyrannized by chemicals to chemically free—will be as much inspiration for newcomers as the dramatic changes in others' lives have been for me. May I—like those other joyous ones in the fellowship—learn how to be "high on life."

Today I Will Remember

Life is the greatest "high" of them all.

Reflection for the Day

My progress in recovery depends in large measure on my attitude, and my attitude is up to me. It's the way I decide to look at things. Nobody can force an attitude on me. For me, a good attitude is a point of view unclouded by self-pity and resentments. There will be stumbling blocks in my path, without a doubt. But the Program has taught me that stumbling blocks can be turned into stepping stones for growth. *Do I believe, as Tennyson put it, "that men may rise on stepping stones of their dead selves to higher things..."?*

Today I Pray

May God help me cultivate a healthy attitude toward myself, the Program, and other people. God, keep me from losing my spiritual stabilizers, which keep me level in purpose and outlook. Let me ignore self-pity, discouragement, and my tendency to overdramatize. Let no dead weight burden throw me out of balance.

Today I Will Remember

I can't be discouraged with God on my side.

Reflection for the Day

"Fundamental progress has to do with the reinterpretation of basic ideas," wrote Alfred North Whitehead. When we review the ups and downs of our recovery in the Program, we can see that truth of that statement. We make progress each time we get rid of an old idea, each time we uncover a character defect, each time we become ready to have that defect removed and then humbly ask God to remove it. We make progress, one day at a time, as we shun the first drink, the first pill, the first addictive act that will so quickly swerve us from the path of despair. *Have I considered the progress I've made since I've come to the Program?*

Today I Pray

May I remember that there are few new ideas in this world, only old ones reinterpreted and restated. May I be always conscious that even the big things in life—like love, brotherhood, God, sobriety—become more finely defined in each human life. So may the Twelve Steps of the Program be redefined in each of our lives, as we keep in mind that, basically, these are time-tried principles—which work.

Today I Will Remember

The Twelve Steps work.

Reflection for the Day

All too often I unwittingly—and even unconsciously—set standards for others in the Program. Worse yet, I expect those standards to be met. I go so far, on occasion, to decide what progress other people should make in *their* recoveries, and how *their* attitudes and actions should change. Not surprisingly, when things don't work out the way I expect, I become frustrated and even angry. I have to learn to leave others to God. I have to learn neither to demand nor expect changes in others, concentrating solely on my own shortcomings. Finally, I mustn't look for perfection in another human being until I've achieved perfection myself. *Can I ever be perfect?*

Today I Pray

May God ask me to step down immediately if I start to climb up on any of these high places: on my podium, as the know-it-all scholar; on my soapbox, as the leader who's out to change the world; into my pulpit, as the holier-than-thou-could-possibly-be messenger of God; into the seat of judgment, as the gavel-banging upholder of the law. May God please keep me from vesting myself with all this unwarranted authority and keep me humble.

Today I Will Remember

A heavy hand is not a helping hand.

Reflection for the Day

Someone once said that the mind's direction is more important than its progress. If my direction is correct, then progress is sure to follow. We first come to the Program to receive something for ourselves, but soon learn that we receive most bountifully when we give to others. If the direction of my mind is to give rather than to receive, then I'll benefit beyond my greatest expectations. The more I give of myself and the more generously I open my heart and mind to others, the more growth and progress I'll achieve. *Am I learning not to measure my giving against my getting, accepting that the act of giving is its own reward?*

Today I Pray

May I not lose sight of that Pillar of the Program—helping myself through helping others in our purpose of achieving comfortable sobriety. May I feel that marvel of giving and taking and giving back again from the moment I take the First Step. May I care deeply about others' maintaining their freedom from chemicals, and may I know that they care about me. It is a simple—and beautiful—exchange.

Today I Will Remember

Give and take and give back again.

Reflection for the Day

Now that we're sober and living in reality, it's sometimes difficult to see ourselves as others see us and, in the process, determine how much progress we've made in recovery. In the old days, the back-of-the-bar mirror presented us with a distorted and illusory view of ourselves: The way we imagined ourselves to be and the way we imagined ourselves to appear in the eyes of others. A good way for me to measure my progress today is simply to look about me at my friends in the Program. As I witness the miracle of their recoveries, I realize that I'm part of the same miracle—and will remain so as long as I'm willing. *Am I grateful for reality and the Divine miracle of my recovery?*

Today I Pray

May God keep my eyes open for miracles—those marvelous changes that have taken place in my own life and in the lives of my friends in the group. May I ask no other measurement of progress than a smile I can honestly mean and a clear eye and a mind that can, at last, touch reality. May my own joy be my answer to my question, "How am I doing?"

Today I Will Remember

Miracles measure our progress. Who needs more?

Reflection for the Day

Not in my wildest dreams could I have imagined the rewards that would be mine when I first contemplated turning my life and will over to the care of God as I understand Him. Now I can rejoice in the blessing of my own recovery, as well as the recoveries of countless others who have found hope and a new way of life in the Program. After all the years of waste and terror, I realize today that God has always been on my side and at my side. *Isn't my clearer understanding of God's will one of the best things that has happened to me?*

Today I Pray

May I be thankful for the blessed contrast between the way my life used to be (Part I) and the way it is now (Part II). In Part I, I was the practicing addict, adrift among my fears and delusions. In Part II, I am the recovering addict, rediscovering my emotions, accepting my responsibilities, learning what the real world has to offer. Without the contrast, I could never feel the joy I know today or sense the peaceful nearness of my Higher Power.

Today I Will Remember

I am grateful for such contrast.

Reflection for the Day

There are countless ways by which my progress and growth in the Program can be measured. One of the most important is my awareness that I'm no longer compelled, almost obsessively, to go around judging everything and everybody. My only business today is to work on changing myself, rather than other people, places, and things. In its own way, the obsession of being forever judgmental was as burdensome to me as the obsession of my addiction; I'm grateful that both weights have been lifted from my shoulders. *When I become judgmental, will I remind myself that I'm trespassing on God's territory?*

Today I Pray

Forgive me my trespasses, when I have become the self-proclaimed judge-and-jury of my peers. By being judgmental, I have trespassed on the rights of others to judge themselves—and on the rights of God in the Highest Court of all. May I throw away all my judgmental tools—my own yardstick and measuring tapes, my own comparisons, my unreachable standards—and accept each person as an individual beyond compare.

Today I Will Remember

Throw away old tapes—especially measuring tapes.

Reflection for the Day

Before I admitted my powerlessness over alcohol and other chemicals, I had as much self-worth as a "peeled zero." I came into the Program as a nobody who desperately wanted to be a somebody. In retrospect, my self-esteem was shredded, seemingly beyond repair. Gradually, the Program has enabled me to achieve an ever stronger sense of self-worth. I've come to accept myself, realizing that I'm not so bad as I had always supposed myself to be. *Am I learning that my self-worth is not dependent on the approval of others, but instead is truly an "inside job"?*

Today I Pray

When I am feeling down and worthless, may my Higher Power and my friends in the group help me see that, although I was "fallen," I was not "cast down." However sick I might have been in my worst days, with all the self-esteem of an earthworm, may I know that I still had the power of choice. And I chose to do something about myself. May that good choice be the basis for my reactivated self-worth.

Today I Will Remember

I will not kick myself when I'm down.

Reflection for the Day

There's a world of difference between the idea of self-love and love of self. Self-love is a reflection of an inflated ego, around which—in our distorted view of our own self-importance—everything must revolve. *Self-love* is the breeding ground for hostility, arrogance, and a host of other character defects which blind us to any points of view but our own. *Love of self,* in contrast, is an appreciation of our dignity and value as human beings. Love of self is an expression of self-realization, from which springs humility. *Do I believe that I can love others best when I have gained love of self?*

Today I Pray

May God, who loves me, teach me to love myself. May I notice that the most arrogant and officious humans are not so completely sure of themselves, after all. Instead, they are apt to have a painfully low self-image, an insecurity which they cloak in pomp and princely trappings. May God show me that when I can like myself, I am duly crediting Him, since every living thing is a work of God.

Today I Will Remember

I will try to like myself.

Reflection for the Day

"Not all those who know their minds know their hearts as well," wrote La Rochefoucauld. The Program is of inestimable value for those of us, formerly addicted, who want to know ourselves and who are courageous enough to seek growth through self-examination and self-improvement. If I remain honest, open-minded, and willing, the Program will enable me to rid myself of my self-deceptive attitudes and character flaws that for so long prevented me from growing into the kind of person I want to be. *Do I try to help others understand the Program and Twelve Steps? Do I carry the message by example?*

Today I Pray

I ask God's blessing for the group, which has shown me so much about myself that I was not willing to face on my own. May I have the courage to be confronted and to confront, not only to be honest for honesty's sake—which may be reason enough—but to allow myself and the others in the group to grow in self-knowledge.

Today I Will Remember

We are mirrors of each other.

Reflection for the Day

"One's own self is well hidden from one's own self," a renowned philosopher once wrote. "Of all mines of treasure, one's own is the last to be dug up." The Twelve Steps have enabled me to unearth my "own self," the one that for so long was buried beneath my desperate need for approval from others. Thanks to the Program and my Higher Power, I've begun acquiring a true sense of self and a comfortable sense of confidence. No longer do I have to react chameleon-like, changing my coloration from one moment to the next fruitlessly trying to be all things to all people. *Do I strive, at all times, to be true to myself?*

Today I Pray

I pray that I may be honest with myself, and that I will continue—with the help of God and my friends—to try to get to know the real me. May I know that I cannot suddenly be a pulled-together, totally defined, completely consistent personality; it may take a while to develop into that personality, to work out my values and my priorities. May I know now that I have a good start on being who I want to be.

Today I Will Remember

I'm getting to be who I want to be.

Reflection for the Day

So many of us in the Program went through childhood—as well as part of our adult lives—emotionally shackled with the terrible burden called shyness. We found it difficult to walk into crowded rooms, to converse with even our friends, to make eye contact with *any-one*. The agonies we suffered! We learn in the Program that shyness is just another manifestation of self-centered fear, which is the root of all our character defects. Shyness, specifically, is fear of what others think or might think about us. To our enormous relief, our shyness gradually leaves us as we work the Program and interact with others. *Am I aware that I'm okay as long as I don't concentrate on me?*

Today I Pray

God, may I be grateful that I am getting over my shyness, after years of pulling back from people, squirming, blushing, blurting out all the "wrong things" or saying nothing at all—then reliving the agonies and imagining what I *should* have said and done. May I know that it has taken a full-blown addiction and a lot of caring people to convince me that I'm okay—and you're okay, he's okay and so is she.

Today I Will Remember

A cure for shyness is caring about somebody else.

Reflection for the Day

My addictions were like thieves in more ways than I can count. They robbed me not only of money, property, and other material things, but of dignity and self-respect, while my family and friends suffered right along with me. My addictions also robbed me of the ability to treat myself properly, as God would treat me. Today, in total contrast, I'm capable of true love of self—to the extent that I'm able to provide myself with more love than even I need. So I give that love away to other people in the Program, just as they have given their love to me. *Do I thank God for bringing me to a Program in which sick people are loved back to health?*

Today I Pray

Thanks be to God for a way of life which generates such love and caring that we in the Program can't help but learn to love ourselves. When I see that someone cares about me, I am more apt to be convinced that perhaps I am, after all, worth caring about. May I be conscious always of the love I am now able to give—and give it.

Today I Will Remember

Someone caring about me makes me feel worth caring about.

Reflection for the Day

From time to time when I see the slogan, *But for the Grace of God*, I remember how I used to mouth those words when I saw others whose addictions had brought them to what I considered a "hopeless and helpless" state. The slogan had long been a cop-out for me, reinforcing my denial of my own addiction by enabling me to point to others seemingly worse off than I. "If I ever get like that, I'll quit," was my oft-repeated refrain. Today, instead, *But for the Grace of God* has become my prayer of thankfulness, reminding me to be grateful to my Higher Power for my recovery, my life, and the *way* of life I've found in the Program. *Was anyone ever more "hopeless and helpless" than I?*

Today I Pray

May I know that but for the grace of God, I could be dead or insane by now, because there have been others who started on addictive paths when I did who are no longer here. May that same grace of God help those who are still caught in the downward spin, who are heading for disaster as sure as gravity.

Today I Will Remember

have seen God's amazing grace.

Reflection for the Day

The Program's Fourth Step suggests that we make a fearless moral inventory of ourselves. For so many of us, especially newcomers, the task seems impossible. Each time we take pencil in hand and try to look inward, Pride says scoffingly, "You don't have to bother to look." And Fear cautions, "You'd better *not* look." We find eventually that pride and fear are mere wisps of smoke, the cloudy strands from which were woven the mythology of our old ideas. When we push pride and fear aside and finally make a fearless inventory, we experience relief and a new sense of confidence beyond description. *Have I made an inventory? Have I shared its rewards so as to encourage others?*

Today I Pray

May I not be stalled by my inhibitions when it comes to making a moral inventory of myself. May I not get to the Fourth Step and then screech to a stop because the task seems overwhelming. May I know that my inventory today, even though I try to make it "thorough" and honest, may not be as complete as it will be if I repeat it again, for the process of self-discovery goes on and on.

Today I Will Remember

Praise God for progress.

Reflection for the Day

"Pride, like a magnet, constantly points to one object, self; unlike the magnet, it has no attractive pole, but at all points repels," wrote *Colton*.

When the earliest members of the Program discovered just how spiritually prideful they could be, they admonished one another to avoid "instant sainthood." That old-time warning could be taken as an alibi to excuse us from doing our best, but it's really the Program's way of warning against "pride blindness" and the imaginary perfections we don't possess. *Am I beginning to understand the difference between pride and humility?*

Today I Pray

May God, who in His mercy has saved our lives, keep us from setting ourselves up as the saints and prophets of the Program. May we recognize the value of our experiences for others without getting smug about it. May we remember with humility and love the thousands of other "old hands" who are equally well-versed in its principles.

Today I Will Remember

I will avoid "instant sainthood."

Reflection for the Day

Virtually all of us suffered the defect of pride when we sought help through the Program, the Twelve Steps, and the fellowship of those who truly understood what we felt and where we had been. We learned about our shortcomings—and of pride in particular—and began to replace self-satisfaction with gratitude for the miracle of our recovery, gratitude for the privilege of working with others, and gratitude for God's gift, which enabled us to turn catastrophe into good fortune. *Have I begun to realize that "pride is to character as the attic to the house—the highest part, and generally the most empty..."?*

Today I Pray

God, please tell me if I am banging my shins on my own pride. Luckily for me, the Program has its own built-in check for flaws like this—the clear-eyed vision of the group, which sees in me what I sometimes cannot see myself. May I know that any kind of success has always gone straight to my head, and be watching for it as I begin to reconstruct my confidence.

Today I Will Remember

"Success" can be a setback.

Reflection for the Day

When I'm motivated by pride—by bondage of self—I become partly or even wholly blind to my liabilities and shortcomings. At that point, the last thing I need is comfort. Instead, I need an understanding friend in the Program—one who knows where I'm at—a friend who'll unhesitatingly chop a hole through the wall my ego has built so that the light of reason can once again shine through. *Do I take time to review my progress, to spot-check myself on a daily basis, and to promptly try to remedy my wrongs?*

Today I Pray

God I pray that the group—or just one friend—will be honest enough to see my slippery manifestations of pride and brave enough to tell me about them. My self-esteem was starved for so long, that with my first successes in the Program, it may swell to the gross proportions of self-satisfaction. May a view from outside myself give me a true picture of how I am handling the triumph of my sobriety—with humility or with pride.

Today I Will Remember

Self-esteem or self-satisfaction?

Reflection for the Day

If I'm to continue growing in the Program, I must literally "get wise to myself." I must remember that for most of my life I've been terribly self-deceived. The sin of pride has been at the root of most of my self-deception, usually masquerading under the guise of some virtue. I must work continually to uncover pride in all its subtle forms, lest it stop me in my tracks and push me backward once again to the brink of disaster. *When it comes to pride, do I believe, in Emerson's words, that "it is impossible for a man to be cheated by anyone but himself..."?*

Today I Pray

May I know that button-popping pride is inappropriate for me as a recovering addict. It hides my faults from me. It turns people off and gets in the way of my helping others. It halts my progress because it makes me think I've done enough self-searching and I'm cured. I pray to my Higher Power that I may be realistic enough to accept my success in the Program without giving in to pride.

Today I Will Remember

Pride halts progress.

Reflection for the Day

Those whom I most respect in the Program—and, in turn, those from whom I've learned the most—seem convinced that pride is, as one person put it, the "root-sin." In moral theology, pride is the first of the seven deadly sins. It is also considered the most serious, standing apart from the rest by virtue of its unique quality. Pride gets right into our spiritual victories. It insinuates itself into all our successes and accomplishments, even when we attribute them to God. *Do I struggle against pride by working the Tenth Step regularly, facing myself freshly and making things right where they've gone wrong?*

Today I Pray

May I be on guard constantly against the sneakiness of pride, which can creep into every achievement, every triumph, every reciprocated affection. May I know that whenever things are going well for me, my pride will be on the spot, ready to take credit. May I watch for it.

Today I Will Remember

Put pride in its place.

Reflection for the Day

The more self-searching we do, the more we realize how often we react negatively because our "pride has been hurt." Pride is at the root of most of my personal problems. When my pride is "hurt," for example, I almost invariably experience resentment and anger—sometimes to the point where I'm unable to talk or think rationally. When I'm in that sort of emotional swamp, I must remind myself that my pride—and nothing but *my pride*—has been injured. I have to pause and try to cool off until such time as I can evaluate the problem realistically. *When my pride is injured or threatened, will I pray for humility so that I can rise above myself?*

Today I Pray

May I know that if my pride is hurt, the rest of me may not be injured at all. May I know that my pride can take a battering and still come back stronger than ever for more. May I know that every time my pride takes a blow, it is liable to get more defensive, nastier, more unreasonable, more feisty. May I learn to keep my upstart pride in another place, where it will not be so easily hurt—or so willing to take credit.

Today I Will Remember

Humility is the only authority over pride.

Reflection for the Day

The Program's Twelve Steps comprise a body of *living* spiritual wisdom. To the degree that we continue to study the Steps and apply them to our daily lives, our knowledge and understanding expands without limitation. As we say in the Program, "It gets better...and better...and better." The Eleventh Step speaks of prayer and meditation, urging us to apply our minds quietly to the contemplation of spiritual truth. By its nature, the Eleventh Step illuminates for us the purpose and value of the other Steps. As we seek through prayer and meditation to improve our conscious contact with God, the remaining Steps become ever more useful in our new way of life. *Do I take the time each day to pray and meditate?*

Today I Pray

May I seek—as the Eleventh Step says—to know God better through prayer and meditation, talking to and listening for God. As my life becomes more full of the realities of earth—and the goodness thereof—may I always keep aside a time for communion with God. May this communion define my life and give it purpose.

Today I Will Remember

Take time out for God.

Reflection for the Day

We're taught in the Program that debate has no place in meditation. In a quiet place and time of our own choosing, we simply dwell on spiritual matters to the best of our capability, seeking only to experience and learn. We strive for a state of being which, hopefully, deepens our conscious contact with God. We pray not for things, but essentially for knowledge and power. *If you knew what God wanted you to do, you would be happy. You are doing what God wants you to do, so be happy.*

Today I Pray

May I find my own best way to God, my own best technique of meditation—whether I use the oriental mantra, substitute the name of Jesus Christ, or just allow the spirit of God, as I understand Him, to settle into me and give me peace. By whatever means I discover my God, may I learn to know Him well and feel His presence—not only at these quiet times, but in everything I do.

Today I Will Remember

Meditation is opening myself to the spirit of God.

Reflection for the Day

For many months after I came to the Program, I paid little attention to the practice of serious meditation and prayer. I felt that it might help me meet an emergency—such as a sudden craving to return to my old ways—but it remained among the lowest levels on my list of priorities. In those early days, I equated prayer and meditation with mystery and even hypocrisy. I've since found that prayer and meditation are more rewarding in their results than I could have ever imagined. For me today, the harvest is increasingly bountiful, and I continue to gain peace of mind and strength far beyond my human limitations. *Is my former pain being replaced by tranquility?*

Today I Pray

May I discover that prayer and meditation make up the central hall of my life's structure—the place where my thoughts collect and form into order. May I feel God's mystery there, and an overwhelming resource of energy.

Today I Will Remember

Fantasy is mine. Mystery is God's.

Reflection for the Day

There are no boundaries to meditation. It has neither width, depth, nor height, which means that it can always be further developed without limitation of any sort. Meditation is an individual matter; few of us meditate in the same way, and in that sense, it is truly a *personal* adventure. For all of us who practice meditation seriously, however, the purpose is the same: to improve our conscious contact with God. Despite its lack of specific dimensions and despite its intangibility, meditation is, in reality, the most intensely practical thing that we can do. One of its first rewards, for example, is emotional balance. What could be more practical than that? *Am I broadening and deepening the channel between myself and God?*

Today I Pray

As I seek God through daily prayer and meditation, may I find the peace that passes understanding, that balance that gives perspective to the whole of life. May I center myself in God.

Today I Will Remember

My balance comes from God.

Reflection for the Day

There are those in the Program who, at the beginning, shun meditation and prayer as they would avoid a pit filled with rattlesnakes. When they do finally take the first tentative and experimental step, however, and unexpected things begin to take place, they begin to feel different. Invariably, such tentative beginnings lead to true belief, to the extent that those who once belittled prayer and meditation become nothing less than walking advertisements for its rewards. We hear in the Program that "almost the only scoffers at prayer are those who never really tried it." *Is there an obstinate part of me that still scoffs?*

Today I Pray

May I learn, however irreverent I have been, that prayer is not to be mocked; I see the power of prayer effecting miracles around me, and I wonder. If I have refused to pray, may I look to see if pride is in my way—that old pride that insists on doing things on its own. Now that I have found a place for prayer in my life, may I reserve that place—religiously.

Today I Will Remember

Whoever learns to pray keeps on praying.

Reflection for the Day

My conscious contact with God depends entirely on me and on my *desire* for it. God's power is available for me to use at all times; whether I decide to use it or not is my choice. It has been said that "God is present in all His creatures, but all are not equally aware of His presence." I'll try to remind myself every day of how much depends on my awareness of God's influence in my life. And I'll try to accept His help in everything I do. *Will I remember that God knows how to help me, that He can help me, and that He wants to help me?*

Today I Pray

May I be aware always that God's power and peace are a bottomless well within me. I can draw bucket after bucket from it to refresh and purify my life. All I need to supply are the buckets and the rope. The water is mine—free, fresh, healing, and unpolluted.

Today I Will Remember

The well is God's; I bring the buckets.

Reflection for the Day

As time passes, daily communion with God is becoming as essential to me as breathing in and out. I don't need a special place to pray, because God always hears my call. I don't need special words with which to pray, because God already knows my thoughts and my needs. I have only to turn my attention to God, aware that His attention is always turned to me. *Do I know that only good can come to me if I trust God completely?*

Today I Pray

May my communion with God become a regular part of my life, as natural as a heartbeat. May I find, as I grow accustomed to the attitude of prayer, that it becomes less important to find a corner of a room, a bedside, a church pew, or even a special time of day, for prayer. May my thoughts turn to God automatically and often, whenever there is a lull in my day or a need for direction.

Today I Will Remember

Let prayer become a habit.

Reflection for the Day

When I first came to the Program, I thought that humility was just another word for weakness. But I gradually learned that there's nothing incompatible between humility and intellect, just as long as I place humility first. As soon as I began to do that, I was told, I would receive the gift of faith—a faith which would work for me as it has worked and continues to work for countless others who have been freed of their addictions and have found a new way of life in the Program. *Have I come to believe, in the words of Heine, that "the actions of men are like the index of a book; they point out what is most remarkable in them..."?*

Today I Pray

May I never let my intelligence be an excuse for lack of humility. It is so easy, if I consider myself reasonably bright and capable of making decisions and handling my own affairs, to look down upon humility as a property of those less intelligent. May I remember that intelligence and humility are both God-given.

Today I Will Remember

If I have no humility, I have no intelligence.

Reflection for the Day

What, exactly, is humility? Does it mean that we are to be submissive, accepting everything that comes our way, no matter how humiliating? Does it mean surrender to ugliness and a destructive way of life? On the contrary. The basic ingredient of all humility is simply a desire to seek and do God's will. *Am I coming to understand that an attitude of true humility confers dignity and grace on me, strengthening me to take intelligent spiritual action in solving my problems?*

Today I Pray

May I discover that humility is not bowing and scraping, kowtowing, or letting people walk all over me—all of which have built-in expectations of some sort of personal reward, like approval or sympathy. Real humility is awareness of the vast love and unending might of God. It is the perspective that tells me how I, as a human being, relate to that Divine Power.

Today I Will Remember

Humility is awareness of God.

Reflection for the Day

There are few "absolutes" in the Program's Twelve Steps. We're free to start at any point we can, or will. God, as we understand Him, may be defined as simply a "Power greater"; for many of us in the Program, the group itself was the first "Power greater." And this acknowledgment is relatively easy to make if a newcomer knows that most of the members are sober and otherwise chemically free and he or she isn't. This admission is the beginning of humility. Perhaps for the first time, the newcomer is at least willing to disclaim that he himself—or she herself—is God. *Is my behavior more convincing to newcomers than my words?*

Today I Pray

May I define and discover my own Higher Power. As that definition becomes clearer and closer to me, may I remember not to insist that my interpretation is right. For each must find his or her own Higher Power. If a newcomer is feeling godless and alone, the power of the group may be enough for now. May I never discredit the power of the group.

Today I Will Remember

Group power can be a Higher Power.

Reflection for the Day

We hear it said that all progress in the Program can be boiled down and measured by just two words: humility and responsibility. It's also said that our entire spiritual development can be precisely measured by our degree of adherence to those standards. As AA co-founder Bill W. once put it, "Ever deepening humility, accompanied by an ever greater willingness to accept and to act upon clear-cut obligations—these are truly our touchstones for all growth in the life of the spirit." *Am I responsible?*

Today I Pray

I pray that of all the good words and catch phrases and wisps of inspiration that come to me, I will remember these two above all: humility and responsibility. These may be the hardest to come by—humility because it means shooing away my pride, responsibility because I am in the habit of using my addiction as a thin excuse for getting out of obligations. I pray that I may break these old patterns.

Today I Will Remember

First humility, then responsibility.

Reflection for the Day

First search for a little humility, my sponsor urged me. If you don't, he said, you're greatly increasing the risk of going out there again. After a while, in spite of my lifelong rebelliousness, I took his advice; I began to try to practice humility, simply because I believed it was the right thing to do. Hopefully, the day will come when most of my rebelliousness will be but a memory, and then I'll practice humility because I deeply want it as a way of life. *Can I try today, to leave my self behind and to seek the humility of self-forgetfulness?*

Today I Pray

Since I—like so many chemically or otherwise dependent people—am a rebel, may I know that I will need to practice humility. May I recognize that humility does not come easily to a rebellious nature, whether I am out-and-out defiant, dug-in negative, or, more subtly, determined in a roundabout way to change everything else but myself. I pray that by practicing humility it will become instinctive for me.

Today I Will Remember

Get the humble habit.

Reflection for the Day

As a newcomer, I was told that my admission of my powerlessness over alcohol was my first step toward freedom from its deadly grip; I soon came to realize the truth of that fact. In that regard, surrender was a dire necessity. But for me that was only a small beginning toward acquiring humility. I've learned in the Program that to be willing to work for humility—as something to be desired for itself—takes most of us a long, long time. *Do I realize that a whole lifetime geared to self-centeredness can't be shifted into reverse in a split second?*

Today I Pray

May I search for my own humility as a quality that I must cultivate to survive, not just an admission that I am powerless over my compulsive behavior. Step One is just that—step one in the direction of acquiring an attitude of humility. May I be realistic enough to know that this may take half a lifetime.

Today I Will Remember

Pride blew it; let humility have a chance.

Reflection for the Day

We sometimes hear humility defined as the state of being "teachable." In that sense, most of us in the Program who are able to stay free of active addiction have acquired at least a smattering of humility, or we never would have learned to stay away from the first drink, the first tranquilizer, the first "side bet," and similar destructive acts for those of us who are powerless over our respective addictions. *Do I see increasing humility as a pathway to continuing improvement?*

Today I Pray

Now that I have made a start at developing humility, may I keep it up. May I open myself to the will of God and the suggestions of my friends in the group. May I remain teachable, confrontable, receptive, and conscious that I must stay that way in order to be healthy.

Today I Will Remember

To remain confrontable.

Reflection for the Day

Many of us in the Program stubbornly cling to false ideas and positions simply because we fear we'd be left defenseless if we admitted having been wrong. The thought of "backing down" still seems distasteful to some of us. But we come to learn that our self-esteem soars when we're able to push pride into the background and truly face the facts. Chances are that people with true humility have more genuine self-esteem than those of us who are repeatedly victimized by pride. *Does pride deviously keep me from thorough and continuing attention to the Tenth Step?*

Today I Pray

May pride stay out of my way, now that I've found a road to follow. May I avoid that familiar, destructive cycle of pride—the ego that balloons up out of all proportion and then deflates with a fizzle. May I learn the value of "backing down."

Today I Will Remember

Pride is the arch-enemy of self-esteem.

Reflection for the Day

"Nothing is enough to the man for whom enough is too little," wrote the Greek philosopher Epicurus. Now that we're free from addiction, rebuilding our self-respect and winning back the esteem of family and friends, we have to avoid becoming smug about our new-found success. For most of us, success has always been a heady brew; even in our new life, it's still possible to fall into the dangerous trap of "big-shot-itis." As insurance, we ought to remember that we're free today only by the grace of God. *Will I remember that any success I may be having is far more His success than mine?*

Today I Pray

May I keep a constant string-on-the-finger reminder that I have found freedom through the grace of God—just so I don't let my pride try to convince me I did it all myself. May I learn to cope with success by ascribing it to a Higher Power, not to my own questionable superiority.

Today I Will Remember

Learn to deal with success.

Reflection for the Day

I no longer argue with people who believe that satisfaction of our natural desires is the primary purpose of life. It's not our business in the Program to knock material achievement. When we stop and think about it, in fact, no group of people ever made a worse mess of trying to live by that "la dolce vita" formula than we did. We always insisted on more than our share—in all areas. And even when we seemed to be succeeding, we fueled our addictions so that we could dream of still greater successes. *Am I learning that material satisfactions are simply by-products and not the chief aim of life? Am I gaining the perspective to see that character-building and spiritual values must come first?*

Today I Pray

May I recognize that I never did handle excesses very well, based on my past experience. I have been apt to "want more" of whatever it is I have—love, money, property, things, chemicals, foods, winnings. May the Program teach me that I must concentrate on my spiritual, rather than my material bounty.

Today I Will Remember

It's okay to be spiritually greedy.

NOVEMBER 20

Reflection for the Day

I've come to measure success in a whole new way. My success today isn't limited by social or economic benchmarks. Success is mine today, no matter what the undertaking, when I tap the power of God within me and allow myself to be an open channel for the expression of His good. The spirit of success works through me as increased vision and understanding, as creative ideas and useful service—as efficient use of my time and energy, and as cooperative effort with others. *Will I try to keep my mind centered in the realization that within me is the God-implanted power to succeed?*

Today I Pray

May I develop a new concept of success, based on measurements of the good qualities which come from God's treasure-filled bank of good. To draw from that bank, all I have to do is look within myself. May I know that God's riches are the only kind that are fully insurable, because they are infinite. May I look in God's bank for my security.

Today I Will Remember

Spiritual "success" is my security.

Reflection for the Day

Adversity introduces man to himself, a poet once said. For me, the same is true of even *imagined* adversity. If I expect another person to react in a certain way in a given situation—and he or she fails to meet my expectation—well, then I hardly have the right to be disappointed or angry. Yet I occasionally still experience feelings of frustration when people don't act or react as I think they should. Through such imagined—or, better yet, *self-inflicted*—adversity, I come face to face again with my old self, the one who wanted to run the whole show. *Is it finally time for me to stop expecting and to start accepting?*

Today I Pray

May I stop putting words in people's mouths, programming them—in my own mind—to react as I expect them to. Expectations have fooled me before: I expected unbounded love and protection from those close to me, perfection from myself, undivided attention from casual acquaintances. On the adverse side, I expected failure from myself, and rejection from others. May I stop borrowing trouble—or triumph either—from the future.

Today I Will Remember

Accept. Don't expect.

Reflection for the Day

"We succeed in enterprises which demand the positive qualities we possess," wrote de Tocqueville, "but we excel in those which can also make use of our defects." We learn in the Program that our defects do have value—to the extent that we use them as the starting point for change and the pathway to better things. Fear can be a stepping stone to prudence, for example, as well as to respect for others. Fear can also help us turn away from hate and toward understanding. In the same way, pride can lead us toward the road of humility. *Am I aware of my direction today? Do I care where I'm going?*

Today I Pray

I pray that my Higher Power will show me how to use my defects in a positive way, because nothing—not even fear or selfishness or greed—is all bad. May I trust that every quality that leads me into trouble has a reverse side that can lead me out. Pride, for instance, can't puff itself up unduly without bursting and demonstrating that it is, in essence, only hot air. May I learn from my weaknesses.

Today I Will Remember

Good news out of bad.

Reflection for the Day

Before I came to the Program, I was like an actor who insisted on writing the script, producing, directing, and, in short, running the whole show. I had to do it *my* way, forever trying to arrange and re-arrange the lights, lines, sets, and, most of all, the other players' performances. If only my arrangements would stay put, and people would behave as I wished, the show would be fantastic. My self-delusion led me to believe that if *they* all would just shape up, everything would be fine. Of course, it never worked out that way. *Isn't it amazing how others seem to be "shaping up" now that I've stopped trying to manage everything and everybody?*

Today I Pray

May I talk myself out of that old urge to control everything and everybody. Time was, if I couldn't manage directly, I would do it indirectly, through manipulation, secret conferences, and asides. May I know that if I am the one who is always pulling the strings on the marionettes, then I am also the one who feels the frustration when they collapse or slip off the stage.

Today I Will Remember

I can only "shape up" myself.

Reflection for the Day

Although we came into the Program to deal with a specific problem, we soon became aware that we would find not only freedom from addiction, but freedom to live in the real world without fear and frustration. We learned that the solutions are within ourselves. With the help of my Higher Power, I can enrich my life with comfort, enjoyment, and deep-down serenity. *Am I changing from my own worst enemy to my own best friend?*

Today I Pray

May I praise my Higher Power for my freedoms—from addiction, from spiritual bankruptcy, from loneliness, from fear, from the seesaw of pride, from despair, from delusions, from shallowness, from doom. I give thanks for the way of life that has given me these freedoms and replaces the empty spaces with extra goodness and peace of mind.

Today I Will Remember

To give thanks for *all* my freedoms.

Reflection for the Day

"What you have may seem small; you desire so much more. See children thrusting their hands into a narrow necked jar, striving to pull out the sweets. If they fill the hand, they cannot pull it out and then they fall to tears. When they let go a few, they can draw out the rest. You, too, let your desire go; covet not too much...", wrote *Epictetus*.

Let me expect not too much of anyone, particularly myself. Let me learn to settle for less than I wish were possible, and be willing to accept it and appreciate it. *Do I accept gratefully and graciously the good that has already come to me in the Program?*

Today I Pray

May I search my soul for those little hankerings of want which may keep me from delighting in all that I have. If I can just teach myself not to want too much, not to expect too much, then when those expectations are not satisfied, I will not be let down. May I accept with grace what the grace of God has provided.

Today I Will Remember

I, alone, can grant myself the "freedom from want."

Reflection for the Day

During our first days in the Program we got rid of alcohol and pills. We had to get rid of our chemicals, for we knew they surely would have killed us. We got rid of the addictive substances, but we couldn't get rid of our addictions until we took further action. So we also had to learn to toss self-pity, self-justification, self-righteousness, and self-will straight out the window. We had to get off the rickety ladder that supposedly led to money, property, and prestige. And we had to take personal responsibility. To gain enough humility and self-respect to stay alive at all, we had to give up our most valued possessions—our ambition and our pride. *Am I well rid of the weights and chains that once bound me?*

Today I Pray

May I give credit to my Higher Power not only for removing my addiction, but for teaching me to remove my old demanding, pushy "self" from all my spiritual and earthly relationships. For all the things I have learned and unlearned, for my own faith and for the grace of God, I am fully and heartily thankful.

Today I Will Remember

Gratitude for the grace of God.

Reflection for the Day

The Program shows us how to transform the pipe-dreams of our pasts into reality and true sense of purpose, together with a growing consciousness of the power of God in our lives. It's all right to keep our heads in the clouds with Him, we're taught, but our feet should remain firmly planted here on earth. Here's where other people are; here's where our work must be accomplished. *Do I see anything incompatible between spirituality and a useful life in the here and now?*

Today I Pray

May my new "reality" include not only the nuts and bolts and pots and pans of daily living, but also my spiritual reality, my growing knowledge of the presence of God. May this new reality have room, too, for my dreams—not the drug-induced, mind-drifting fantasies of the past or the remnants of my delusions, but the products of a healthy imagination. May I respect these dreams, anchor them in earth's possibilities, and turn them into useful creativity.

Today I Will Remember

Heaven has a place in the here and now.

Reflection for the Day

Our faith in God's power—at work in us and in our lives—doesn't relieve us of responsibility. Instead, our faith strengthens our efforts, makes us confident and assured, and enables us to act decisively and wisely. We're no longer afraid to make decisions; we're not afraid to take the steps that seem called for in the proper handling of given situations. *Do I believe that God is at work beyond my human efforts, and that my faith and trust in Him will bring forth results far exceeding my expectations?*

Today I Pray

May my trust in my Higher Power never falter. May my faith in that Power continue to shore up my optimism, my confidence, my belief in my own decision making. May I never shut my eyes to the wonder of God's work or discount the wisdom of His solutions.

Today I Will Remember

Our hope in ages past, our help for years to come.

Reflection for the Day

Contrary to what some people think, our slogan, *Let Go and Let God*, isn't an expression of apathy, an attitude of defeatism, or an unwillingness to accept responsibility. Those who turn their backs on their problems are not "letting go and letting God," but, instead, are abandoning their commitment to act on God's inspiration and guidance. They neither ask for nor expect help; they want God to do it *all*. *In seeking God's guidance, do I realize that the ultimate responsibility is mine?*

Today I Pray

May I not allow myself to be lazy just because I think God is going to do everything anyway. (Such apathy reminds me of my old powerless self, the one that moaned that the world was going up in smoke, civilization was going down the drain, and there wasn't a thing I could do about it.) Neither may I use "letting God" do it as an excuse for shrugging off my problems without even trying. May God be my inspiration; may I be an instrument of God.

Today I Will Remember

God guides those who help themselves.

Reflection for the Day

If you're a negative thinker and are not yet ready to do an about-face, here are some guidelines that can keep you miserable for just as long as you wish to remain so. First, don't go to meetings of the Program, especially discussion groups. If you somehow find yourself at a meeting, keep your mouth shut, your hands in your pockets, and your mind closed. Don't try to solve any of your problems, never laugh at yourself, and don't trust the other people in the Program. Above all, under no conditions should you try to live in the Now. *Am I aware that negative thinking means taking myself deadly serious at all times, leaving no time for laughter—and for living?*

Today I Pray

If I am feeling negative, may I check myself in the mirror that is the group for any symptoms of a closed mind: tight lips, forced smile, set jaw, straight-ahead glance—and no glimmer of humor. God, grant me the ability to laugh at myself—often—for I need that laughter to cope with the everyday commotion of living.

Today I Will Remember

To laugh at myself.

DECEMBER 1

Reflection for the Day

It has truly been said that "We become what we do." It's emphasized to us over and over in the Program that our thoughts and actions toward others color and shape our spiritual lives. Words and acts of kindness, generosity, thoughtfulness, and forgiveness serve to strengthen those qualities within us that heighten our consciousness of God's love. *In asking God to direct and guide my life, am I also asking love to take over and lead me where it will?*

Today I Pray

May I make a resolute attempt at acting out the way I want to be—loving, forgiving, kind, thoughtful. May I be aware that each small, attentive act carries with it an echo of God's all-caring. For God so loved the world...may we make His love our example.

Today I Will Remember

We become what we do.

Reflection for the Day

Once at a meeting held in a church, I saw a stained glass window on which was written, "God Is Love." For some reason, my mind transposed the words into "Love is God." Either way is correct and true, I realized, looking about me and becoming even more conscious of the spirit of love and Power in the small meeting room. I'll continue to seek out that love and Power, following the Program as if my life depended upon it—as indeed it does. *Does life to me today mean living—in the active sense—joyously and comfortably?*

Today I Pray

May I feel the spirit of love that gives our prayers their energy. May I feel the oneness in this room, the concentration of love that gives the group its power. May I feel the exemplary love of a Higher Power, which our love echoes.

Today I Will Remember

Love is God.

Reflection for the Day

Our ancient enemy, self-will, wears a mask, confronting me with this sort of rationalization: "Why do I have to lean on God? Hasn't He already given me the intelligence to think for myself?" I have to pause when such thoughts creep into my mind, remembering that I've never really been able to bring about the results I wanted simply by relying on my own devices. I'm not self-sufficient, nor do I know all the answers; bitter experience alone teaches me that. *Do I know that I need God's guidance? Am I willing to accept it?*

Today I Pray

I pray that, as I become stronger in my conviction and in my sobriety, I will not begin to shrug off my dependence on a Higher Power. May I continue to pray for guidance, even when things seem to be going along smoothly. May I know that I need my Higher Power as much in times of triumph as in times of trauma.

Today I Will Remember

Self-sufficiency is a godless myth.

Reflection for the Day

Most of us in the Program are far more comfortable with the determination that we won't take the first drink *today*, than we are with the "vow" that we'll *never drink again*. Saying "I intend never to drink again" is quite different from saying "I'll never drink again." The last statement is far too reflective of self-will; it doesn't leave much room for the idea that God will remove our obsession to drink if we practice the Program's Twelve Steps one day at a time. *Will I continue to fight against complacency, realizing that I'll always be just one drink away from disaster?*

Today I Pray

"Never again" demands too binding a commitment, even for the strongest among us. Our past lives were full of "never agains" and "won't evers," promises that were broken before the next dawn. May I, for now, set my sights on just one straight, sober day at a time.

Today I Will Remember

Never say "never again."

DECEMBER 5

Reflection for the Day

"It is of low benefit to give me something. It is of high benefit to enable me to do something for myself," wrote *Emerson*.

I've been taught in the Program that I begin to use my will properly when I try to make it conform with God's will. In the past, most of my problems resulted from the *improper* use of will power. I'd always tried to use it, in sledgehammer fashion, as a way of solving my problems or changing the conditions of my life. *Do I see that a primary purpose of the Twelve Steps is to help me channel my will into agreement with God's intentions for me?*

Today I Pray

May I direct my will power into a channel where it can pick up the will of God. May I no longer use my will power—which has not proved mighty in the past—as willfulness. May I think of my will only as an extension of God's will, listening always for direction.

Today I Will Remember

To use my will power as willingness, not willfulness.

Reflection for the Day

When I finally convince myself to let go of a problem that's been tearing me apart—when I take the action to set aside my will and let God handle the problem—my torment subsides immediately. If I continue to stay out of my own way, then solutions begin to unfold and reveal themselves. More and more, I'm coming to accept the limitations of my human understanding and power. More and more, I'm learning to let go and trust my Higher Power for the answers and the help. *Do I keep in the forefront of my mind the fact that only God is all-wise and all-powerful?*

Today I Pray

If I come across a stumbling-block, may I learn to step out of the way and let God remove it. May I realize my human limitations at problem-solving, since I can never begin to predict God's solutions until I see them happening. May I know that whatever answer I come to, God may have a better one.

Today I Will Remember

God has a better answer.

Reflection for the Day

As long as I stubbornly hang on to the conviction that I can live solely by my individual strength and intelligence, a working faith in my Higher Power is impossible. This is true, no matter how strongly I believe that God exists. My religious beliefs—no matter how sincere —will remain forever lifeless if I continue trying to play God myself. What it comes down to, we find, is that, as long as we place self-reliance first, true reliance upon a Higher Power is out of the question. *How strong is my desire to seek and do God's will?*

Today I Pray

I pray that I may not place my self-reliance above reliance on God. May I know that there is no conflict between taking responsibility for my own actions, which I have been taught is the essence of maturity, and looking to God for guidance. May I remember that if I stick to the "do it myself" rule, it is like refusing to ask for a road map from a tourist information bureau —and wandering around forever lost.

Today I Will Remember

Maturity is knowing where to go for help.

Reflection for the Day

We often see people in the Program—devoutly and with seeming sincerity—ask for God's guidance on matters ranging from major crises to such insignificant things as what to serve at a dinner party. Though they may be well-intentioned, such people tend to force their wills into all sorts of situations—with the comfortable assurance that they're following God's specific directions. In reality, this sort of prayer is nothing more than a self-serving demand of God for "replies"; it has little to do with the Program's suggested Eleventh Step. *Do I strive regularly to study each of the Steps, and to practice them in all my affairs?*

Today I Pray

May I not make the common mistake of listing my own solutions for God and then asking for a stamp of Divine approval. May I catch myself if I am not really opening my mind to God's guidance, but merely laying out my own answers with a "what do You think of these?" attitude.

Today I Will Remember

Am I looking for God's rubber stamp?

Reflection for the Day

"Difficulties are God's errands, and when we are sent upon them, we should esteem it a proof of God's confidence," wrote *Beecher*.

I've come to realize that my past troubles were really of my own making. Although I hardly thought so at the time, I was a primary example of what the Program calls "self-will run riot." Today I'll accept my difficulties as signposts to growth and as evidence of God's confidence in me. *Do I believe that God will never give me more than I can handle?*

Today I Pray

May I believe strongly that God has confidence in me to handle my troubles, that the difficulties I must face are in direct proportion to my strength and ability to bear up and keep a cool head in a crisis. May I also understand that it is my faith in God which keeps me from crumbling.

Today I Will Remember

God has faith in me, because I have faith in God.

Reflection for the Day

Have I ever stopped to think that the impulse to "blow off steam" and say something unkind or even vicious will, if followed through, hurt me far more seriously than the person to whom the insult is directed? I must try constantly to quiet my mind before I act with impatience or hostility, for my mind can be—in that very real way —an enemy as great as any I've ever known. *Will I look before I leap, think before I speak—and try to avoid self-will to the greatest extent possible?*

Today I Pray

May I remember that my blow-ups and explosions, when they are torrents of accusations or insults, hurt me just as much as the other person. May I try not to let my anger get to the blow-up stage, simply by recognizing it as I go along and stating it as a fact.

Today I Will Remember

Keep a loose lid on the teapot.

Reflection for the Day

Before I came to the Program—in fact, before I knew of the Program's existence—I drifted from crisis to crisis. Occasionally, I tried to use my will to chart a new course; however, like a rudderless ship, I inevitably foundered once again on the rocks of my own despair. Today, in contrast, I receive guidance from my Higher Power. Sometimes, the only answer is a sense of peace or an assurance that all is well. *Even though there may be a time of waiting before I see results, or before any direct guidance comes, will I try to remain confident that things are working out in ways that will be for the greatest good of everyone concerned?*

Today I Pray

May I not expect instant, verbal communication with my Higher Power, like directions on a stamped, self-addressed post-card. May I have patience, and listen, and sense that God is present. May I accept my new feeling of radiant warmth and serenity as God's way of assuring me that I am, finally, making some good choices.

Today I Will Remember

Patience: God's message will come.

Reflection for the Day

These days, if I go through an experience that is new and demanding, I can do so in a spirit of confidence and trust. Thanks to the Program and Twelve Steps, I've come to know that God is with me in all places and in all endeavors. His Spirit is in me as well as in the people around me. As a result, I feel comfortable even in new situations and at home even among strangers. *Will I continue to flow along and grow along with the Program, trusting in the power and love of God at work in me and in my life?*

Today I Pray

May God's comfort be with me in all situations, familiar or new. May He rebuild the sagging bridge of my confidence. May I acknowledge God in me and in others around me. May that mutual identity in God help me communicate with people on a plane of honesty. If I can learn to trust God, I can learn to trust the ones who share this earth with me.

Today I Will Remember

God teaches me how to trust.

Reflection for the Day

A friend in the Program told me of a favorite hymn from her childhood: "Open my eyes that I may see glimpses of truth Thou hast for me." In actuality, that is what the Program has done for me—it has opened my eyes so that I have come to see the true nature of my addiction, as well as the true nature of the joyous life that can be mine if I practice the principles embodied in the Program's Twelve Steps to recovery. *Through prayer and meditation, am I also improving my inner vision, so that I can better see God's love and power working in me and through me?*

Today I Pray

May each glint of truth that I catch sight of as I work the Steps begin to take on the steadier shine of a fixed star. May I know that these stars are all that I need to chart my course and navigate safely. May I no longer feel the frantic need to put in to every unknown port along the way in search of direction. These stars are always mine to steer by.

Today I Will Remember

Find the fixed stars and fix on them.

Reflection for the Day

Some of us in the Program are inclined to make the mistake of thinking that the few moments we spend in prayer and meditation—in "talking with God"—are all that count. The truth is that the attitude we maintain throughout the entire day is just as important. If we place ourselves in God's hands in the morning, and throughout the day hold ourselves ready to accept His will as it is made known through the events of our daily life, our attitude of acceptance becomes a *constant* prayer. *Can I try to cultivate an attitude of total acceptance each day?*

Today I Pray

May I maintain contact with my Higher Power all through my day, not just check in for a prayer now and then. May my communion with God never become merely a casual aside. May I come to know that every time I do something that is in accord with God's will I am living a prayer.

Today I Will Remember

Prayer is an attitude.

Reflection for the Day

Some people are such worriers that they feel sorry about the fact that they have nothing to worry about. Newcomers in the Program sometimes feel, for example, "This is much too good to last." Most of us, however, have plenty of real things to worry about—old standbys like money, health, death, and taxes, to name just a few. But the Program tells us that the proven antidote to worry and fear is confidence—confidence not in ourselves, but in our Higher Power. *Will I continue to believe that God can and will avert the calamity that I spend my days and nights dreading? Will I believe that if calamity does strike, God will enable me to see it through?*

Today I Pray

May I realize that the worry habit—worry that grows out of broader, often unlabeled fears—will take more than time to conquer. Like many dependent people, I have lived with worry so long that it has become my constant, floor-pacing companion. May my Higher Power teach me that making a chum out of worry is a waste of my energy and fritters away my constructive hours.

Today I Will Remember

Kick the worry habit.

Reflection for the Day

Sometimes, on those bad days we all have from time to time, it almost seems that God doesn't want us to be happy here on earth and, for those of us who believe in an afterlife, that He demands pain and suffering in this life as the price of happiness in the next. The Program teaches me that just the opposite is the case. God wants me to be happy right here on earth—right now. When I allow Him to, He will even point out the way. *Do I sometimes stubbornly refuse to look where God is pointing?*

Today I Pray

I pray that I am not playing the perennial sufferer, dragging around in the boots of tragedy and acting as if suffering is the only ticket to heaven. May I look around, at the goodness and greenery of earth, which is testimony enough that our life here is meant to be more than just one pitfall after another. May no misconception of God as a master trapper, waiting in every thicket to snare us, distort my relationship with a loving, forgiving Higher Power.

Today I Will Remember

There is more to life than suffering.

DECEMBER 17

Reflection for the Day

More and more these days, as I progress in my recovery, I seem to do a lot of *listening*—quietly waiting to hear God's unmistakable voice within me. Prayer is becoming a two-way street—of seeking and listening, of searching and finding. A favorite bit of Scripture for me is, "Be still and know that I am God." *Do I pay quiet and loving attention to Him, evermore confident of an enlightened knowledge of His will for me?*

Today I Pray

As I seek to know my Higher Power, may I learn the best ways—for me—to reach and hear Him. May I begin to *feel* prayer, not just listen to the sound of my own verbalizing. May I feel the sharp outlines of my humanness fading as His Godliness becomes a part of me. May I feel that I am one with Him.

Today I will Remember

Feel the stillness of God.

Reflection for the Day

I'm learning—all too slowly, at times—that when I give up the losing battle of trying to run my life in my own way, I gain abiding peace and deep serenity. For many of us, that learning process is a painfully slow one. Eventually, however, I understand that there are only two wills in the world, my will and God's. Whatever is within my direct control is my will, whatever is beyond my direct control is His will. So I try to accept that which is beyond my control as God's will for me. *Am I beginning to realize that by surrendering my will to the Divine Will, I am for the first time living without turmoil and without anxiety?*

Today I Pray

May I hope that my will can be congruent with the all-encompassing will of God. I pray that I will know immediately if my will is in a useless tug of war with His Divine Will. May I trust God now to guide my will according to His Master Plan—and to make His purpose mine.

Today I Will Remember

Achievement comes when my will is in harmony with God's.

DECEMBER 19

Reflection for the Day

The Program teaches me to work for progress, not perfection. That simple admonition gives me great comfort, for it represents a primary way in which my life today is so different from what it used to be. In my former life, *perfection*—for all its impossibility—was so often my number one goal. Today I can believe that if I sometimes fail, *I'm* not a failure—and if I sometimes make mistakes, *I'm* not a mistake. And I can apply those same beliefs to the Program's Twelve Steps as well as to my entire life. *Do I believe that only Step One can be practiced with perfection, and that the remaining Steps represent perfect ideals?*

Today I Pray

God, teach me to abandon my erstwhile goal of superhuman perfection in everything I did or said. I know now that I was actually bent on failure, because I could never attain those impossible heights I had established for myself. Now that I understand this pattern, may I no longer program my own failures.

Today I Will Remember

I may strive to be a super person, but not a superperson.

Reflection for the Day

When we compulsively strive for perfection, we invariably injure ourselves. For one thing, we end up creating big problems from little ones. For another, we become frustrated and filled with despair when we're unable to meet the impossible goals we've set for ourselves. And finally, we decrease our capability to deal with life and reality as they are. *Can I learn to yield a little, here and there? Can I apply myself with a quiet mind only to what is possible and attainable?*

Today I Pray

May I see that striving for an impossible accomplishment provides me with an ever-ready excuse for not making it. It is also an indication of my loss of reality sense, which ought to involve knowing what I can do and then doing it. With the help of the group and my Higher Power, may I learn to set "reasonable goals." These may seem ridiculously small to me, after years of thinking big. But, by breaking down my projects into several smaller ones, may I find that I actually can accomplish some high goals.

Today I Will Remember

Break down large goals into smaller ones.

DECEMBER 21

Reflection for the Day

Each of us in the Program can, in our own time and own way, reach the triumphant spiritual awakening that is described in the Twelfth Step. The spiritual awakening is a deep-down knowledge that we are no longer alone and helpless. It's also a deep-down awareness that we've learned certain truths which we cannot transmit to others so that perhaps they, too, can be helped. *Am I keeping myself in constant readiness for the spiritual awakening which is certain to come to me as I practice the Steps and surrender my will to God's will?*

Today I Pray

May I be steady, not expecting that my spiritual awakening will startle me like an alarm clock into sudden awareness of a Higher Power. It may settle on me so quietly that I may not recognize precisely when my moment of awareness comes. The clue may come in my desire to Twelfth-Step others. May I realize, then, that I have accepted the principles of the Program and am at home with the spiritual transformation I feel in myself.

Today I Will Remember

My spiritual awakening is my first private moment with God.

Reflection for the Day

Through our own experiences and the experiences of others in the Program, we see that a spiritual awakening is in reality a gift—a gift which in essence is a new state of consciousness and being. It means that I'm now on a road which really leads somewhere; it means that life is really worth living, rather than something to be endured. It means that I have been transformed in the sense that I have undergone a basic personality change—and that I possess a source of strength which I had so long denied myself. *Do I believe that none come too soon to the Program, and that none return too late?*

Today I Pray

I pray that I may attain that state of consciousness which transcends my everyday reality—but is also a part of it. May I no longer question the existence of God because I have touched His Being. For us who are recovering from addictions, the words reborn in the Spirit have a special, precious meaning. May I be wholly grateful to a Higher Power for leading me to a spiritual rebirth.

Today I Will Remember

Renaissance through my Higher Power.

Reflection for the Day

How can I tell if I have had a spiritual awakening? For many of us in the Program, a spiritual awakening manifests itself in simple, rather than complicated, evidences: emotional maturity; an end to constant and soul churning resentments; the ability to love and be loved in return; the belief, even without understanding, that something lets the sun rise and set, brings forth and ends life, and gives joy to human hearts. *Am I now able to do, feel, and believe that which I could not previously do through my own unaided strength and resources alone?*

Today I Pray

May my spiritual confidence begin to spread over my attitudes towards others, especially during holiday times, when anticipations and anxieties are high. As an addictive person, I have not handled holidays well—greeting those who gather at home, missing those who are not here. I pray for serenity to cope with the holiday brew of emotions.

Today I Will Remember

Spirit without "spirits." Cheer without "cheer."

Reflection for the Day

We came to the Program as supplicants, literally at the ends of our ropes. Sooner or later, by practicing the principles of the Twelve Steps, we discover within ourselves a very precious thing. We uncover something with which we can be comfortable in all places and situations. We gain strength and grow with the help of God as we understand Him, with the fellowship of the Program, and by applying the Twelve Steps to our lives. *Can anyone take my new life from me?*

Today I Pray

May my prayers of desperate supplication, which I brought to my God as a newcomer to the Program, change to a peaceful surrender to the will of God. Now that I have seen what can be done through the endless might of a Higher Power, may my gift to others be that strong conviction. I pray that those I love will have the faith to find their own spiritual experiences and the blessings of peace.

Today I Will Remember

Peace—inner and outer—is God's greatest blessing.

Reflection for the Day

Today is a special day in more ways than one. It's a day that God has made, and I'm alive in God's world. I know that all things in my life this day are an expression of God's love—the fact that I'm alive, that I'm recovering, and that I'm able to feel the way I feel at this very instant. For me, this will be a day of gratitude. *Am I deeply thankful for being a part of this special day, and for all my blessings?*

Today I Pray

On this day of remembering God's gift, may I understand that giving and receiving are the same. Each is part of each. If I give, I receive the happiness of giving. If I receive, I give someone else that same happiness of giving. I pray that I may give myself—my love and my strengths—generously. May I also receive graciously the love and strengths of others' selves. May God be our example.

Today I Will Remember

The magnitude of God's giving.

Reflection for the Day

None of us can claim to know God in all His fullness. None of us can really claim to understand our Higher Power to any extent. But this I do know: there is Power beyond my human will which can do wonderful, loving things for me that I can't do for myself. I see this glorious power at work in my own being, and I see the miraculous results of this same power in the lives of thousands upon thousands of other recovering people who are my friends in the Program. *Do I need the grace of God and the loving understanding any less now than when I began my recovery?*

Today I Pray

May I never forget that my spiritual needs are as great today as they were when I came into the Program. It is so easy to look at others, newer to the recovery process, and regard them as the needy ones. As I think of myself as increasingly independent, may I never overlook my dependence on my Higher Power.

Today I Will Remember

I will never outgrow my need for God.

Reflection for the Day

"The central characteristic of the spiritual experience," wrote AA co-founder Bill W., "is that it gives the recipient a new and better motivation out of all proportion to any process of discipline, belief, or faith. These experiences cannot make us whole at once; they are a rebirth to a fresh and certain opportunity." *Do I see my assets as God's gifts, which have been in part matched by an increasing willingness on my part to find and do His will for me?*

Today I Pray

I pray for the wholeness of purpose that can come only through spiritual experience. No amount of intellectual theory, pep-talking to myself, disciplined deprivation, "doing it for" somebody else can accomplish the same results. May I pray for spiritual enlightenment, not only in order to recover, but for itself.

Today I Will Remember

Total motivation through spiritual wholeness.

Reflection for the Day

The Program, for me, is not a place nor a philosophy, but a highway to freedom. The highway leads me toward the goal of a "spiritual awakening as the result of these Steps." The highway doesn't get me to the goal as quickly as I sometimes wish, but I try to remember that God and I work from different timetables. But the goal is there, and I know that the Twelve Steps will help me reach it. *Have I come to the realization that I and anyone can now do what I had always thought impossible?*

Today I Pray

As I live the Program, may I realize more and more that it is a means to an end rather than an end in itself. May I keep in mind that the kind of spirituality it calls for is never complete, but is the essence of change and growth, a drawing nearer to an ideal state. May I be wary of setting time-oriented goals for myself to measure my spiritual progress.

Today I Will Remember

Timetables are human inventions.

Reflection for the Day

The success of the Program, I've been taught, lies in large measure in the readiness and willingness of its members to go to any lengths to help others tyrannized by their addictions. If my readiness and willingness cools, then I stand in danger of losing all that I've gained. I must never become unwilling to give away what I have, for only by so doing will I be privileged to keep it. *Do I take to heart the saying, "Out of self into God into others..."?*

Today I Pray

May I never be too busy to answer a fellow addict's call for help. May I never become so wound up in my pursuits that I forget that my own continuing recovery depends on that helping—a half-hour or so on the telephone, a call in person, a lunch date, whatever the situation calls for. May I know what my priorities must be.

Today I Will Remember

Helping helps me.

Reflection for the Day

My life before coming to the Program was not unlike the lives of so many of us who were cruelly buffeted and tormented by the power of our addictions. For years, I had been sick and tired. When I became sick and tired of being sick and tired, I finally surrendered and came to the Program. Now I realize that I had been helped all along by a Higher Power; it was this Power, indeed, that allowed me to live so that I could eventually find a new way of life. *Since my awakening, have I found a measure of serenity previously unknown in my life?*

Today I Pray

May I realize that my Higher Power has not suddenly come into my life like a stranger opening a door when I knocked. The Power has been there all along, if I will just remember how many brushes with disaster I have survived by a fraction of time or distance. Now that I have come to know my Higher Power better, I realize that I must have been saved for something—for helping others like me.

Today I Will Remember

I am grateful to be alive and recovering.

Reflection for the Day

God grant me the SERENITY to accept the things I cannot change; COURAGE to change the things I can; and WISDOM to know the difference—living one day at a time; accepting hardships as the pathway to peace; taking, as He did, this sinful world as it is, not as I would have it; trusting that He will make all things right if I surrender to His Will; that I may be reasonably happy in this life and supremely happy with Him forever in the next. Amen.

Today I Pray

May I look back at this past year as a good one, in that nothing I did or said was wasted. No experience—however insignificant it may have seemed—was worthless. Hurt gave me the capacity to feel happiness; bad times made me appreciate the good ones; what I regarded as my weaknesses became my greatest strengths. I thank God for a year of growing.

Today I Will Remember

Hope is my "balance brought forward"—into a new year's ledger.

THE TWELVE STEPS
OF ALCOHOLICS ANONYMOUS

1. We admitted we were powerless over alcohol—that our lives had become unmanageable.

2. Came to believe that a Power greater than ourselves could restore us to sanity.

3. Made a decision to turn our will and our lives over to the care of God *as we understood Him.*

4. Made a searching and fearless moral inventory of ourselves.

5. Admitted to God, to ourselves, and to another human being the exact nature of our wrongs.

6. Were entirely ready to have God remove all these defects of character.

7. Humbly asked Him to remove our shortcomings.

8. Made a list of all persons we had harmed, and became willing to make amends to them all.

9. Made direct amends to such people wherever possible, except when to do so would injure them or others.

10. Continued to take personal inventory and when we were wrong promptly admitted it.

11. Sought through prayer and meditation to improve our conscious contact with God *as we understood Him,* praying only for knowledge of His will for us and the power to carry that out.

12. Having had a spiritual awakening as the result of these steps, we tried to carry this message to alcoholics, and to practice these principles in all our affairs.

---

* The Twelve Steps of A.A. are taken from *Alcoholics Anonymous,* 3rd ed., published by A.A. World Services, Inc., New York, N.Y., 59-60. Reprinted with permission of A.A. World Services, Inc.

THE TWELVE TRADITIONS
OF ALCOHOLICS ANONYMOUS*

1. Our common welfare should come first; personal recovery depends upon A.A. unity.

2. For our group purpose there is but one ultimate authority—a loving God as He may express Himself in our group conscience. Our leaders are but trusted servants; they do not govern.

3. The only requirement for A.A. membership is a desire to stop drinking.

4. Each group should be autonomous except in matters affecting other groups or A.A. as a whole.

5. Each group has but one primary purpose—to carry its message to the alcoholic who still suffers.

6. An A.A. group ought never endorse, finance or lend the A.A. name to any related facility or outside enterprise, lest problems of money, property and prestige divert us from our primary purpose.

7. Every A.A. group ought to be fully self-supporting, declining outside contributions.

8. Alcoholics Anonymous should remain forever nonprofessional, but our service centers may employ special workers.

9. A.A., as such, ought never be organized; but we may create service boards or committees directly responsible to those they serve.

10. Alcoholics Anonymous has no opinion on outside issues; hence the A.A. name ought never be drawn into public controversy.

11. Our public relations policy is based on attraction rather than promotion; we need always maintain personal anonymity at the level of press, radio and films.

12. Anonymity is the spiritual foundation of all our Traditions, ever reminding us to place principles before personalities.

* The Twelve Traditions of A.A. are taken from *Alcoholics Anonymous*, 3rd ed., published by A.A. World Services, Inc., New York, N.Y., 564. Reprinted with permission of A.A. World Services, Inc.

KEEP IT SIMPLE

DAILY MEDITATIONS FOR TWELVE-STEP BEGINNINGS & RENEWAL

A Day at a Time

Words to Live By

HAZELDEN

MJF BOOKS

NEW YORK

Published by MJF Books
Fine Communications
Two Lincoln Square
60 West 66th Street
New York, NY 10023

A Day at a Time/Keep It Simple
Library of Congress Catalog Card Number 97-75632
ISBN 1-56731-258-6

10   9   8   7   6   5   4   3   2   1

WE DEDICATE THIS BOOK TO ALL
THOSE WHO'VE GONE BEFORE US AND
CARRIED THE MESSAGE; WE THANK
YOU WITH OUR LIVES

INTRODUCTION

We, the authors of this book, believe a recovery program should be made up of meditation, prayer, and action. This book will try to help readers in each of these areas.

On each page you'll find three sections. The first section will be a quote followed by a few paragraphs on the spiritual message we have found within the quote. We suggest reading the quote and our thoughts on it; then take a few minutes and reflect on your own spiritual journey. How does this quote and our thoughts on the quote speak to your recovery program? Is your program where you want it to be? If so, take pride. If not, think about which of the Twelve Steps you need to work, and what action needs to be taken. We are firm believers that the Steps plus action will solve most problems.

Next on the page, you'll find a Prayer for the Day. We see prayer as an important action. Prayer is an act of reaching outside of yourself. Prayer is an act of asking for help in the task of being human. We suggest reading the Prayer for the Day, and if it fits for you, repeat it throughout the day. If it doesn't, take a few moments and come up with a personal prayer that fits for you. If none comes to mind, use the prayer suggested in Step Eleven, "Thy will be done." Remember, each day we are to turn our self-will over to our Higher Power. In

doing so, we get the serenity the program promises.

Finally, you'll find a section named Action for the Day. Our illness was fed by a set of actions. Harmful, destructive actions. A recovery program is also about action. Daily spiritual action. Spiritual action helps us feel better about ourselves and safer in the world. In this section, you'll be asked to take an action that is, we hope, made to strengthen your program. Again, if the action fits, do it. If not, think of one that fits for you.

Also in this book, you'll see that we use words like *addict* and *addiction*. As time changes, so does language. When we use these terms, we are speaking to both the alcoholic and the drug dependent person. We see no difference between the two. We believe both suffer from the same deadly disease. We ask you to see yourself in the pages, and not in any one word.

Recovery is a process of finding balance between mind, body, and soul. Hopefully, this book will help you find or strengthen this balance.

We thank you for letting us share a part of our spiritual journey with you. We wish you well on your spiritual journey. May you and your Higher Power have a wonderful relationship!

THE AUTHORS

*W*e admitted we were powerless over alcohol—that our lives had become unmanageable.

— *Step One*
from Alcoholics Anonymous

We admitted we were
powerless over alcohol. . .
— From Step One of
Alcoholics Anonymous

In Step One, we accept our powerlessness over alcohol and other drugs. But we are powerless over many parts of life. We are powerless over other people. We are powerless over what our Higher Power has planned for us.

Before recovery, we only believed in control. We tried to control everything. We fought against a basic truth, the truth that we are powerless over much of life.

When we accept this truth, we begin to see what power we do have. We have the power to make choices. When we're lonely, we have the power to reach out to others. We have power over how we live our own lives.

Prayer for the Day

Higher Power, help me to know that it's You who is running my life. Help me to know that power comes from accepting I am powerless.

Action for the Day

I am powerless over much of life. Today I'll look to see how this is true. I'll look to see what I really have control over and what I don't.

. . .our lives had become
unmanageable.
— Second half of Step One

The First Step tells us a lot about addiction. We were out of control. Our addiction was in control. Addiction managed everything. It managed our relationships. It managed how we behaved with our families. As Step One says, ". . .our lives had become unmanageable."

But we pretended we managed our lives. What a lie! Addiction ran our lives—not us. We weren't honest with ourselves. Our program heals us through self-honesty. We feel better just speaking the truth. We are becoming good people with spiritual values. Our spiritual journey has begun.

Prayer for the Day

Higher Power, I give You my life to manage. When I'm faced with a choice, I'll ask myself, "What would my Higher Power choose for me?"

Action for the Day

Today, I'll be honest with a friend about how unmanageable my life had become.

*Never play leapfrog with a
unicorn.*

— *Unknown*

As we work Step One, we accept that alcohol
and other drugs are poison to us. We accept
our limits. This means we know that hanging around our drinking or using "buddies"
can remind us of "the good old days." Hanging around "slippery places" means we could
"slip" back into our old ways. This isn't testing
our sobriety; it's being reckless with it.

So, let's accept our limits. Everybody has
limits. When we know our limits, we protect
our recovery against the people and places
that pull us from our spiritual center. This is
what true acceptance means.

Prayer for the Day

I pray for true acceptance. Higher Power, help me
to stay away from slippery places. I will protect the
gift You've given me.

Action for the Day

Today, I'll list the people and places that are risky
for me to be around. I will share this list with my
sponsor, my group, and my sober friends.

*He who is swift to believe is
swift to forget.*
— *Abraham Joshua Herschel*

Life is full of questions. Many people tell us
they have the answers. We have to be careful
of who and what we believe. Other people's
ideas may not fit us.

The program doesn't tell us much about
what to believe. It teaches us *how* to believe.
How well the program works for us depends
on what we believe and how well we live it.

When we face all the facts, we can really
believe. We believe we are powerless over our
addiction. We believe we must and can
change some things in our lives. We believe
we can trust a Higher Power to care for us.
When we choose to believe, we want to choose
the best beliefs we can. And once we believe,
we must not forget.

Prayer for the Day

Higher Power, help me know You, and help me
know the truth.

Today's Action

Today I'll think about my First Step. Do I truly
believe I'm powerless over my disease?

The journey of a thousand miles begins with a single step.

— Chinese proverb

Life holds so many choices now that we are sober. We'd like to go so many places. We'd like to see so many things. We have so much to do.

We are slowly learning how to trust our dreams and reach for them. Our program teaches us that we live One Day at a Time. We make progress by doing First Things First. Easy Does It.

Our dreams may seem very big and far away. We wonder if we'll ever get there. But our faith tells us to go for it. And we know how: one step at a time.

Prayer for the Day

Higher Power, help me know this gentle truth: my life matters. Help me set goals that I can grow toward, one step at a time.

Action for the Day

Today I'll think about one of my goals. I will list ten little steps that will help me get there.

We.
— First word of the Twelve
Steps

We. This little word says a lot about the Twelve Steps. Our addiction made us lonely. The "we" of the program makes us whole again. It makes us a member of a loving, growing group of people.

Our addiction isolated us from others. We couldn't be honest. We felt a lot of shame. But all this is in the past. The "we" of the program helps us live outside ourselves. Now we tell each other about our pasts. We comfort each other. We try to help each other.

Prayer for the Day

Higher Power, help me to join the *we* of the program. Help me to admit and accept my illness, so the healing can begin.

Action for the Day

Today, I'll work to make the *we* of the program even stronger. I'll find someone to help.

*A good scare is worth more
to a man than good advice.*
—*E. W. Howe*

Do you let yourself be afraid of your illness?
You'd better. Many of us were scared into
sobriety. Often, a spiritual awakening directly
follows a good scare. Fear seems to improve
our vision.

Are you smart enough to run from your addiction? The First Step should create fear
inside us. It's about looking honestly at our
addiction and what would happen to us if we
kept using. Looking at Step One regularly will
give us the respectful fear we need to stay
sober. Often fear is seen as bad, but it can be
good, if we listen to it. It can be a great mover.
When you're afraid, your spirit is trying to tell
you something.

Prayer for the Day

God, direct my fear. Have me go to You, family,
friends, and others who love me. Help me see my
fear and listen to its message.

Action for the Day

I'll list five ways that my fear has taught me important lessons. I'll see that my fear can help me
as long as I listen to it and not live in it.

*Believe more deeply. Hold
your face up to the Light,
even though for the
moment you do not see.*
— Bill W.

At times, we'll go through pain and hard-
ship. At times, we'll have doubts. At times,
we'll get angry and think we just don't care
anymore. These things can spiritually blind
us. But this is normal. Hopefully, we'll be
ready for those times. Hopefully, we will have
friends who will be there for us.

Thank God for these moments! Yes, hard
times can make our spirits deep and strong.
These moments tell us who we are as sober
people. These moments help us grow and
change. Spirituality is about choice. To be
spiritual, we must turn ourselves over to the
care of our Higher Power.

Prayer for the Day

God, help me find You in my moments of blindness. This is when I really need You.

Today's Action

Today I'll get ready for the hard times ahead. I
will list my friends who will be there for me.

*Everything is funny as long
as it is happening to
someone else.*
— *Will Rogers*

We laugh when others do something silly.
We're amused when something funny happens
to them. But if the same happens to us and
people laugh, we might give them the evil eye.

Yet, when others laugh, it can free us. It
frees us to see the world through new eyes.
Likewise, when we laugh at ourselves, we're
free to see ourselves with new eyes. Instead
of trying to be perfect, we accept we're human.
To laugh at ourselves is to accept ourselves.
There's no room for shame when we laugh.
We enjoy ourselves just as we are. Can I accept
the fact I'm human and I have limits?

Prayer for the Day

Higher Power, when I refuse to accept that
I'm only human, be gentle with me. I know that,
when I least expect it, You will remind me that I'm
only human.

Action for the Day

I will share with a friend one or two stories about
funny mistakes I've made.

*I'm always ready to learn,
although I do not always
like being taught.*
— *Winston Churchill*

We addicts are used to learning the hard
way. Many of us think we're different and can
do things our own way. But then we get in too
much trouble or pain. The first A.A. members
were just like us. They knew how it is to hate
being told what to do. So they suggested we
follow the Twelve Steps. They didn't say we
have to do anything. They didn't say working the Steps is the *only* way to live sober.
They just said the Steps worked for them.

We're finding out that the Steps work for us
too. We don't *have* to work them. We don't
have to stay sober. We just like our new sober
life better than our old drinking or drugging
life. And we're learning how to live this new
life by working the Steps.

Prayer for the Day
Higher Power, help me be open to your lessons.
Teach me gently and help me listen.

Action for the Day
I will list five ways that I get in the way of my
own learning.

*If there's a harder way of
doing something, someone
will find it.*
— *Ralph E. Ross*

When we used alcohol or other drugs, we
did most things the hard way. We could turn
a simple task into a day-long project. We
could turn a simple problem into an argument. We were creative giants in doing things
the hard way!

We need to change this. We deserve easier
lives. It's okay to take the smooth road. In our
program, we have slogans for this: Keep It
Simple, Let Go and Let God, First Things
First, and Easy Does It. These slogans remind
us that it's okay to live with as little trouble
as possible.

Prayer for the Day

Higher Power, show me how to live a simple life.
I don't have to do everything the hard way if I listen
better to You.

Action for the Day

I'll list three or four things I do that make my
life harder than it needs to be. I'll share them with
a friend.

*Remember always that you
have not only the right to
be an individual, you have
an obligation to be one.*
— *Eleanor Roosevelt*

When we were using alcohol and other
drugs, we often thought that we were different
from others. We secretly thought that no one
could understand us. Maybe we tried to be
one of the group, but we were lonely.

Now we know for sure—we *are* different
from others. Everyone's unique. We all have
this in common. Being like others helps us
feel safe and normal. But we need to feel good
about the ways we're different from others too.
We think a little different, act a little different, and look a little different from anyone
else. We each have our own way to make life
better for others.

Prayer for the Day

Higher Power, help me be an individual. Help me
use my special gifts, not hide them.

Action for the Day

Today, I'll make a list of the things I'm good at.
I'll think about how I can use these gifts.

*The junkie can never start to
cure himself until he
recognizes his true condition.*
— *Malcolm X*

Now we know what the problem is. Now we
can do something about it. The truth of our
problem is, we can't handle alcohol or other
drugs. They handle us. They control us. The
Steps ask us to face the truth. And the truth
sets us free. What a wonderful gift! We feared
the truth, but now it's our friend. It's a relief.
Facing the truth means we're honest. And
honesty is our best friend in recovery. It's like
a cozy fire on a winter's night. Honesty is how
we get well. It's also what will keep us well.
Do I truly believe I can't use alcohol or other
drugs?

Prayer for the Day
Higher Power, help me see my illness for what
it is. It's my enemy. Help me see that honesty is
my best friend.

Action for the Day
Today, I'll take fifteen minutes to think about
what my *true* condition was when I was drinking
and drugging. And I'll think about what my true
condition is now.

*If you play with a thing
long enough, you will
surely break it.*
— *Anonymous*

Some things shouldn't be played with. Our recovery program is one of these things. When we play with our program, we're taking a risk. We play with the program by missing meetings. Or by not calling our sponsors. Or by skipping the Steps we think are too hard.

It's okay to play. But it's not okay to play with our recovery program. When we play with our program, we risk our lives.

Prayer for the Day

Higher Power, help me know that I must work this program with care and respect.

Action for the Day

Today, I'll make two lists. On one list, I'll write ways I *work* on my program. On the other list, I'll write ways I *play* with my program. And I'll put my energy into working the program.

*I shall tell you a great
secret, my friend. Do not
wait for the last judgment,
it takes place every day.*
— *Albert Camus*

"Later." How often have we said this? This trick helps us avoid the tasks of the day. Life is full of tasks—many fun, some boring, others hard. Can I accept the tasks my Higher Power gives me, easy or hard?

When we used alcohol or other drugs, we'd avoid tasks, if they became hard for us. We believed we had more control than we really did. We started to believe we could control outcomes. What we really were doing was setting ourselves up for a great fall. We had to face the fact that when our Higher Power had given us a task, we said no, and turned away. Thus, we turned away from the guiding hand of our Higher Power.

Prayer for the Day

God, help me face You and the tasks You give me. Make me a grateful student of life.

Today's Action

Today I will talk with friends. I will tell them what tasks I'm working on.

*Fair play is primarily not
blaming others for anything
that is wrong with us.*
— *Eric Hoffer*

It's tempting to blame others for our problems. Recovery asks us to answer for our actions. Admitting we are powerless over our alcohol and other drugs is a start. Each of the Twelve Steps asks us to answer for our actions in some way. And the program shows us how to do this.

Over time, we see that being responsible for our actions is the best way to live. Our self-confidence grows as we become more responsible. We start to see just how much we can do. We have gone from being drunks to being responsible people. If we can do this, then we can do anything!

Prayer for the Day

I pray to remember that I'm responsible for my actions. Blaming puts distance between me and other people. Higher Power, help me to play fair.

Action for the Day

Today, I'll list four times I've blamed someone else for a problem that was really *my* problem.

*When all else fails, read
the instructions.*
— *Agnes Allen*

The instructions for recovery are in our Twelve Step program. Yet, there are times when we feel our program isn't working. At these times, we need to read the instructions.

Have you followed the "instructions," the wise words found in The Big Book, The Twelve and Twelve, and other recovery literature? When we do, we recover.

It's hard at times, and easy at others. Our problems go deeper than just staying sober. No matter what our problems, our program can help us start fixing them, if we follow the instructions. Don't use alcohol or other drugs. Go to meetings. Talk often with sponsors and program friends. Work the Steps. Think. Easy Does It. First Things First. Listen. Let Go and Let God. One Day at a Time.

Prayer for the Day
Higher Power, tell me which instructions to read today. If I'm headed for trouble, help me out.

Today's Action
I'll read the instructions today.

*The reality is that changes
are coming....They must
come. You must share in
bringing them.*
— *John Hersey*

Change. It's scary. It's hard. It's needed. Sometimes it feels good; other times it feels bad. But one thing is for sure: it keeps on happening.

Just when our life seems settled, it changes. We can't stop life. We can't stay this age forever. The world changes. Life moves on. There are always new things to do and learn.

Change means we're always beginners in some ways. We need to ask for wisdom and courage. We get it by listening, by praying, by meditating. When we ask, our Higher Power will teach us to be part of good changes.

Prayer for the Day

Higher Power, help me believe that Your plans call for good changes.

Action for the Day

Today I'll think about the changes in my life. I've lived through a lot. I'll be okay when more changes come, with God's help. I can keep on growing.

*Study sickness when you
are well.*
— *Thomas Fuller*

Now is the time to learn about our sickness—chemical dependency. It is a *chronic* illness. That means it never goes away. We have to live with it the best we can. Luckily, we *can* live with it—very well! Our program of recovery is so simple, and it feels so good, that we think we'll never give it up. But we can't take our recovery for granted.

Our disease is "cunning, baffling, powerful." The more we know about it, the less we'll let it fool us. Some days we may find we're headed toward a slip. We must learn to recognize the first trouble signs in ourselves so we can get help to stay sober.

Prayer for the Day

Higher Power, my addiction is "cunning, baffling, powerful." Don't let me use alcohol or other drugs again. Thank you for my sobriety today.

Action for the Day

Today, I'll learn my warning signs: I'll list ten old thoughts, feelings, and actions that were part of my illness. I'll share this with my sponsor.

*SERVICE—A beautiful word
fallen upon bad days.*
— *Claude McKay*

Service is really a beautiful word. Service means *respect*. When we serve others we're part of the human race. We all need to help each other.

Service is a sure way to stay sober. Helping someone else stay sober helps us stay sober. And service frees us from self-will. It teaches us about how to care for ourselves and others. It teaches us that we're worthwhile. It teaches us that we make a difference. Service keeps us feeling good.

Am I quiet when the topic of service comes up at meetings? If so, how can I change this?

Prayer for the Day

Higher Power, show me where I can be of help. Give me the courage to make a difference. Give me the courage to really serve others in need.

Action for the Day

I'll list five ways service has made or can make my life better.

*What is defeat?. . .Nothing
but the first step to
something better.*
— *Wendell Phillips*

A man walks into a meeting. He says, "I surrender. I can't drink like other folks." We smile and welcome him. We know that feeling. All of us in the program must admit defeat. Our illness is more powerful than we are. We begin recovery when we surrender.

Admitting defeat is our first step into a beautiful world. Like all first steps, it's hard. But what a world we find ourselves in! A world where we count! A world where all are really equal!

This first step brings us into God's world of care. We get love. We give love. We stay sober because daily we admit defeat.

Prayer for the Day

I surrender. I can't drink and use other drugs. I'm different. Higher Power, help me surrender daily.

Action for the Day

Every so often, I need to admit defeat and talk about what it was like, what happened, and where I am now.

*Go often to the house of
your friend: for weeds soon
choke up the unused path.*
— *Scandinavian proverb*

Our program has two parts: the Steps, and
the fellowship. Both keep us sober. We can't
stay sober if we go it alone. We need to work
the Steps. We also need people—the help of
our friends daily.

Recovery is about relationships. We get new
friends. We get involved. We give. We get. In
times of need, we may not want to ask our
new friends for help. Maybe we don't want to
"burden them." Maybe we're afraid to ask for
help. Well, go ahead. Make that call. Ask your
new friend to spend time with you. You
deserve and need it. They deserve it; they
need it.

Prayer for the Day
Higher Power, help me to get help from my
friends as if my life depends on it.

Action for the Day
Today, I'll see or call two program friends and let
them know how I'm doing.

*Sex, like all else between
human beings, is never
perfect.*
— *Theodore Isaac Rubin*

Addiction made our sex lives a mess. Maybe we wanted perfect sex or we wanted no sex. We were afraid. Maybe we wanted a high from sex we just couldn't seem to get. Some of us had lots of sex partners; some of us had none.

What now?

We're doing what we need to do by being in recovery. We're getting to know ourselves. We're living by our real values. We're being honest with ourselves and others. We're learning to love and care about others. It's open, honest caring we express with our bodies. Thus, sex can be trusting and safe.

Prayer for the Day

Higher Power, I turn over my sex life and my will to You—just for today. I know You want me to be happy.

Action for the Day

What do I believe about sex? How does it match with what's said in the third paragraph above?

*Few people can be happy
unless they hate some
other person, nation, or
creed.*

— *Bertrand Russell*

In recovery we learn to give up hate. We must stand for justice, not for hate. We must learn to respect people. They, in turn, will respect us in most cases. We begin to see how important it is to give up hate—if we want others to care for us.

Hate is often our secret. Hate is found deep in our hearts and minds. It eats at our souls. It hurts our spiritual growth. Sometimes people are public about their hate. There are even dangerous groups based on hate. But, the most dangerous hate is the private and unspoken. Do I have public hates? Do I have secret hates?

Prayer for the Day

Higher Power, search my heart and show me any hates I have. Help me rid myself of them.

Action for the Day

I'll list any people, nations, or creeds I hate. I'll pray to have this hate removed. I'll pray for these people, nations, or creeds.

*The best place to find a
helping hand is at the end
of your own arm.*
— *Swedish proverb*

During our illness, we hurt others. We hurt
ourselves. We messed up a lot. So, a lot of us
come into recovery not trusting ourselves
very much. The truth is, as addicts, we
couldn't be trusted.

But in recovery, we can be trusted again.
We can again live and love ourselves. We do
this by finding our spiritual center. This is the
place inside of us where our Higher Power
lives. We turn our will and our lives over to
this spiritual center. We do as our spiritual
center tells us. And from our spiritual center,
we'll find our values. We'll live better lives.
We'll come to trust ourselves again.

Prayer for the Day

Higher Power, thank-you for helping me believe
in myself again. I'll treat myself with love and kindness. I know You want me to.

Action for the Day

Today, I'll list four ways I couldn't be trusted during my addiction. I'll also list four ways I can now
be trusted.

One forgives to the degree
that one loves.
— La Rochefaucould

We all get hurt by other people sometimes. When this happens, we have choices. We can get angry and stay that way. We can act like it didn't hurt and try to forget it. We can act like a sad sack and hold a grudge. Or we can forgive.

We first have to think about how someone hurt us. It often helps to talk to the person, to tell the person that he or she hurt us. We then tell the person what we'd like from him or her to help set our relationship straight. Then we let go.

This is what forgiveness is: (1) loving ourselves enough to stand up for ourselves, (2) loving others enough to point out their behavior, and (3) letting go.

Prayer for the Day

Higher Power, help me lovingly forgive those who have hurt me.

Action for the Day

I will list five persons who have hurt me. Have I forgiven them? I will talk to my sponsor about it today.

They are able because they
think they are able.
— *Virgil*

For most of us, addiction was full of doubt. We stopped believing in ourselves. Our thoughts had turned to "stinkin' thinkin'." We didn't believe in much of anything. We didn't take risks. We always looked for the easier, softer way.

In recovery, we start to believe again. We believe in the program. We believe in a Higher Power. We believe in people. And, over time, we believe in ourselves again. We become better at taking risks.

We are able to stay sober because we believe, because we take risks. As we stay sober, we can face almost anything—with the help of others.

Prayer for the Day

Higher Power, I have learned to believe in You. Help me believe in myself. I have something to give to this world. Help me give it freely.

Action for the Day

Today, I'll list ten good points about myself. I'll go over these good points with a friend.

There is no they, only us.
 — *Bumper sticker*

We're now part of a fellowship we call "the program." Let's also remember that we're part of a larger fellowship called "the human race." We all hurt the same. We all love the same. We all bleed the same. We all need understanding and care.

Yet, in other ways, we are *not* all the same. Let's remember to understand differences among people. If not, we'll be afraid of anyone who's not like us. And this isn't God's way.

Prayer for the Day

Higher Power, help me to love all people. Help me be open to others who are different from me. Help me love my neighbor.

Action for the Day

Do I think I'm better than others? If that's true, I'll pray that my Higher Power will remove this shortcoming of mine.

*An alcoholic spends his life
committing suicide on the
installment plan.*
— *Laurence Peter*

None of us woke up one morning and found
we had suddenly turned into an addict. We
got to be one by practice. And we practiced
often. We ignored our families—we left work
early—and went drinking and drugging.
Daily, we chose chemicals over anything else.

Likewise, getting sober is no accident. We
use the Steps. We work the program. At meetings, we're reminded to help others. We all get
sober on the installment plan. A day at a time.
We got sick one day at a time; we recover one
day at a time.

Prayer for the Day

Today, with my Higher Power's help, I'll be happier, more honest, more sober. Sobriety is like a
good savings account. Higher Power, help me to
put in more than I take out.

Action for the Day

I'll go over my Step One to remind myself it's no
accident I'm an addict.

Go and wake up your luck.
— Persian proverb

We've been given recovery. For this, we're lucky. And we're grateful. Now it's up to us. We must accept our choices. When we're afraid, do we choose to be alone? Or do we choose to go to an extra meeting? When we're not honest, do we keep it secret? Or do we admit it and try to be more honest? No matter what we choose, we're responsible for that choice. Through choices, we either make our program strong or weak.

We can choose to be lucky. Or we can choose not to be. The choice is ours. Our addiction robbed us of choice. It taught us to blame others. Now we see ourselves as responsible.

Prayer for the Day

Higher Power, help me to choose wisely. Help me remember I'm responsible for my choices.

Today's Action

Today I'll work at being responsible for my choices. I'll see myself as one of the lucky ones.

*Do not cut down the tree
that gives you shade.*
— *Arabian proverb*

We need to remember what got us well. The Twelve Steps heal us. The meetings we attend heal us. Reading and listening to program tapes heal us. Talking with our sponsor heals us. The time we spend with program friends heals us.

Sometimes we're pressed for time. As a result, we have to make choices about how to use our time. We may think we know enough about the program. We may feel like cutting down on meetings. These are danger signs. We only know how to stay sober One Day at a Time: by working the Steps. Let's not forget them as we grow in this program. It may seem like we've been recovering a long time, but we're all beginners.

Prayer for the Day

Higher Power, I've found You in the program. Help me find ways to stay a "beginner" in the program.

Action for the Day

Today, I'll take time to read the Twelve Steps. I'll meditate on how much these Steps have given me.

*C*ame to believe
that a Power greater
than ourselves could
restore us to sanity.

— *Step Two*
from Alcoholics
Anonymous

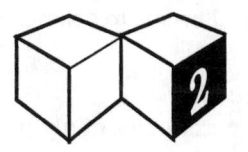

Came to believe that a
Power greater than
ourselves could restore us
to sanity.

— *Step Two*

The Second Step directs us to believe there is hope for us. It may take time to believe this. Many of us had given up hope. But look around. Hope fills our meeting rooms. We are surrounded by miracles. This Power greater than ourselves has healed many. Listen as others tell their stories. They speak of how powerful this Power is.

At times, we will not want to believe. This is normal. But in recovery, "coming to believe" means opening ourselves up to healing power found in the program.

Prayer for the Day

Higher Power, allow me to believe. Help me stay open to recovery.

Action for the Day

I will list three examples of my past insanity. I will share these examples with my group, sponsor, a program friend, or with my Higher Power. I will remember that I'm a miracle.

FEBRUARY 2

We must believe the things
we teach our children.
— *Woodrow Wilson*

It may be easy to say the words and phrases we've heard without really meaning them. Someone says something at a meeting that sounds good. Our counselor has a favorite saying. We may say these words, but are we taking the time to ask the question, Do I believe what I'm saying?

Step Two speaks of, "Came to believe...." By really believing in the Twelve Steps, we let them become part of us. The more we believe in the Steps the more we turn our lives over to them. Hopefully, over time, the Twelve Steps will guide us more and more. We'll speak to our family with the respect we've found in the Twelve Steps. Our spirit must truly believe. Then we can work the Steps.

Prayer for the Day
Higher Power, believing is something that lasts a lifetime. Give me the power to believe even when doubt creeps in.

Action for the Day
My beliefs are changing. Today, in my inventory, I'll ask: Do I believe what I said today?

*Never go to a doctor whose
office plants have died.*
— *Erma Bombeck*

We often hear, "Stick with the winners."
Not everyone in Twelve Step meetings is
there for recovery. But many members follow
a Twelve Step way of living. We need to find
those people. This is really true when it
comes to finding a sponsor.

Look for a sponsor who gets good things
from his or her program. Why pick a sponsor who isn't happy in the program? Recovery is hard work. You deserve the best. Find
the best sponsor you can. Remember, ours is
a selfish program. We're fighting for our lives.

Prayer for the Day

Higher Power, help me find the best in my program. Help me find a good sponsor, so we can get
as much from each other and this program as
we can.

Today's Action

Today I'll think about what it means to have a
good sponsor.

We do not remember days,
we remember moments.
— *Cesare Pavese*

It's the moment that's important. Each moment holds choice. Our spirits grow through working our program moment to moment. Moments lead to days, days to years, and years to a life of honest recovery.

It will be the moments of choice that we remember. The moment we call a friend instead of being alone. The moment we decide to go for a walk instead of arguing with our partner. The moment we decide to go to an extra meeting instead of drinking or using other drugs. These moments lead us to our Higher Power. These moments teach us that we're human, that we need others. At these moments, we know others care about us— our joys, and our struggles.

Prayer for the Day

Higher Power, help me remember that my recovery is made up of many moments of choice.

Today's Action

I'll look back over the last twenty-four hours. What moments come to mind? Why were they important to me?

*Do not bite at the bait of
pleasure til you know there
is no hook beneath it.*
— *Thomas Jefferson*

Pleasure is important in recovery. But at
times we think pleasure is the answer to life's
pains. Alcohol and other drugs were what we
liked best. We need to watch out so we don't
switch to another addiction—such as gambling, food, sex, or work.

The real answer to life's pains is in having
a strong spiritual center. It is also our best
way to avoid another addiction. Recovery lets
us turn our pain over to the *care* of our Higher
Power. Our Higher Power can handle any
problem we may have. Our program can help
us with our problems too. Recovery is a three-
way deal—Higher Power, program, and us.

Prayer for the Day

Higher Power, help me avoid another addiction.
When I have problems, have me come to You and
to my program before anything else.

Action for the Day

Today, I'll set aside time and ask the question,
"Am I headed for another addiction?" I'll also ask
my sponsor what he or she thinks.

We will not know unless we begin.
— *Howard Zinn*

Let us begin! Whether it be working on our First Step, finding a sponsor, or talking to someone we've hurt—let us begin. Doubt will set in if we wait too long. Fear will follow. So, let us begin.

We learn by doing. Recovery is for doers. Sobriety doesn't just happen. We create it. We create it by working the Steps and learning from them. We'll never totally understand the Steps unless we work them. In the same way, we'll never learn how to have friends unless we try. So, call your friends, instead of waiting to be called. Begin and begin again. Each day *is* a new beginning.

Prayer for the Day

Higher Power, today I'll begin. I begin by asking for Your help and love. Be with me as I go through my day. Help me work for progress, not perfection.

Action for the Day

Today, I'll not sit on the sidelines. I'll be a doer. I'll decide what to do to move closer to friends, family, Higher Power, and myself.

*I thank God for my
handicaps, for through
them, I have found myself,
my work and my God.*
— *Helen Keller*

None of us ever wanted to be addicts. It's
not what we would choose to be—just as no
one would choose to be blind and deaf. Helen
Keller, who was blind and deaf, told of how
her problems became her biggest gift.
Through them, she found true meaning in
her life.

We can accept our handicap—our addiction—
and learn from it. The truth is, we're all handicapped in some way. Recovery is about facing
our addiction and learning to live with it.
When we see we can't do things alone, we see
the need for a Higher Power.

Prayer for the Day

Higher Power, help me see myself as I really am.
Give to me the serenity that comes from accepting
my handicaps.

Action for the Day

Today, I'll list all the ways I am handicapped. I'll
ask myself, "What gift does each of these hold for
me?"

*You must find the ideas
that have some promise in
them...it is not enough to
just have ideas.*
— *George E. Woodberry*

Each day we're flooded with ideas. Everyone seems to have found the truth, and now they want to share it. We may feel loaded down with all these ideas. Who and what do we believe?

We've fallen on a set of ideas that hold great promise: The Twelve Steps. The ideas of the program have much promise because they're simple. They ask nothing that isn't good for us. They have been proven to work. Now we're people with more than ideas. We're people with good ideas that *work*. When we find ourselves wondering how to live, all we need to do is look to the Steps.

Prayer for the Day

Higher Power, help me to put my energy into working the Steps.

Action for the Day

Today, I'll list what is right about the Steps for me. What promises do the Steps hold for me?

H.A.L.T.

> — *AA Slogan*

H.A.L.T. stands for Hungry, Angry, Lonely, and Tired. These feelings can be of danger to us. They can lead us away from our program.

We need to eat regular meals. When we get too hungry, we get cranky. Then we say and do things we regret.

We need to turn anger over to our Higher Power, or else our anger can turn into rage.

We need friends to help us in recovery. If we get too lonely, we may turn to our addictive ways for friendship. We don't stay sober by ourselves.

We need a clear mind to deal with life. If we get too tired, we tend to feel sorry for ourselves. Being tired gets us into crazy thinking.

Prayer for the Day

Higher Power, remind me to H.A.L.T. Help me to not get too Hungry, Angry, Lonely, or Tired.

Action for the Day

Today, I'll review the four parts of H.A.L.T. In which areas do I practice good self-care? In which areas do I not? How can I improve?

*Life didn't promise to be
wonderful.*
— *Teddy Pendergrass*

Life doesn't promise us anything, except a chance. We have a chance to live any way we like. No matter how we choose to live, we'll have pain and we'll have joy. And we can learn from both.

Because of our recovery program, we can have life's biggest wonder—love. We share it in a smile, a touch, a phone call, or a note. We share it with our friends, our partners, our family. Life didn't promise to be wonderful, but it sure is full of little wonders! And we only have to open up and see them, feel them, and let them happen.

Prayer for the Day

Higher Power, help me see the wonders of life today, in nature, in people's faces, in my own heart.

Action for the Day

I can help make wonderful things happen for others, with a smile, a greeting, a helping hand. What "little" things will I do for someone today?

Sanity is madness put to
good use.
— *George Santayana*

In Step Two we come to believe a Power greater than ourselves can restore us to sanity. In a way, as we work Step Two, we're praying that our madness can be put to good use. This is just what happens. Addiction was wrecking our life. But it's also our addiction that forced us into a new way of life.

As long as we remember what our madness was like, we can put it to good use. When we feel like giving up, let's remember our madness. It will help us go on. When we see someone suffering from the illness of addiction, let's remember our own days of madness. It will help us be there for that person. It's also good to remember that our madness is only a pill or a drink away.

Prayer for the Day

Higher Power, I believe You can put my madness to good use. I give up my madness; do with it what You want.

Action for the Day

I'll list a couple ways my Higher Power and I have changed my madness into sanity.

We are always the same
age inside.
— *Gertrude Stein*

Deep inside, we each have a child's spirit. We still have many of the feelings we had when we were young. Some of us have a hurting child inside. There's sadness, fear, or anger that hasn't gone away. We're still lonely, no matter how many people care about us.

Our inner child needs special help to heal. We can be good parents to our inner child. We do this by being gentle and caring with ourselves. In time, this child can be a happy center in our hearts.

Prayer for the Day

Higher Power, please heal the child inside me a little more each day. Help my inner child be alive, free, and full of joy.

Action for the Day

Right now, I'll close my eyes for a minute. I'll think kind thoughts about myself. Then I'll say out loud, "Inner child, I love you. I'll take good care of you." I'll do this two more times today.

Tomorrow doesn't matter,
for I have lived today.
— *Horace*

Life is found in the present. One of the first things we hear when we enter the program is, One Day at a Time. We break life into short time periods. This gives us the power to change. We're not sure we can stay sober for a lifetime. But we know that with God, and our program, we can stay sober for today.

This holds true for many other things in our lives. We're not sure we can go a lifetime without feeling self-pity, but we can give it up for the day. By living One Day at a Time, we become more sure of our strength. We have the power to change things only in the present. The present holds much for us, if we get a hold on it.

Prayer for the Day

Higher Power, You are found in the moment. You are here. I will stay with You minute by minute.

Action for the Day

I will ground myself in the present. Today, I'll not worry about the past or the future.

*Some things have to be
believed to be seen.*
— *Ralph Hodgson*

In recovery, we learn to trust. We trust that
our Higher Power is on our side. Maybe we
can't *see* our Higher Power, but once we start
trusting, things change. Step Two says,
"Came to believe. . ." Once we come to believe, we start to see our Higher Power working in many ways. We make new program
friends. We find new peace. Our family and
friends trust us again.

Life won't always be fair. We won't get all
we want. But we'll find the love and care we
need. If we're open to believing in love, the
easy times will be easier and the harder times
a bit softer. Do I believe in love?

Prayer for the Day

Higher Power, help me believe, especially when
times are hard. Help me not blame You for the hard
times.

Action for the Day

I will write what I believe the program and my
Higher Power want for me.

Easy Does It.
— *Twelve Step slogan*

We are people who push ourselves too hard. We try to be perfect. Well, we need to lighten up. Easy Does It. We need to slow down our pace.

Why? Because our program teaches us to give up trying to be perfect. We begin to love ourselves for who we are. *We are enough.* Over and over we hear this as we live the Steps. It's the message of God's love.

Our Higher Power wants us to live at a pace that's not fast and hard, so we always know we're loved. Remember, we've turned our life over to the *care* of God. And our life is a wonderful gift. As recovering people, we may know that better than others.

Prayer for the Day

Higher Power, teach me to live at Your pace, not mine. Help me keep in mind that life isn't a race. It's a spiritual journey. Walk with me.

Action for the Day

Today, I'll take two hours just to relax and do loving things for myself. I'll take time to count my blessings.

*Friendships, like
marriages, are dependent on
avoiding the unforgivable.*
— *John D. MacDonald*

We need to remember that relationships are made up of people—people who are strong, but also fragile. We don't break easily, but we do break. We need to be aware of how fragile relationships are. Don't say something that will hurt others even if it's honest. It's mean to be honest with someone, without showing that you care for the person's feelings.

We can learn to be honest without being cruel. The backbone of any relationship is this: we need to honor the rules and agreements we make. If we promise to be faithful to someone, we follow this rule. And we need to trust the other person to do the same. When we see that our agreements don't work, we need to go to that person and talk about them.

Prayer for the Day

Higher Power, help me become a person who honors rules and agreements in my relationships.

Action for the Day

I'll make no promises today that I will not keep.

*. . . no one who learns to
know himself remains just
what he was before.*
— *Thomas Mann*

Deep inside, we all know that we're changing. It started when we took Step One. We learned and accepted something new about ourselves. That changed us, just a little.

We no longer wanted to live as addicts. That meant we had to change and to learn to live sober. It's been nonstop ever since: learn about ourselves, change a little, learn about ourselves, change a little more, and so on.

All we know is that each step of learning and changing makes life better. How long can it keep getting better? As long as we keep learning to know ourselves.

Prayer for the Day

Higher Power, teach me about myself today. Teach me gently.

Action for the Day

Today, I'll think about what I've learned about myself by working the program. I'll list five things.

*Whoever gossips to you will
gossip about you.*
— *Spanish proverb*

Gossip can kill the trust in a Twelve Step program. We all need to feel safe when we share our personal lives with others. We need to know our private business won't be spread around.

We can do two things to help keep the trust in our groups, and in the rest of our lives too. First, don't gossip. Second, don't listen to gossip about others.

Prayer for the Day

Higher Power, help me mind my own business today. Help me honor the trust of my friends by not gossiping.

Action for the Day

Today, I'll think of two ways to stop someone from telling me gossip. Then, I'll put those ways to use.

*Changing brings questions,
and questions bring
change.*

— *Anonymous*

What am I becoming? How do I know if what I'm doing is right? Is it best for me? We are full of questions. Often, times of questions are times of change. We are becoming something new, and there is always a little fear of change.

Luckily, we don't *need* to know what we are becoming to find peace. What we need to know is what we believe in. And we'll become what we believe in. If we believe in sobriety, we'll be sober. If we believe in honesty, we'll struggle to be more honest.

We must give ourselves the freedom of becoming. Becoming means we're on a trip, a journey. Over time, becoming takes on a comfort of its own.

Prayer for the Day

Higher Power, what am I becoming? I give up having to know the answer. All I need to believe is that You love me and will do what is best for me.

Action for the Day

I'll ask lots of questions. Often, the question is more important than the answer.

Let Go and Let God.
— Twelve Step slogan

Some days we might ask ourselves, *Is it worth it?* We feel alone. No one seems to care. Life seems hard. Recovery seems hard.

This is when we need to slow down and take a look at what's going on. We're feeling this way because we're off our recovery path. We may be back into wanting people to see things our way, or do things our way. We want control.

Remember, all problems are not *our* problems. All work is not *our* work. We can't have everything the way we want it. But we can do our part and let go of the rest. Then we can feel better.

Prayer for the Day

Higher Power, help me remember my only work today is to do Your will for me. It is not my job to be You.

Action for the Day

I'll talk with my sponsor or a program friend today. I'll talk about how to deal with things that seem to pull me down.

To thine own self be true.
— AA medallions

Sometimes we hear that we have a "selfish program." Being "selfish" means that we ask for help when we need it. We only go to places that are safe for us, no matter what others are doing. Being selfish comes to mean *safety* for us.

Being selfish doesn't mean we act like brats. We must act in ways that show respect and love—for ourselves and for others. Being selfish means we do what is *good* for us.

What is good for us? First, we have to save our lives by stopping our drinking and drugging. Next, we start working the Steps. We come to know a loving Higher Power. This is how we come to know our true self.

Prayer for the Day

Higher Power, help me be true to myself and my values. Help me be "selfish" about spending time to talk with You each day.

Action for the Day

I'll list ten ways I need to be "selfish" in recovery. If I get stuck, I'll be "selfish" and ask for help.

It's easier to speak of love,
than to practice it.
— *Anonymous*

Do we help our neighbor who is in need? We must help when we see the need, not just when it fits our schedule. In the program, this becomes our goal. We work at helping out. For example, when someone is needed to run the meeting, we offer. We see that the needs of the group are also our needs. We are the group.

Over time, the idea of service spreads to the rest of our lives. Maybe we help a family down the street. We start to see that we have something to offer the world: ourselves. We start to see that the needs of the world are also our needs. We are an important part of the world.

Prayer for the Day

Higher Power, make me quick to act when I see a need. Please don't let my fear stop me.

Action for the Day

Today, I'll list what I have to offer the world. I will think of two ways I can use these gifts my Higher Power has given me.

Hitch your wagon to a star.
— Ralph Waldo Emerson

Millions of people are sober and have peace of mind through the Twelve Steps. Like the stars, the Steps are always there. At times, clouds block our view of the stars, but we know they're still there. Let's view the Twelve Steps the same way.

It is said that the stars are the gate to heaven, that we pass through their beauty to get ready to enter heaven. The Twelve Steps are the gate to spirituality here on earth. We travel through their beauty on our way to a spiritual awakening. Hitch your wagon to the Steps, and get ready for the ride of a lifetime!

Prayer for the Day

I pray to remember that the Steps keep me sober. I pray that I will follow where the Steps take me.

Action for the Day

I'll look at the stars tonight. I'll think of them as symbols of my life touched by the Twelve Steps.

Failure is impossible.
— *Susan B. Anthony*

Failure is an attitude. Having an attitude of failure can't help us. It can only hurt us. If we're not careful, it can grow into a way of life. So, when we feel like failures, we'd better look at our attitudes.

An attitude of failure often comes from making mistakes. But we can learn to see our mistakes as lessons. This turns mistakes into gains, not failures. Sometimes, we try to do things that just can't be done. When we act like we can control others, we're going to fail. When we act like we know everything, we're going to fail. If we try to act like God, we're going to fail.

We can't control others. We can't know everything. We're not God. We're human. If we act human, we've already won.

Prayer for the Day

Higher Power, help me to learn from my attitudes. Whatever the outcome, help me learn.

Action for the Day

Facing our past "failures" is the first step to learning from them. I'll talk to my sponsor about a past "failure" and the good that came from it.

*Believe that life is worth
living and your belief will
help create the fact.*
— *William James*

Step Two speaks of believing. For many years, we had given up believing in ourselves, in a Higher Power, and in others. We believed in getting high.

Now our program tells us to believe in love. We *are* lovable, and we can love others without hurting them.

Of course, believing is an important part of recovery. To believe means to put aside our doubts. To believe means to have hope. Believing makes the road a little smoother. So, believing lets the healing happen a little faster.

All of this is how we get ready to let in the care of our Higher Power.

Prayer for the Day

I pray for the courage to believe. I'll not let doubt into my heart. I can recover. I can give myself totally to this simple program.

Action for the Day

I'll list four times doubt got in my way. And I'll think of what I can do to not let that happen again.

Forewarned, forearmed;
being prepared is half the
victory.
— *Miguel de Cervantes*

There will be hard times in our program. There will be hard times in our life. That's the way life is. It helps if we accept this. Then we can prepare for tough times.

We can prepare by getting a good set of habits and sticking to them. We can make it a habit to give time to our program each day.

Sticking to good habits is like having a savings account: when hard times come, we can take the "investment" we've made and overcome our problems.

Prayer for the Day

Higher Power, help me accept that there will be hard times. Help me prepare for them. With Your help, I'll stay close to You, my friends, and the program.

Action for the Day

I'll put something into my program "savings account" today. I'll make that extra call. I'll read a little longer or go to an extra meeting.

*Without work all life goes
rotten.*
— *Albert Camus*

Work is more than earning money. Work means using our time and skills to make life better for those around us. Our work can be our hobbies. Growing food or growing flowers can be our work. Raising children or caring for older people who need help can be our work. Building homes or helping people live in them can be our work.

Thanks to our program of recovery, we can do our best work again. What a change from the drugged-up and hung over days when we didn't do anything well. We are sober, and we have something to offer.

Prayer for the Day

Higher Power, help me see that work makes me part of the human family. Help me do Your will in my work today.

Action for the Day

Good work teaches us good habits. How do the things I've learned in my work help me in my recovery program? I'll list five ways.

Leave yourself alone.
        — Jenny Janacek

We often pick on ourselves. We put ourselves down. But doing this isn't part of our recovery. In fact, it goes against our program. Our program is based on loving care. We have turned our lives over to a caring, loving Higher Power who will give us the answers.

We are told Easy Does It. We back off. As recovering addicts, we learn not to judge. Instead, we learn to be kind to ourselves. Our job is not to figure out the world, but to add more love to it. Let's start with ourselves.

Prayer for the Day

Higher Power, stop me from judging. Help me know what You want me to do. Help me work Steps Two and Three.

Action for the Day

Today, I'll leave myself alone. I will remember that picking on myself is another form of control.

In my friend, I find a
second self.
— *Isabel Norton*

We are all part of each other. *We* are part of others. When we can't see ourselves, maybe we need to look at others in our group. We can learn from them. We can learn how to stand firm, even when our knees are shaking and we want to run away. We can learn to speak gently to ourselves, even when our heart is full of tears. We can learn how to take pride in the simple things we do. Our friends in the program can teach us all these things.

We will learn to love again as others come to love us. We will become the heaven that keeps others from the hell of addiction. Through us, others will believe that a Power greater than themselves can restore them to sanity.

Prayer for the Day

Higher Power, please watch over the members of my Twelve Step group. Keep them safe and sober, for they have helped to keep me safe and sober.

Action for the Day

I will take time to find some way to say thank-you to my group.

March

***M**ade a decision to turn our will and our lives over to the care of God as we understood Him.*

— *Step Three*
from Alcoholics
Anonymous

*Made a decision to turn our
will and our lives over to
the care of God as we
understood Him.*
— *Step Three*

Care. This is what we turn our will and lives
over to the care of our Higher Power. What
peace follows! We see our God as caring, as
loving. We turn everything over to this Higher
Power, who can take better care of us than we
can by ourselves.

Care can guide us. If we want to do something, we can ask ourselves, "Would my
Higher Power see this as an act of care?" If
the answer is yes, then we go ahead. If the
answer is no, we don't do it. If we can't be sure,
we wait and talk it over with our friends and
sponsor. We wait until we know whether it
would be an act of care or not. What wonderful guidance!

Prayer for the Day
Higher Power, I give to You my will. I give to You
my life. I gladly jump into Your loving arms.

Action for the Day
Today, I'll care about others. I'll find as many
ways as I can to care for others.

*Love conquers all; let us
surrender to love.*

— *Virgil*

In Step Three, we turn our lives over to
God's care, God's love. If we turn our lives over
to a loving God, we can conquer all.

If you need proof, look around at your next
meeting. The room will be full of people who
know that love conquers addiction. Like them,
we've surrendered to love. Once we've done
this, we can't use again. For us, using alcohol or other drugs is an act of hate, not love.

To face the hard things in life, we'll need a
lot of love. We'll find love in our Higher Power,
groups, and friends. We're now part of a community based on love. We're all working at
turning our lives over to love.

Prayer for the Day

There was a time that love scared me. It still
does, at times. Higher Power, help me see that You
are love, and I must follow where love takes me.

Action for the Day

I'll meditate on the question, "How has Step
Three changed my life?"

*But the alcoholic. . .will be
absolutely unable to stop
drinking on the basis of
self-knowledge.*
— *Alcoholics Anonymous*

Our program says three things are more important than knowing ourselves: (1) admitting we have no control over our addiction, (2) believing in a Higher Power, and (3) turning our lives over to the care of that Higher Power.

Knowing ourselves makes our lives better in recovery. But it does not give us sobriety. Sobriety starts with surrender to our Higher Power. We now know we need the faith and strength we get from a Higher Power. We also need the support of others in our program.

Prayer for the Day
Higher Power, thank you for my sobriety today. Teach me what I need to know about myself to do Your will today.

Action for the Day
Today, I'll talk with my sponsor about the change in my spirit that keeps me sober.

Better bend than break.
— Scottish proverb

Our program is based on bending. We call it "surrender." We surrender our self-will to the care of God. We do what we believe our Higher Power wants us to do. We learn this as an act of love.

Many of us believed surrender was a sign of weakness. We tried to control everything. But we change as we're in the program longer and longer. We learn to bend. We start to see that what is important is learning. We learn to do what's best for us and for others. To learn, we need an open mind. To bend, we must stay open. Love and care become the center of our lives.

Prayer for the Day

Higher Power, teach me that strength comes from knowing how and when to bend.

Action for the Day

Today, I'll check on myself. How open am I? Do I bend when I need to?

I am not afraid of
tomorrow, for I have seen
yesterday and I love today.
— William Allen White

Big changes are happening to us, but we can trust that changes will bring good things. After all, what have we got to lose? We have lived through the days and years of our addiction. Now, with the help of our Higher Power, the pain of those days has ended. We have no reason to worry.

Yet, recovery won't make our lives perfect. Hard things still happen. But we never have to lose hope again. We never have to feel alone with our problems again.

What will come next? We don't know the details, but we can be sure the future will be good if we stay on our path of recovery.

Prayer for the Day

Higher Power, I know life holds many new things for me. Help me and protect me as I live in Your care today.

Action for the Day

Today, I'll trust that each day of my life will bring me good. I will share this idea with one friend.

*When I see a bird that
walks like a duck and
swims like a duck, and
quacks like a duck, I call
that bird a duck.*
— *Richard Cardinal Cushing*

Remember how we tried to make others think we were not in trouble? We walked and talked like addicts. We acted like addicts. Most everyone knew the truth but us. We were like ducks pretending to be eagles.

We need to see ourselves as we really are. But sometimes we can't see ourselves that way. This is normal. That's why we need others to help us see what we can't. We were *addicts*. We are now *recovering addicts*. We need friends, sponsors, and family members to tell us when we may be acting like *addicts* again. It may save our lives.

Prayer for the Day

Higher Power, give my friends and family members the strength to tell me when I'm acting like an addict.

Action for the Day

I'll go to people whom I trust and ask them to tell me when I'm acting like an addict.

To make the world a
  friendly place
One must show it a
  friendly face.
  — James Whitcomb Riley

We are beginning to learn that we get what we expect. Why? If we believe that people are out to get us, we'll not treat them well. We will think it's okay to "get them" before they "get us." Then, they'll be angry and want to get even. And on it goes.

It's great when we can meet the world with a balance. We are now honest people. We can expect others to be fair with us. We get the faith, strength, and courage to do this because of our trust in our Higher Power.

Prayer for the Day

Higher Power, I put my life in Your care. Use me to spread Your love to others.

Action for the Day

Today, I'll spread friendliness. I will greet people with a smile.

*We lose the fear of making
decisions, great and small,
as we realize that should
our choice prove wrong we
can, if we will, learn from
the experience.*

— Bill W.

As our disease grew, we often felt like any decision we made was wrong. We felt like *wrong people.* We lost self-respect, because deep inside we knew that, for us, using alcohol and other drugs was wrong. We went against our spirit.

Now we go with our spirit. We follow what we think our Higher Power wants for us. Now we *learn* from our mistakes. Another wonderful gift has been given back to us: the gift of learning. From this gift, we stop playing God. How free it feels!

Prayer for the Day

Higher Power, You have taken away my illness and replaced it with many wonderful gifts. I thank You for everything, even my mistakes.

Action for the Day

Today, I'll share with a friend my mistakes of the past week.

*You've got to do your own
growing, no matter how
tall your grandfather was.*
— *Irish proverb*

Each of us has been given recovery. Now it's up to each of us what we do with it. At times, we'll work hard and grow quickly. At other times, our growth will be slower. This is okay. We're not in a race. Our pace is not important. What is important is that we're always working on our recovery.

We're all part of a fellowship, a caring group. We're one of many. But we're each important. Each one of us will have a special way to work our programs through our readings, friends, meetings, and what we know of how life works. Each of us puts together a miracle of recovery. We then take our miracle and share it with others, so they can build their miracle.

Prayer for the Day

Higher Power, help me work at growing. Help me be a person who is an important part of a group.

Action for the Day

Today, I'll work at seeing myself as very important. I'll remind myself that others' recovery also depends on my recovery. I am needed.

*Little things affect little
minds.*
— *Benjamin Disraeli*

Before recovery, we liked things *our way*.
We thought every new thing we tried should
go right the first time. Little problems could
really upset us. We let little things spoil our
day. We let little things affect big things—our
entire lives. And our bad moods affected
people around us.

Funny how we have fewer of those problems
now. The program is teaching us to let go.
What a relief when we know we don't have to
control every little thing! How nice when
things get done without our "expert advice"!
We are starting to see what's really important,
and what's not. One promise of the program
is coming true: we know how to handle situations better.

Prayer for the Day
Higher Power, help me see what is really important for me today. Help me to stop worrying about
what's not.

Action for the Day
When I'm upset, I'll ask myself, Is this problem
really so bad? If I can't change it, I'll let go.

If it ain't broke, don't fix it.
— AA saying

Before recovery, we never thought we had enough alcohol or other drugs. More would make us feel better, we thought. Sometimes, we are like this in our recovery too. We know we need to change, so we want to do it all *right now.* If we can just change ourselves *totally,* we'll feel better, we think.

But we can't change all at once. If we ask our Higher Power to take charge of our lives, we'll have the chance to change a little at a time. We'll learn the right things when we need to know them.

Prayer for the Day

Higher Power, help me fix what needs fixing today.

Action for the Day

I'll make a list of what is broken. Which things on my list can I fix today?

*The Twelve Step program is
spiritual, based on action
coming from love...*
— Martha Cleveland

To be *spiritual* means to be an active person. It means spending time with others. It means sharing love. It means looking for ways to be more loving to others. It means looking for ways to make the world a better place.

Step Three helps us to look at the world better. We turn our lives over to the *care* of our Higher Power. So let's allow *care* to direct our lives. Let's always be asking ourselves, "Is what I'm doing something that shows I care?"

Prayer for the Day
Higher Power, let me be active in a loving, caring way. Let the love in my heart be my guide.

Action for the Day
Today, I'll do something good for someone and keep it a secret.

*God loves the world
through us.*
— *Mother Teresa*

In Step Three, we turn our will and our lives over to the *care* of God. How do we feel God's care, God's love? We feel God's care and love through how people treat us. Our Higher Power works through people who love us back to life.

With time, we begin returning this care and love to others. We feel this warm love flow right through us and out to others. We're kind without trying to be. We smile at others for no reason. We comfort those who hurt just by holding them.

Prayer for the Day

Higher Power, use me to make Your love real to someone today.

Action for the Day

Fear sometimes keeps me from loving. I'll list three things I'm afraid will happen if I'm "too loving." I'll share these fears with my sponsor.

Archie doesn't know how to
worry without getting
upset.
                              — Edith Bunker

Most of us are like Edith's television hus-
band, Archie. When we worry, we get upset.
Problems seem too big for us. We get afraid.
We feel powerless.

What does the program tell us to do when
we feel powerless and our life is upset? We
look at the problem honestly. Then we ask
our Higher Power to help us with the problem.
We take it One Day at a Time. We believe our
Higher Power will take care of us and help us.

We'll have problems. That's life! But we can
get through them with care and support. We
don't have to get crazy. We don't have to make
things worse. We can be kind to ourselves and
live through problems just fine—with our
Higher Power's help.

Prayer for the Day

Higher Power, help me do what I can today about
my problems. Help me stop worrying.

Action for the Day

If I have a problem today, I'll do what I can—
and I'll leave the outcome to my Higher Power.

*I never loved another
person the way I loved
myself.*

— Mae West

This sums up how we used to live. We were in love with ourselves. We had to be on center stage. Our self-will ran riot.

Recovery pulls us out of that world. We learn to focus on others. We learn to reach out to them with love. This is the best way to love ourselves.

This doesn't mean that we live our lives through others. It means we invite others into our lives. It also means we ask to be invited into their lives. Recovery breaks down our self-will. It makes room for others in our lives.

Prayer for the Day
Higher Power, I give You my self-will. I know You'll do better with it than me.

Action for the Day
I'll list three ways my self-will has messed up my life. How am I doing at turning over these things to my Higher Power?

*Every saint has a past and
every sinner has a future.*
— Oscar Wilde

We all change. We learn, and change, and grow. We once made alcohol or other drugs our Higher Power. Perhaps we had other higher powers too—like money, gambling, food, or sex. But, it's never too late to be in touch with a true Higher Power. Each day we do this, we're saints. Each day we follow a false higher power, we aren't.

Prayer for the Day
Higher Power, help me put my life and will in Your hands today. Help me be a saint, just for today.

Action for the Day
How have my ideas about saints and sinners changed since I got into a Twelve Step program? I'll talk with my sponsor about it today.

Money costs too much.
  — *Ross MacDonald*

Many people are poor and really need money to live better lives. But we're in trouble if we think money will solve all our problems. If money solved all problems, all rich people would be happy.

Consider this: A man talks about his shortcomings in a Twelve Step meeting. He says his main shortcoming is to think being happy means having enough money. But then he says that he has over a million dollars!

This man is lucky—not because he has money, but because he knows greed is a shortcoming. He knows he has a spiritual problem. He doesn't need money; he needs faith in a Higher Power.

Prayer for the Day
Higher Power, help me to really believe I'll be given what I need. This will free me to get on with life.

Action for the Day
Today, I'll read over the promises of the program. They are found at the bottom of page 83 and at the top of page 84 in the Big Book, *Alcoholics Anonymous*, Third Edition.

Skill to do comes of doing.
— *Ralph Waldo Emerson*

Often, we just want to sit and do nothing.
And why not? We go to meetings, work the
Twelve Steps, read, make new friends. All this
takes energy and means taking risks. Haven't
we earned the right to just sit and take a
break from it all?

No! In the past, we avoided life. Now we're
becoming people of action. We take risks.
We're becoming people who get involved in
life. We practice caring about people and caring about ourselves. At times, we may complain, but we do what is needed to stay sober.
We gain skills by doing.

Why? We do it to save our lives. How? By
trusting. We now trust that our Higher Power
and friends will be there for us. They will help
us push past our fears. As we *practice* daily
how to stay sober, our skills grow.

Prayer for the Day
Higher Power, Yours is a spirit of action. Allow
me to become skilled at being active.

Action for the Day
Today, I'll work at being active and alive. Maybe
I'll start a new friendship or try a new meeting.

*Speak when you're angry
and you'll make the best
speech you'll ever regret.*
— Lawrence J. Peter

When we used alcohol or other drugs, most of us were hotheads. We thought we were right. If we were proven wrong, we may have made life hell for everyone. People knew enough to stay away from us.

In recovery, things will still go badly at times. We'll get hurt. And we'll get angry. But now, our anger no longer controls us. We also turn over our anger to our Higher Power. In our groups, we talk about what makes us angry. Then we leave the anger behind when the meeting is over. We find that being at peace is now more important than getting even.

Prayer for the Day

Higher Power, when I'm angry, help me slow down. Help me remember it's okay to be angry, but it's not okay to abuse people.

Action for the Day

I will remember a time when I turned anger into rage and hurt someone. I will also remember a time I was angry in a respectful way.

> *You can make more friends
> in two months by becoming
> interested in other people
> than you can in two years
> of trying to get other people
> interested in you.*
> — *Dale Carnegie*

We wanted friends, but our addiction wanted all our attention. We had no time to be close to others.

Well, stand aside, addiction! The program has taught us that others are important. Our purpose is to help others. People have become what's important to us.

Now we *listen* to others. We help them do what *they* want to do, not what *we* want them to do. We help people instead of use them. Friendship is now a way of life. And another promise of the program becomes a part of us.

Prayer for the Day

Higher Power, help me to know that I'm here to help others, not just myself. Through others, I find myself.

Today's Action

Today I'll help someone in the way he or she wants to be helped.

With each sunrise, we start anew.

— *Anonymous*

Like a tree, our life depends on new growth. There are many ways to bring new ideas and growth into our lives. We can attend Twelve Step retreats. We can study books and tapes on spirituality. We can attend different Twelve Step meetings.

But our spiritual newness may not just come from the Twelve Steps. We can do volunteer work or be active in other types of groups. We need to invite new ideas into our lives. We need to stay open to change. It doesn't matter what renews our spiritual growth. What matters is that we keep our spiritual lives fresh and growing.

Prayer for the Day

Higher Power, spring is one of the four seasons. Help me feel like spring. Help me to be strong but not stuck. Help me be firm yet open to spiritual growth.

Action for the Day

Today I'll try to do something new. When I get stuck or stubborn, I'll see that it's due to my fear of trying new ideas.

*Youth is happy because it
has the ability to see
beauty. Anyone who keeps
the ability to see beauty
never grows old.*
— *Franz Kafka*

Our addiction closed our eyes to the beauty of the world. The longer our disease went on, the uglier we felt and acted. We looked at honesty as an enemy, not as a friend.

In recovery, we start over. As time goes on, we work to stay young in the program. We need to be beginners. We need the eyes of a child to stay sober. We might think we know how to stay sober. This thinking can be full of danger. Instead, we need to see staying sober as a gift. It's a gift that's given one day at a time. We need to stay open to the beauty of the Twelve Steps and the gifts they hold.

Prayer for the Day

Higher Power, help me stay a beginner in this program. Have me see the beauty of the world. My addiction made me old. Help me regain my youth.

Today's Action

Today I'll study the children I meet. I'll learn much from their gentle beauty.

*If anything, we have
tended to be people who
wanted it all now. To hope
is not to demand.*
— *On Hope*

Maybe we were a bit demanding. Maybe we were a bit impatient. Maybe that's why we had such little hope.

Hope is believing good will come, even in bad times. Hope is knowing that "this, too, shall pass." Hope is knowing that no matter how afraid we are, God will be with us. Hope is knowing we never have to be alone again. It is knowing that time is on our side. Hope is giving up control. Hope is knowing we never had control in the first place. Hope is believing in ourselves. Hope is what our program is all about.

Prayer for the Day

Higher Power, in our program we share our experiences, our strengths, and our hopes. Thank you for giving all three of these to me to share.

Action for the Day

I will share my hope for the future with myself, my Higher Power, and my friends. I also will share this with someone who has lost hope.

*Love your enemy—it will
drive him nuts.*
— *Eleanor Doan*

Love your enemy. It's a lot easier on you!
Hating someone takes so much time and
energy.

Loving your enemy means, instead of trying to get even, you let your Higher Power
handle that person. Of course, loving your
enemy is also hard. It means giving up control. It means giving up self-will. We addicts
naturally want to control things and people.

This is where we turn to our program for
help. We learn to love our enemies, not for
some grand reason. We simply do it because
hate can cause us to use alcohol or other
drugs again.

Prayer for the Day

Higher Power, watch over my family, friends, and
my enemies. Take from me my desire to control.
Take from me *all* reasons to get high.

Action for the Day

Today, I'll list all of my enemies. I'll say each of
their names, and then I'll read the Third Step out
loud.

*The artist who aims at
perfection in everything
achieves it in nothing.*
— *Eugene Delacroix*

Trying to be perfect puts distance between
us and our Higher Power. Trying to be perfect
shows we're ashamed of being human. In
recovery, we accept that we're human. We try
to be the best *human* we can be.

We used to get high to feel powerful and
god-like. But God is not just power. God is also
gentleness. Gentleness and love are the power
we look for in recovery. We give up trying to
be perfect. We work to be human. We work
to know the loving, gentle side of ourselves
and our Higher Power. Remember, if we try
to be a god, we'll fail. If we try to be human,
we'll win.

Prayer for the Day

Higher Power, help me give up trying to be perfect. Help me always keep in mind that I'm
human—which means, I'm not perfect.

Action for the Day

Part of being human is making mistakes. Today,
I'll see my mistakes as chances to learn.

*I'm gonna die with my
boots on.*
            — Gene Autry

Most of us don't like to think about death.
But it's a sure thing, and we have to face it.
First, we face the deaths of people around us.
Then, some day, we'll face our own.

Most of us want to go quickly—"with our
boots on"—when we die. We're afraid of illness, of pain, of being helpless. We're afraid
of needing other people.

But being in the program teaches us it's
okay to need other people. It's nice to accept
their care and love for us. And no matter how
we die, our trust in our Higher Power lets us
face our fears with courage.

Prayer for the Day

Higher Power, help me live fully today. Help me
put my life in Your hands.

Action for the Day

Is there anything I need to do before I die? Can
I do it today? If I can, I will.

*The secret of success is
constancy of purpose.*
— Benjamin Disraeli

In Twelve Step meetings, we don't talk about counseling, treatment centers, or non-program reading. Many of us have been helped in these ways, but we shouldn't confuse them with Twelve Step programs.

We must keep our Twelve Step programs pure, no matter what is in style among counselors or at treatment centers, or what the latest books say. Certainly, we should use these sources if they help us, but not in our program meetings. There, we must stick to the basics that have helped addicts recover all over the world for many years. Steps, traditions, meetings, sponsorship—these things work, no matter what is in style.

Prayer for the Day

Higher Power, let me be there to help an addict in need, by sharing my Twelve Step program.

Action for the Day

I will help out today by being a sponsor or by calling a new group member, just to say hello.

*God is not a cosmic
bellboy.*
— *Harry Emerson Fosdick*

We have to laugh when we look back at the times we treated God like our servant. Who did we think we were, ordering God to do something for us? But we got away with it. God even did some of the things we asked.

Now we know that our Higher Power is not a servant. As we work the Steps, we know we don't give orders to our Higher Power. We don't expect God to work miracles every time we'd like one. We're asking our Higher Power to lead us. After all, who knows what is best for us—our Higher Power or us?

Our Higher Power has many wonderful gifts for us. Our Higher Power will show us goals, help us live in love and joy, and give us strength.

Prayer for the Day

Higher Power, show me ways to help others as You've helped me. I'm grateful that You love me and help me.

Action for the Day

Today, I'll make a list of times my Higher Power has helped me out of trouble.

*Whatever is in the heart
will come up to the tongue.*
— *Persian proverb*

During our illness, we wouldn't let people get close to us. We spoke much of what was in our heart. And much of what filled our heart was sadness, anger, and hopelessness. Those who wanted to be close to us heard what was in our heart. In short, we had become our illness.

Recovery is about changing what's in our heart. We open our heart to the program and to its healing. We open our heart up to our Higher Power.

The first three Steps are about opening our hearts. They're about honesty and needing others. They're about turning our will and our lives over to a Higher Power. If you're wondering where you are with these Steps, listen to the words you speak.

Prayer for the Day

Higher Power, keep my heart open to the first three Steps.

Action for the Day

Today, I'll work at really listening to what I have to say.

*Spirituality is...the
awareness that survival is
a savage fight between you
and yourself.*

— *Lisa S.*

As recovering people, we're getting stronger each day. We go to meetings to learn how to be better people. But we also go to remind ourselves of the beast inside us—our addiction. This beast is waiting for us to slip—to go back to our addiction—so it can regain control.

Thus, it's wise to learn all we can about our disease. That's why it's important to do a good job on our Fourth Step. When we work Step Four, we learn how our addiction acts, thinks, and feels. With the help of our program, we can quiet the beast, One Day at a Time.

Prayer for the Day
Higher Power, I'm fighting for my life. Thanks to You, I'm winning today and my life is free.

Action for the Day
I'll talk to a friend about my addiction, the beast inside me. I'll do this so it will have less power over me.

*You grow up the day you
have your first real laugh
at yourself.*
— *Ethel Barrymore*

There was a time when we wouldn't let anyone laugh at us—even ourselves. We had too much shame. We had too much pain. We took the world too seriously. If we laughed, it was at others—not at ourselves.

Over time, real and honest laughter returns to us. Laughter is a way of accepting ourselves as human. To be human means we can make mistakes. It means we can lighten up. It also means growing up. And growing up means being happy with *all* of who we are—even parts of us that may seem odd or funny. If we can't laugh at ourselves, we shut ourselves off from the world. We shut ourselves off from the parts of us we need to accept. Am I willing to accept the fact that I'm human?

Prayer for the Day

Higher Power, You made laughter. Help me use it to make my life easier. Help me accept *all* of me.

Today's Action

Today, I'll share with someone close to me a funny mistake I've made.

Made a searching and fearless moral inventory of ourselves.

— *Step Four*
from Alcoholics
Anonymous

*Made a searching and
fearless moral inventory of
ourselves.*
— *Step Four of Alcoholics
Anonymous*

We avoid the Fourth Step. We put it off.
We're scared of what we will find inside of us.
We may find out we're mean, angry, selfish,
afraid. We might see how badly we've acted
to others, to ourselves. We have power to hurt,
and we've used it. We all have these things
inside of us.

We also have love, trust, faith, and hope. We
love art, music, nature, or sports. We have
power to heal, and we have used it too.

The Fourth Step helps us to know our inner
power. As we learn about our own power, we
can use it carefully, on purpose, to do good.

Prayer for the Day

Higher Power, help me use my power to do Your
will. Let Your power work through me too.

Action for the Day

Today I'll watch my own actions and words. I'll
see how my power affects others. I'll talk about this
with my sponsor.

*To know all things is not
permitted.*

— *Horace*

In recovery, we give up trying to be perfect.
We give up trying to know everything. We
work at coming to know and accept our shortcomings. In Steps Four and Five, we look at
our good points and our bad points. In Step
Six, we become ready to have our Higher
Power remove our "defects of character."
Then in Step Seven we ask our Higher Power
to remove our "shortcomings."

Recovery is about coming to accept that
we're not perfect. We admit that trying to be
perfect got in the way of being useful to ourselves, our Higher Power, and those around
us. Pretending to be perfect doesn't allow us
to be real. It's also boring and no fun—you
never get to mess up.

Prayer for the Day

Higher Power, You will let me know what I need
to know. Allow me to claim my mistakes and shortcomings.

Action for the Day

I will work at being okay today. Not perfect,
just okay.

*Rest is the guardian of
health.*
— *Melba Colgrove*

Now that we're sober, we're feeling better than we have in years. We're busy too. We attend meetings and visit friends. We have work, school, families, and homes to keep up with.

It's easy to forget to rest. We forget that our bodies and minds need time off. We need plenty of sleep each night. And we need a lazy weekend now and then to let our bodies recover from the *go, go, go* of daily life.

Prayer for the Day

Higher Power, help me listen to my body. Remind me to slow down and rest now and then.

Action for the Day

How much have I rested lately? Have I gotten enough sleep each night? What can I do in the next two days to rest my body, mind, and spirit?

*Pray without resentment in
your heart.*
— The Little Red Book

Resentment is anger that we don't want to turn over to our Higher Power. Sometimes, we want to keep our anger. Maybe we want to "get even." It's hard to be spiritual and full of anger at the same time. When we hold on to anger, it turns into self-will.

We all get angry from time to time. This is normal. But we now have a program to help us let go of anger. We also know that stored-up anger can drive us back to alcohol and other drugs. Instead of trying to "get even," let's work at keeping anger out of our hearts.

Prayer for the Day
I pray without anger in my heart. Higher Power, I give You my anger. Have me work for justice, instead of acting like a judge.

Action for the Day
I'll list any resentments I now have. I'll talk about them at my next meeting. This is the best way to turn resentments over to my Higher Power.

*Go outside, to the fields,
enjoy nature and the
sunshine, go out and try to
recapture happiness in
yourself and in God.*
— Anne Frank

Many of us first looked at the joy and beauty of the program with caution. It was different from our addictive joy. Was it to be trusted?

When we started working the Steps, we found inner joy and beauty. As we let go and gave in to the program, we found more happiness. We found joy in ourselves, our friends, our Higher Power, and those around us. Our self-pity changed to self-respect. We were truly out in the sunshine. We were no longer lost in misery. We now know how to walk through misery to find joy.

Prayer for the Day

May I become better friends with my self. Higher Power, let me see the world through Your innocent, yet wise and loving eyes.

Today's Action

Today I'll work to make my life and the lives of others more joyful. I'll greet myself and others with much joy.

APRIL 6

*To know the road ahead,
ask those coming back.*
— Chinese proverb

We're going down a new road—in our recovery and in our lives. We don't know the road. We only know we're on the right one, because our Higher Power led us here.

We ask for help from those who already know the road. We ask our sponsor, "How far is it until I get done feeling guilty?" "How far to self-love?" "How bumpy is the road when I'm at Step Four?"

We need the help of people who have been in the program. They tell us where to slow down because this part of the trip is beautiful.

Someday, maybe today, we too will be called on to guide others.

Prayer for the Day

Higher Power, You've put me on this road. You've also put others on this road. Let them be my guides. Let my guides become my friends.

Action for the Day

Today, I'll find someone who has been in the program two or more years longer than me. I'll ask that person what the road ahead is like.

Better bend than break.
— Scottish proverb

At times, we need to take a stand. But there will be more times when we'll need to bend. Bending means listening to other opinions. Often, we just react instead of listening. Bending means remembering what's really important. Often, we get stubborn just to prove a point. Bending means knowing that, most often, the relationship is more important than the point we want to prove.

Bending is about letting go. Often, what we need to let go of is our self-will. If we live only by self-will, we'll eventually break. Self-will is as fragile as fine china. We need to be more like Tupperware than fine china—we'll last longer and be invited to dinner more often.

Prayer for the Day

Higher Power, You made the trees. They stand, but they also bend, especially when they're young and growing.

Action for the Day

I'll list three times in my life where knowing how to bend would've been helpful.

APRIL 8

*It's a simple formula: "Do
your best and somebody
might like it."*
— *Dorothy Baker*

Our program is a selfish program. It tells us
to let go of what others think. We're staying
sober for ourselves, not for anyone else. Our
body and our spirit are at stake. And we know
what we need to do to stay sober. If we feel
shaky about going to a party, we don't go—
no matter who gets upset. If our job makes
it hard to stay sober, we get a different one—
no matter who gets upset. It's simple.

We must take good care of ourselves before
we can be good to others. In doing this, we
learn how to be a friend, a good parent, a good
spouse. We have to care for ourselves to have
good relationships. Do I believe it's okay to be
selfish when it comes to my program?

Prayer for the Day
Higher Power, help me do what is best for my
recovery, no matter what others think.

Action for the Day
I will remind myself that staying sober is simple.
I don't use chemicals. And I work the program.

*The best thing about the
future is that it comes only
one day at a time.*
— *Abraham Lincoln*

Abraham Lincoln did great things for the
United States. He took life One Day at a Time.
He broke the future into manageable pieces.
We can do the same. We can live in the
present and focus on the task at hand.
Spirituality comes when we focus this way.
When we stay in the present we find choice.
And we worry less about the future.

Still, we must have goals. We must plan for
our future. Goals and plans help us give more
credit to the present than to the future. And
when we feel good about the present, we feel
good about the future.

Prayer for the Day

Higher Power, help me focus. Help me keep my
energy in the present. Have me live life One Day
at a Time.

Action for the Day

When I find myself drifting into the future, I'll
work at bringing myself back to the present.

> *You cannot prevent the*
> *birds of sadness from*
> *passing over your head,*
> *but you can prevent their*
> *making nests in your hair.*
> — *Chinese proverb*

Life is full of feelings. We can be happy, sad, mad, scared. These feelings can come and go quickly. Or we may hang on to them. As recovering addicts, we used to hang on to feelings that made us feel bad. We let them make "nests" in our hair. We used our feelings as an excuse to drink or use other drugs.

Now we're learning to hang on to our good feelings. We can let go of anger, hurt, and fear. We can shoo away the birds of sadness and welcome the birds of happiness.

Prayer for the Day

Higher Power, help me become a "bird watcher." Help me learn from my feelings. And help me let go of the bad ones so I can be happy.

Action for the Day

If I need to get rid of the sadness or anger that I'm hanging on to, I'll get help from my sponsor, a counselor, or a clergyperson.

Fools, through false shame,
conceal their open wounds.
— *Horace*

Many of us, as children, were taught to hide our pain, to act as if we had none. We looked for ways to hide our pain. Alcohol and other drugs helped us do this. But the pain always returned. We were ashamed that we hurt. We thought we were the only ones who hurt so badly. And, worst of all, we thought our pain meant we were bad people.

Ours is a program of honesty. As we live life, there will be troubles, and there will be pain. But now we know that we don't try to hide it. If we hide our wounds, they will not heal. We will listen to others' pains and ask them to listen to ours. This will help us continue our journey in recovery.

Prayer for the Day

God, help me be honest about my pain. Help me see pain not as a personal defect, but as a part of life.

Action for the Day

I'll share my pain with a friend, a family member, my group, or sponsor. I'll ask them to do the same with me. I'll think of pain as part of life.

*Life I love you, all is
groovy.*
— *Paul Simon*

Working the Twelve Steps is more than
recovery from alcohol or other drug addiction.
It's also about how to enjoy life.

Our illness pulled us toward death. Our
spirits were dying, and maybe even our bodies were dying. Now our spirits are coming to
life. We feel more alive than ever before. Our
feelings are coming alive. We feel hope and
faith, love and joy, and even hurt and fear. We
notice the sunshine as well as the clouds. We
know life needs both sunshine and rain, both
joy and pain. We are alive!

Prayer for the Day

Higher Power, help me let go of my fears and enjoy life. I haven't always known how to enjoy life,
but You can teach me. All life is from You, so teach
me to be free in Your light and love.

Today's Action

Right now, I can think of at least three things in
life that make me feel like sunshine. What are
they?

No labor, however humble,
is dishonoring.
— *The Talmud*

Work is good for our hearts. Work is good for our minds. It can give us something to focus on besides ourselves. Labor doesn't just mean having a job. It may mean planting a garden or helping a friend. It certainly means working our program. Hopefully, it's a labor of love.

We can get in trouble if we have too much time on our hands. We can turn it into mischief or self-pity. We can get bored. Being bored is a matter of choice. We'll never be bored if we ask ourselves, "How can I make this world a better place?" We can then turn our answers into action.

Prayer for the Day

Higher Power, teach me to use my time wisely. Help me be well-balanced between labor and fun. I need both.

Action for the Day

I'll list five ways that labor and fun can help me get closer to my Higher Power. And I'll look for people and things to fill my time in positive ways.

It is enough that I am of
value to somebody today.
— *Hugh Prather*

Even in recovery, we addicts often feel we
are not enough. Maybe it's leftover shame
from our using days. But we *are* enough. We
are of great value. We all need each other to
stay sober.

Each of us needs other recovering people
to help us remember the hell of addiction. We
can forget how bad it was, but telling our
stories makes us remember. When you feel
you don't want to stay sober for yourself, then
stay sober for your brothers and sisters in the
program. They need you. You're their recovery, as they're yours. There may be days you
don't feel glad to be sober. But your friends
in this fellowship are glad you're sober. They
thank-you for your sobriety.

Prayer for the Day

Higher Power, may Your will, not mine, be done.

Action for the Day

I'll stop and think of all the people I'm glad for.
I'll start telling them today.

*That day is lost on which
one has not laughed.*
— *French proverb*

For a long time, we didn't really laugh. It's surprising when we think about it: we hadn't really laughed for so long . . . we almost forgot how good we could feel. It feels so good to laugh again!

Now, our spirits come more alive each day. Now, we feel what alcohol and other drugs stuffed deep inside us. Pain, fear, and anger come up. But so do happiness and joy, thankfulness and a sense of humor. In early recovery, we work through the hard feelings. As we grow in the program, we have more and more room for happiness.

Prayer for the Day
Higher Power, wake me up to the joy and laughter that today holds for me. Don't let me miss it!

Action for the Day
Today, I'll spread some laughter. I will learn a joke and tell it to three people.

*No human creature can
give orders to love.*
— *George Sand*

If we're trying to get others to love us, all
we're really doing is trying to be in control.
Trying to control others can be a powerful
drug. Remember, we can't control others. We
can't *make* others love us. Our Higher Power
has control, not us.

So, what do we need to do? Turn things over
to our Higher Power and just be ourselves.

Sure, it can scare us to just be ourselves.
The truth is, not everyone will love us. But if
we're honest about who we are, others will
respect us. We'll like ourselves better. And
we'll have a better chance of loving others and
being loved.

Prayer for the Day

I pray to have my need for control lifted from me.
I pray to be rid of self-will.

Action for the Day

Today, I'll list five ways my self-will—my need to
control—has gotten me in trouble.

*We create revolution by
living it.*
— *Jerry Rubin*

There's a lot wrong in the world—child abuse, homeless and hungry people, pollution. Our old way of dealing with these troubles was to break the rules or to "drop out" by using chemicals.

Now we have a new way to change the world. We're changing ourselves. One Day at a Time, we're acting like the caring, responsible people we want to be. We use the ideas of the program in our lives.

We're kinder. We're more honest. We stand up for ourselves and for others who need our help. What if the whole world started working the Steps? What a wonderful world this would be!

Prayer for the Day
Higher Power, please work through me today. Help me make the world a little better place.

Action for the Day
I'll list one thing that bothers me about the world today. How can using the ideas of the program help solve that problem? Remember, the program tells us to look at our *own* behavior.

*Patience is needed with
everyone, but first of all
with ourselves.*
— St. Francis de Sales

How do you treat yourself? Do you talk to
yourself with a kind and loving voice? We
can't be kind and loving to others until we
learn to be kind and loving with ourselves. To
live this way, we must give ourselves the gift
of patience.

Let's practice patience with ourselves daily.
Practice talking to yourself in a kind, loving
voice. Over time, this will become your everyday voice. Your voice will be that of a loving
parent who helps a child with a new task.
Your Higher Power is willing to be patient
with you. Give yourself the same gift.

Prayer for the Day

Higher Power, I pray that I'll treat myself and
others with the same loving patience You've
shown me.

Action for the Day

I will listen to how I talk to myself. I will practice talking to myself with a kind, loving, and
patient voice.

We give thanks for
unknown blessings already
on their way.
 — *Sacred ritual chant*

Good things keep happening to us. We are sober. We can think clearly. We can see progress on how we handle our problems. We have friends. We have love. We have hope.

We are starting to love ourselves. We are starting to feel joy. Our fears are getting smaller. We are starting to trust our new way of life. Our new life brings good things to us. It brings blessings every day. We are beginning to expect them. But we're still surprised at how good life can be. What a difference from the days before we entered our program!

Prayer for the Day

Higher Power, thank-you for the blessings You keep on giving me. And thanks for whatever today will bring.

Action for the Day

One way to give thanks for my blessings is to share them with others. How can I share my recovery today?

> *A great obstacle to*
> *happiness is to expect too*
> *much happiness.*
> — *Fontenelle*

Our disease is sometimes called the disease of "always wanting more." We pushed ourselves to get as much pleasure as we could. If one was good, two was better. We didn't see that what we were lacking was faith.

At times, in recovery, we still crave "more." We must pay attention to these cravings. When we have a craving, maybe we're scared, and our Higher Power is trying to tell us that, if we have faith, we'll be taken care of. Perhaps our Higher Power just has a message of love for us. All we need to do is listen. It may be that this is the only "more" we really need.

Prayer for the Day

I pray to see my cravings as spiritual needs. I pray to turn to my Higher Power instead of to alcohol or other drugs.

Action for the Day

Today, I'll think about how much recovery has given me. I will share this with a friend and with my Higher Power.

*One of the most important
parts of the A.A. program
is to give our drink problem
to God honestly and fully. . .*
— Twenty-Four Hours a Day,
March 1

We don't *handle* our drinking or other drug problem. We don't *take care* of this problem by ourselves. We *turn* our problem over to *God* as we understand Him. We need to be very clear about this. *We can't handle our drinking or other drug problem!* Our Higher Power keeps us sober through the Steps and the fellowship of the program.

Our job is to hand over our problem to our Higher Power. We do this daily by acting like sober people.

Prayer for the Day

Higher Power, I know I can't handle drinking and using other drugs. I turn my problem over to you. Please take from me the urge to drink or use.

Action for the Day

Today, I'll remember why I *can't* handle or take care of my problem with alcohol or other drugs. And I'll remember why my Higher Power *can.*

*One meets his destiny often
on the road one takes to
avoid it.*
— *French proverb*

None of us, perhaps, ever thought we'd end up in recovery. But we were working at joining recovery years before we got here! Maybe recovery was our fate from the day we first took a drink or a pill. Others around us could see the writing on the wall, but we couldn't. We were too busy trying to avoid pain.

Alcoholism and other drug abuse have to do with us trying to find spiritual wholeness— the kind of spiritual wholeness we're finding now. . . in recovery. So, let's welcome recovery into our lives. We have found our spiritual home.

Prayer for the Day
Higher Power, I got lost because I acted like I knew the way to a good life. You lead the way. Thank-you for putting me on the right track.

Action for the Day
Today, I'll think about why it's my fate to be in recovery. I will list ways that I try to avoid my fate.

*When people talk, listen
completely. Most people
never listen.*
— *Ernest Hemingway*

It's hard to listen in a complete way. Often we listen, but we're still thinking about ourselves. We wonder, "How do their words relate to me? Do I have anything to add?" Often, fear is behind these questions. We fear saying the wrong thing. We fear looking stupid.

Good listeners know how to let go. They let go of their fears. To listen completely, we step outside ourselves, and we're totally there for someone else. Sometimes we listen for only a few moments. Sometimes we don't even agree with the people we're listening to. But we let them know that they count. What a gift we give when we listen in a complete way!

Prayer for the Day

Higher Power, teach me to listen in a complete way. Teach me to step outside myself and be there for others.

Action for the Day

Today, I'll *listen* to what the person says.

*The hardest thing to learn
in life is which bridge to
cross and which bridge to
burn.*
— David Russell

Making big decisions is like crossing bridges. Sometimes, these decisions change our lives. We find that turning back will be very hard. This is why we have to be very careful when we decide to burn bridges.

When we decide to make changes, we act carefully. We don't want to make decisions out of anger or envy. Instead, we can think about what we want and how our program can help us make wise decisions.

Prayer for the Day

Higher Power, help me cross those bridges that are on my path.

Action for the Day

What do I really want in life? What decisions do I need to make to get there?

You're never too old to
grow up.
— *Shirley Conran*

Some of us have spent many years trying *not* to grow up. As children, we watched the adults around us. They may not have seemed happy. "Is life all hard work for grown-ups?" we wondered.

No, it's not all hard work. There are lots of good things about growing up. We can take charge of our life. We can learn to take care of ourselves. We can learn to share our feelings with good friends. We can make our world safe enough for us to express feelings again. We can learn how to love others. We *do* have choices.

Prayer for the Day

Higher Power, help me grow up into a happy, grateful adult.

Action for the Day

There are happy grown-ups. I'll find one to be my sponsor.

*Too many people miss the
silver lining because
they're expecting gold.*
— *Maurice Setter*

Silver shines just as bright as gold does. So often we forget this. So often we push, push, push. We forget to live for the moment. Trying too hard can be a defect of character. It can be a way we avoid life.

Gratitude, being thankful, is a key part of recovery. Not just gratitude for getting our self-respect back. Not just gratitude for having a Higher Power. But gratitude for the moment. We're alive again. Let's see each moment as a time to explore life.

Prayer for the Day
Higher Power, thanks for helping me to enjoy each moment. I have gratitude for being alive.

Action for the Day
I'll list ten gifts of recovery for which I have gratitude.

*I noticed my hopelessness
was because I had lost my
freedom of choice.*
— *AA member*

By doing a Fourth Step, we start to see ourselves more clearly. We see how we've acted
against ourselves. Soon, we hear a little voice
inside telling us to *stop* before we act. "Are
you sure you want to say or do that?" the
little voice asks. Then we make a choice: we
do something the same old way, or we try a
new way.

One part of us will always want to do things
the old, sick way. This is natural. But we're
getting stronger every day. Our spirit wants
to learn new ways so we can be honest and
loving. Sometimes we don't know how. But
we still have a choice. We can ask for help.

Prayer for the Day
Higher Power, help me listen to the little voice
inside that helps me see that I have choices.

Action for the Day
Today, I'll make a choice between old ways and
new ways of acting. I will call my sponsor this evening to talk about my choices.

*Unless I accept my faults I
will most certainly doubt
my virtues.*
— *Hugh Prather*

Before recovery, we saw only a blurry picture
of ourselves, like we were looking through an
out-of-focus camera lens. We couldn't see the
good in ourselves because we wouldn't look
close enough.

Step Four helps us look more closely. We
see a clear picture of ourselves, with our good
points and our faults. We don't like everything
we see. But we can't change until we accept
ourselves as we are. Then we can start getting ready to change.

Prayer for the Day

Higher Power, help me see the good in me and
love myself.

Action for the Day

Today, I'll make a list of four of my good points
and four of my faults. Am I getting ready to have
my Higher Power remove these defects of
character?

*I'm as pure as the driven
slush.*
— *Tallulah Bankhead*

The Steps are filled with words and phrases
like *shortcomings, exact nature of our wrongs,
persons we had harmed,* and *when we were
wrong.* The Steps help us accept *all* parts of
who we are.

Our program asks us to share these parts
of ourselves with others. We heal by doing
this. It's hard to talk about how wrong we can
be, but we must. It's part of how we recover.
Remember, all of us have bad points. At
times, we all act like jerks. When we can talk
about our mistakes, we end up having less
shame inside of us.

Prayer for the Day

Higher Power, help me to love and accept
myself—as You love and accept me. Give me the
courage to share *all* my secret wrongs.

Action for the Day

Today, I'll review my Fourth Step. If I haven't
done this Step, I'll start today.

*When you want to be
something, it means you
really love it.*
— *Andy Warhol*

At times, we turned to chemicals because
we couldn't love ourselves. Our addiction gave
a promise of relief, but it gave us self-hate. We
wanted to love, but couldn't.

What is it we really love? Where should we
put our energy? In raising children? In creating art? In helping addicts who still suffer?
There's much in this world that needs our
love. We can be many things in our lives. Let's
be people we believe in. Let's be people we're
proud of. Let's be people we can love.

Prayer for the Day
Higher Power, help me know myself through my
inventories. My skills, talents, values, and my loves
must be clear to me so I can use them to do Your
will.

Today's Action
Today I'll think about what I'd really love to do
through my work.

Admitted to God,
to ourselves, and to
another human being the
exact nature of our wrongs.

— *Step Five*
from Alcoholics
Anonymous

Admitted to God, to ourselves, and to another human being the exact nature of our wrongs.
— *Step Five*

Step Five can be scary. We're to take the wrongs we listed in our Fourth Step and share them with God, ourselves, and another person. We may look for an easier, softer way. But Step Five stops us.

We're to share the *exact* nature of our wrongs. Why? So we can take a load off ourselves. So we won't use again. By totally sharing our past wrongs, we can belong once more. We can heal. We can start to forgive ourselves. We become more humble. When you share your Fifth Step, hold nothing back. You deserve the peace this Step will bring you.

Prayer for the Day
Higher Power, give me courage to tell it all. Give me courage to admit just how wrong I had become.

Action for the Day
Step Five teaches me that sharing is important. I will find a friend and share my wrongs with that friend. I will hold nothing back.

*Happiness is not a goal; it
is a by-product.*
— Eleanor Roosevelt

Most of us want to be happy. We just don't know how. We aren't sure what happiness is. We've learned the hard way that some things we wanted didn't make us happy.

We're learning that happiness comes when we live the way our Higher Power wants us to live. That's when we're honest. When we do our best work. When we are a true friend. We make happiness; we don't find it.

Sometimes we don't even know we're happy. We're too busy with our work, our recovery program, our friends and family. We need to slow down and know that when we do what we need to, happiness comes.

Prayer for the Day

Higher Power, help me know that I'm most happy when I listen to You and do Your will. You know better than I do what will make me happy.

Today's Action

What parts of my program am I most happy about? Today I'll think of these and enjoy myself.

When I have listened to my
mistakes, I have grown.
— Hugh Prather

Everyone makes mistakes. We all know that. So why is it so hard to admit our own? We seem to think we have to be perfect. We have a hard time looking at our mistakes. But our mistakes can be very good teachers.

Our Twelve Step program helps us learn and grow from our mistakes. In Step Four, half of our work is to think of our mistakes. In Step Five, we admit our mistakes to God, ourselves, and another person. We learn, we grow, and become whole. All by coming to know our mistakes. The gift of recovery is not being free of mistakes. Instead, we do the Steps to claim our mistakes and talk about them. We find the gift of recovery when we learn from our mistakes.

Prayer for the Day

Higher Power, help me to see my mistakes as chances to get to know myself better.

Today's Action

Today I'll talk to a friend about what my mistakes taught me. Today I'll feel less shame.

I am the greatest!
— *Muhammad Ali*

We need to believe in ourselves. We're sober. We're honest. We're trustworthy. We're not making so many problems for other people anymore. We do our share. We can even help others sometimes.

We're glad that others help us. We thank our Higher Power every day. But we also give ourselves credit. We're working our program. We handle life as best we can. And as long as we ask our Higher Power to work through us, we *are* the greatest!

Prayer for the Day

Higher Power, help me feel proud of the changes in my life.

Action for the Day

Today, I'll talk with my sponsor about pride. What is good pride? What should I watch out for?

Forgiveness is all-powerful.
Forgiveness heals all ills.
— Catherine Ponder

We need to forgive so we can heal. Forgiveness means not wanting to get even. Forgiveness means letting go of self-will. Anger and hate are forms of self-will that take up room in our heart. Yet, a still, small voice inside of us wants to forgive. Just as others have forgiven us, we need to forgive them. When we forgive, we give our will to our Higher Power. When we forgive, we make room in our heart for our Higher Power. By giving up our anger and our hate, we let that still, small voice come through a little louder. This is how we heal. This is why forgiving is so powerful for us.

Prayer for the Day

Higher Power, help me let go of self-will. Help me forgive people.

Action for the Day

I will list any anger or hate I have. I will think about how this gets in my way, and I'll pray to have this removed.

*Anyone who follows a
middle course is called a
sage.*

— *Maimonides*

Much of the wisdom of our program is about how to live in the middle. We learn how to pause and think before we act. We ask, "What is the best way to handle this?" We look for the smooth part of the road.

Our actions tell us who we are. We listen to our actions, and we think about them. This listening and thinking takes time. This slows us down. It's good for us. It gives us time to talk with our Higher Power. After all, we want our actions to come from the new values our Higher Power has given us. Thus, over time we act and feel wiser. The wisdom of the program becomes part of who we are.

Prayer for the Day
I pray that I don't get caught up in the rush of the day. Higher Power, teach me to stop and think, to seek Your wisdom.

Action for the Day
Today, I'll set aside time to think, meditate, and be alone. I will listen to what's inside me.

*So live that you wouldn't be
ashamed to sell the family
parrot to the town gossip.*
— *Will Rogers*

Secrets help keep us sick. In our drinking
and using days, we did things we weren't
proud of. We lived in a secret world we were
ashamed of. This is part of the power of addiction. Our behavior and our secrets kept us
trapped.

Recovery offers us a way out of this secret
world. In our groups, we share our secrets,
and they lose their power over us. There may
be things we're too ashamed to talk about in
our groups. When we share these things in
our Fifth Step, they lose their power over us.

We have a new way of life that we're not
ashamed to talk about. When shame leaves,
pride enters our hearts. We know we're good
people!

Prayer for the Day

Higher Power, help me live a good life.

Action for the Day

Do I have any secrets that get in my way? Do I
need to do a Fifth Step? If so, I'll pick a date—today.

*The only way to speak the
truth is to speak lovingly.*
— *Thoreau*

Recovery teaches us to tell the truth. We must be honest if we want to save our lives. We must learn to speak with care—care for ourselves and for others.

To be honest means to speak in a fair and truthful way. To be honest and loving means learning *when* to speak, and *how* to speak, in a caring way. We can help others by honestly telling them what we think and feel and see—but only when we do this with love.

We must be careful when we speak. Speaking the truth is like using a very sharp knife—it can be used for good, or it can be used to hurt others. We should never handle it carelessly or use it to hurt someone.

Prayer for the Day

Higher Power, help me know the truth. Help me speak the truth to others with love.

Action for the Day

I'll make a list of three times I've hurt someone by being honest, but not with love. I'll also list three times I've helped someone by being truthful, with love.

*The longer I live the more
beautiful life becomes.*
— Frank Lloyd Wright

For many of us, life was a burden while using alcohol and other drugs. As our illness went on, life was more ugly. We grew further from our friends, family, and Higher Power.

In recovery, our eyes and hearts open a little more each day. We see the beauty that life holds. We now see that before recovery, we weren't living—we were dying. In recovery, we again may feel happy when we hold a baby. We again may feel joy when we see a sunset. This happens mainly because we've chosen to be with people who love life, people who've been given a second chance.

Once we've almost lost something important, it becomes more precious. We almost lost our lives. Now our lives are special.

Prayer for the Day

Higher Power, thank-you for a second chance. Thank-you for opening my eyes and heart. Give me the strength to keep them open.

Action for the Day

I'll list the most beautiful parts of my life. I'll open my heart today to the joy in store for me.

> *As I grow older, I pay less*
> *attention to what men say.*
> *I just watch what they do.*
> — *Andrew Carnegie*

Doing something with our lives, not just talking about it, is important. When we were sick with our addiction, what we did was drink or use other drugs. We only talked about what we wanted to do. Now that we are sober, we can really live our lives.

We've already done a lot. We've gotten help for our chemical dependency. We're facing the harm we did to our families. We've let other people into our lives.

Before recovery, we didn't have to tell people we were alcoholics and addicts. Our actions showed it, if people knew what to look for. Now we don't have to tell people we are recovering, because our actions will show it.

Prayer for the Day

Higher Power, let my actions show that I am getting better every day.

Action for the Day

Today, I'll let my actions speak louder than my words. I'll do one thing that I have been saying I want to do.

*An honest man's the
noblest work of God.*
— *Alexander Pope*

Step Five says, "Admitted to God, to ourselves, and to another human being the exact
nature of our wrongs." When we did this Step,
the person we admitted our wrongs to didn't
run away or reject us. That person stuck with
us. Chances are, we were told that we are
quite human. And working Step Five helped
us to see that we can change, now that we're
sober.

The most important part of Step Five is the
act of being totally honest about ourselves.
Then we know that relationships—with our
Higher Power, ourselves, and others—can be
built. We have faced the truth. Now we know
we never have to lie.

Prayer for the Day

Higher Power, I know no Fifth Step is perfect.
Please help me be as honest as I can in doing my
Fifth Step and at other times.

Action for the Day

If I've avoided doing a Fifth Step, I'll talk to my
sponsor about it today.

*You can observe a lot just
by watching.*
— *Yogi Berra*

When we watch others, we learn how to "act as if." We watch a patient person, and then we "act as if" we're a patient person. The result? Over time, we'll become a patient person. We watch how good listeners listen, and we "act as if" we know how to listen. Then one day, we realize we're really listening! We watch people who have faith, and we "act as if" we have it. Then over time, we become spiritual people!

Prayer for the Day

Higher Power, help me find You in the people and events of my day.

Action for the Day

I will "act as if" my Higher Power is standing next to me all through the day.

*Hating people is like
burning down your own
house to get rid of a rat.*
— *Harry Emerson Fosdick*

Hate is like an illness. It steals our hope, our love, our relationships. Hate puts distance between people. Hate can give us a false sense of power. Do I use hate to make myself feel important?

Our program tells us to let go of hate. Hate and sobriety don't mix. Hate doesn't let us connect with our Higher Power.

Ours is a program of love and respect. We're taught that if someone treats us wrong, we still should be respectful in our response. Why? Because we're changed by our actions. If we act with hate, we become hateful. If we act in a respectful way, we become respectable.

Prayer for the Day

Hate is the drug of those who are afraid. Higher Power, help me to be free from hate today.

Action for the Day

It's self-centered to hate. Today, I'll read pages 60-62 of *Alcoholics Anonymous* (Third Edition) about being self-centered.

Make yourself an honest
[person], and then you may
be sure that there is one
rascal less in the world.
— *Thomas Carlyle*

Honesty does not mean saying all we think
or feel. Many of our thoughts and feelings are
only with us for a minute. They are not always
the truth. For example, saying to someone
you love, "I hate you!" in the middle of an
argument can destroy things.

Honesty means living by what is true to us.
Then we choose when and how to say things
to others. Think of honesty as the air we
breathe; it's what keeps us alive, but it can
get polluted and kill. It must be treated with
respect and care.

Prayer for the Day

Higher Power, help me know the power of
honesty. Help me speak it with care and respect.

Action for the Day

Before I speak today I'll ask myself: "Is this true?
Am I speaking because this needs to be said?"

*That day is lost on which
one has not laughed.*
— *French proverb*

For a long time, we didn't really laugh. It's surprising when we think about it: we hadn't really laughed for so long . . . we almost forgot how good we could feel. It feels so good to laugh again!

Now, our spirits come more alive each day. Now, we feel what alcohol and other drugs stuffed deep inside us. Pain, fear, and anger come up. But so do happiness and joy, thankfulness and a sense of humor. In early recovery, we work through the hard feelings. As we grow in the program, we have more and more room for happiness.

Prayer for the Day
Higher Power, wake me up to the joy and laughter that today holds for me. Don't let me miss it!

Action for the Day
Today, I'll spread some laughter. I will learn a joke and tell it to three people.

*The time to relax is when
you don't have time for it.*
— Sydney J. Harris

Relaxing is one of the little joys of life. We can learn to take time from our busy day to chat with a friend, take a hot bath, or spend a few moments sitting alone under a tree. The busier we are, the more we need to take time to relax.

When we rest, we stop fussing about the outside world. We find out how we're doing *inside.* While relaxing, we can best listen to our Higher Power. Our minds calm down. We put busy thoughts aside. Sometimes, we can almost hear our Higher Power say, "Stay quiet and listen! I have something to tell you!"

Prayer for the Day

Higher Power, remind me to relax. My spirit needs rest and quiet so I can hear You.

Action for the Day

Today, I'll list five ways I like to relax. I'll do one of them today.

*Each day provides its own
gifts.*
— *Ruth P. Freedman*

Spiritual growth is the greatest gift we can
receive. And we earn it through taking risks.
There is much risk involved in working the
Steps: The risk of admitting that we're out of
control. The risk of turning our will and our
lives over to a Power greater than ourselves.
The risk of letting go of character defects. The
risk of making amends to people we've
harmed. The risk of admitting our wrongs. The
risk of telling our stories as we carry the message of hope. To grow spiritually, we need these
adventures. These challenges. These risks.

Prayer for the Day
Higher Power, help me to take the risks that I
need in order to grow.

Action for the Day
I will look at today as an adventure with my
Higher Power. I will list the fears I'll need to let go of.

You cannot plan the future
by the past.
— *Edmund Burke*

We got tired of how we were living. We honestly looked at our life. We saw that alcohol and other drugs controlled our life. We met others who understood us. And we came to believe that a Power greater than ourselves could help us. We turned our will and our life over to this Power. In so doing, we learned that life doesn't take place in the past or in the future. We find life in the present. We find our program in the present.

Prayer for the Day
I pray that I'll leave the past in the past. I pray that I'll walk into each new moment with my Higher Power.

Action for the Day
The only time we revisit the past is when we tell our story. Today, I'll tell my story to someone. I'll tell what really happened. I'll tell what life is like now.

*The art of living is more like
wrestling than dancing.*
— *Marcus Aurelius*

The struggles of life teach us a lot. They challenge our beliefs. As we struggle, we come to believe that our friends, family, and Higher Power will be there for us in hard times. But we must do our part. We need to call and honestly let people know how we're doing. We need to pray and ask our Higher Power for help. If we do these things, we'll come to respect and learn from hard times.

Prayer for the Day

I pray for the wisdom to see that struggles are part of life. Higher Power, I pray for Your help in not taking struggles too personally.

Action for the Day

I'll list four times I've struggled and what I learned from each struggle. I'll share this with a friend.

*And if the blind lead the
blind, both shall fall into
the ditch.*
— *Matt. 15:14*

Twelve Step programs are sometimes called
self-help programs. But they're not really, because we all help each other. We don't stay
sober by ourselves. Sometimes we call Twelve
Step programs *peer programs.* And they are.
All of us are equal. No one is an expert. But
we need to be careful who we choose for a
sponsor. We each need to find someone who
has been sober longer than us. Someone who
understands the Steps. Someone who lives by
them. Someone we want to be like. We need
to stick with the winners.

Prayer for the Day
Higher Power, I know I'm like a blind person who
is just beginning to see. Help me follow the path
of those who see better than I do.

Action for the Day
Today, I'll list the people in my program I go to
for help. Am I sticking with the winners?

*Be not afraid of growing
slowly, be afraid only of
standing still.*
— *Chinese proverb*

All of us are a little afraid of growth. We wonder how growth will change our lives. Who will we be? Will our friends still love us? Can't we grow up and get it over with? Why does it take so long?

All of us have a need to keep growing. There is no age when we're "all grown up" and all done learning. But we don't need to rush our growth. Like a child on a too-big bicycle, at times we'll find ourselves out of control. We'll tip over. We can grow at our own pace, but we must grow. We must make changes. Or else, like an athlete on a too-small bicycle, we won't get far. We'll tip over too!

Prayer for the Day

Higher Power, help me grow. And help me know my own strength as I grow.

Action for the Day

Am I fully using my strength, my mind, my talents? I will list one way that I can do this better.

*Showing up is 80 percent
of life.*
> — *Woody Allen*

Life is full of things we don't want to do. Yet when *all* parts of us (mind, body, spirit) show up, things go okay. By being there, we can learn about ourselves and help others.

Showing up means we care about our program. It means we speak up at meetings. It means we care about our family, our friends, the world. It means we listen when a friend has a bad day. It means seeing ourselves in others. It means we talk to someone who bothers us. Showing up means we laugh when something seems funny. It means we cry when we feel sad. We're important, and we need to bring our mind, body, and spirit with us—wherever we go. Have I learned to show up, all of me?

Prayer for the Day

Higher Power, help me show up for my life. Help me show up to do my part in Your plan today.

Today's Action

As I go through my day, I'll think about how I'm showing up for my life. I'll be proud of myself for doing my part.

*The present will not long
endure.*

— *Pindar*

At certain moments, our best friend is time.
Time is a gift given to us. Time helps us heal.
We need to know that when things are tough,
these times will pass, and peace will return.
Our Higher Power can be like a parent who
comforts a child when there's a storm outside.
The parent gently reminds the child the sun
will shine again.

Tough times come and go. There will be
times when life is ugly and very painful. We
can't be happy all the time. Remember, our
Higher Power is always there. We must have
faith in this. A saying often heard in the program is, "This too shall pass."

Prayer for the Day

Higher Power, remind me that things will get
better. Even if they get worse for a while, they will
get better. Let this be my prayer in hard times.

Action for the Day

Today, I'll list times in my life when I thought
I couldn't go on. I'll remember the pain, but I'll also
remember how time was my friend.

*The way to love anything
is to realize it might be
lost.*
— G. K. Chesterton

Every day we take so much for granted. But we can count certain blessings: a roof over our head, food, clothing, family and friends, freedom, a Higher Power we trust. These things are special. Thinking about them wakes up our happiness. Our recovery program shows us how to be happy. We just have to remember to do what it tells us!

Step Ten helps us wake up our happiness. Each evening, as we think about our day, we can give thanks for the things we love: our recovery, our health, and the special people in our lives. If we spend part of our day thinking about these important areas, we won't lose them.

Prayer for the Day
Higher Power, help me make the most of my blessings today.

Action for the Day
Today, I'll tell five people I love that I'm glad to have them in my life. And I'll tell each of them one reason why.

*In all the world, there is no
one else exactly like me.*
— *Virginia Satir*

Let's keep this in mind: each one of us is
special in our own way. Often, we're hard on
ourselves because we're different.

Our Twelve Step groups pull our differences
together. We listen and learn from our differences. We learn to see that each one of us is
different—and this is important. Our program
and the Steps stay alive for us, because each
new person brings a different way of seeing
things. Let's celebrate our differences instead
of trying to be alike.

Prayer for the Day
Today is a day to celebrate that, in all of the
world, there is only one me. Thank-you, Higher
Power, and help me see clearly how special I am.

Action for the Day
I'll make a list of what makes me special. I'll
share this with a friend or my sponsor and my
Higher Power.

When I look at the future,
it's so bright, it burns my
eyes.
— *Oprah Winfrey*

During our illness, it was as if our spirit lived in a deep, dark cave. Our spirit became gloomy, cold, and lonely. Our spirit didn't know how to get out of the cave. We were dying.

Recovery brings us into the sunlight. At first, we can't see a thing—it's too bright! The world stretches around us—it's so big! There are so many ways to go! We don't know what to do.

But then our eyes get used to the light, and we feel the warm rays of the sun. We see we aren't alone anymore. We relax. We know our spirit is in a better place—a place where we can *live!*

Prayer for the Day

Higher Power, help me feel at home in the sunlight of my new life.

Action for the Day

Addiction made my world so small. It made my future so dark. Today, I'll list three new choices I want to make to better my life.

*It's only by forgetting
yourself that you draw
near to God.*
— *Henry David Thoreau*

The biggest danger we face as recovering people is self-will. Do we try to control others? Do we always put ourselves before others? Are we full of self-pity? These are all ways that bind us to our self-will.

In recovery, we put our lives in the hands of a loving God. Here, we find a new home. Our goal is to lose as much of our self-will as we can. We then put love in place of self-will. Recovery is truly about love.

Prayer for the Day

Higher Power, I pray and offer my self-will to You. Self-will is a danger to my sobriety. I pray that I may be closer to You than to myself.

Action for the Day

I'll list all the areas that self-will gets in my way. I'll read my list every day next week, and I'll try to put love in place of self-will.

Who dares nothing, need
hope for nothing.
  — Johann Friedrich von
    Schiller

As we grow in recovery, we'll need to change our behaviors, values, and beliefs to stay sane. This takes courage. Courage is doing what is needed in spite of fear.

Courage means facing what we can't change. We can't change the fact that we have hurt people. We can't change the fact that we have an illness. And we can't change the fact that we need help from others.

Courage also means facing those things we can change. We need courage to be honest, to have faith, and to be humble. And we need courage to let people know how important they are.

Prayer for the Day

Courage is more than being tough. Courage means being human. Higher Power, grant me the courage to stay sober and live a spiritual life.

Action for the Day

Today I'll have an attitude of courage. I'll talk in my meeting. I'll offer help where it is needed. I'll have the courage to say no when needed.

*The more one judges the
less one loves.*

— *Balzac*

At times we need to make judgments about
people's behavior. We stand back and look at
how their lives affect our sobriety. We have to
do this to choose people whose friendships
will be good for us. We have to do this before
we trust someone in business. We should take
a good look at the other person before we fall
in love. But once we decide to trust or love
someone, we have to stop always judging.

When we love someone, we don't stand
back. We move in close. We give them all our
love can offer. We don't just think and judge.
We feel. We are on their side. We look for the
good in them. We don't pick them apart. We
love the whole person.

Prayer for the Day

Higher Power, help me to judge a little and love
a lot. Help me accept the people I love, faults and
all. Help me love them better.

Action for the Day

Today, I'll catch myself when I start to judge
others. I will accept them as they are.

One Day at a Time
— A.A. program slogan

One Day at a Time reminds us to live in a sane, natural way. It reminds us we can't control the past. It reminds us we can't control the future. We can live only in the present. We have only the moment. We have only today.

Before recovery, our worries about the past and the future put stress in our lives. We need to live in a way that doesn't put us in danger. We need to live in a way that lets us enjoy things. We need to live in a way that lets us stay close to others, ourselves, and our Higher Power.

Prayer for the Day

Higher Power, teach me to really live One Day at a Time.

Action for the Day

Today, I'll keep reminding myself that I have the moment. No more, no less. Am I using my moments the way my Higher Power wants me to?

Nobody ever died of laughter.
— Max Beerbohm

We're not getting sober so we can be more serious. We're getting sober to live. To be free. To laugh and to add more joy to the world. Recovery is about having an even balance between hard work and fun. We work at turning over our will. We do inventories. We drop what we're doing to help a friend in need. We're honest even when it's hard to do. And we learn to have fun. Sobriety needs to be fun.

What are the things you've always wanted to do but were afraid of? Maybe you want to know how to dance. Maybe you want to write poems. Maybe you want to go on a long canoe trip. But you've acted like you don't have the time. Make the time. Have fun! Push yourself to stay fresh in the world! This is the program.

Prayer for the Day
Higher Power, help me to see the funny side of life. Allow me to see humor and fun in my life.

Action for the Day
Today, I'll list the things I like to do for fun. I'll add three fun things I'd like to try over the next few months.

Were entirely ready
to have God remove all
these defects of character.

— *Step Six*
from Alcoholics
Anonymous

*Were entirely ready to have
God remove all these
defects of character.*
— Step Six

Character defects include being stubborn,
feeling self-pity, and wanting to always be in
control. We must be ready to give up these
defects, or they will hurt us. Being ready is
our part of Step Six.

Our Higher Power will remove these defects.
We don't need to know how. We just need to
be ready to give them up when God asks for
them. We don't need to know when. We just
have to be ready.

Prayer for the Day

Higher Power, take away my self-pity, fears,
anger, and anything else that hurts my recovery.
Help me make room for peace.

Action for the Day

Today, I'll get ready to have my character defects
removed. I will list them and ask myself, "What
do I get from keeping them?"

> *God, just for today, please*
> *remove my defects of*
> *character that would keep*
> *me from doing Your will.*
> — *Cyndy T.*

Many of us can't let go of all our character defects at once. So every day, we can ask our Higher Power to remove only the ones that will hurt us today. For example, a character defect such as laziness won't surface each day. But on some days, we don't do our Higher Power's will because of laziness. These are the times we need to have our laziness removed, just for the day.

We may not be entirely ready to have our defects removed forever. But we can give up a few of them—just for today.

Prayer for the Day
God, just for today, please help me remove my defects of character that would keep me from doing Your will.

Action for the Day
I'll say today's prayer three more times during the day.

*Those whom the gods love
grow young.*
— *Oscar Wilde*

Addiction forced us to grow old fast. Recovery helps us slow down. We regain a youthful spirit. Over time, our excitement for life returns. We are like children on the first day of summer break. We see the world as a place to explore. It won't scare us anymore. We don't run from life. We run into it.

Look around at your meeting; you'll see smiles. Look again and you'll see joy and hope. Look again and you'll see people who are growing younger every day.

Prayer for the Day
Thank you, Higher Power, for allowing me to regain my youthful spirit. Help me grow young.

Action for the Day
Today, I'll watch the children. I will look at their excitement for living and try to be like them.

We cannot solve life's problems except by solving them.
— *M. Scott Peck*

Before getting into the program, we ran from problems at all costs. As time went on, we had more problems. As our problems grew, we became afraid of life.

The program—the Twelve Steps—teaches us how to face and solve our problems. We stop running and stand up to problems. That way, life's problems scare us less and less over time.

In fact, life's problems help us better know our Higher Power and ourselves. We now know our Higher Power is with us every step of the way.

Prayer for the Day

I pray for the courage to stand and face life's problems. I pray for the wisdom to ask my Higher Power for help.

Action for the Day

Today, I'll list all the problems I now have. I will talk about them with friends and with my Higher Power. I will make plans to solve them (sometimes solving problems means accepting them).

Life is only this place, this
time, and these people
right here and now.
— *Vincent Collins*

Staying in the present can be hard. This busy world pulls our focus from the present. We often wonder if the future will bring good times or bad times.

Life is right before us. Look around. Life is happening—now! The more we live in the moment, the better we feel. Why? Because we can do something about the present. We can't do anything about the future. We have *choices* in the present, and we can do something with our lives. Addiction ran our lives before. Now, with the help of others and our Higher Power, we run our own lives again. This gives us peace of mind.

Prayer for the Day

Higher Power, thank-you for giving back my life. Teach me how to run my life. Have me seek others when I need help. It's okay to ask for help.

Action for the Day

Today, I'll list five things I do well. Then I'll list three things I don't do well. I'll think of people who can help me, and I'll call them.

Fortunate are the people
whose roots are deep.
— Agnes Meyer

A tree's roots seek water and minerals. Though the roots can't be easily seen, they are there. The life of the tree depends on them. The stronger a tree's roots, the higher a tree can grow.

We need to set deep roots into the soil of recovery. The soil of recovery is made up of the Twelve Steps, fellowship, and service to others. We'll have to get through storms and high winds in our return to health. In so doing, we'll become beautiful, strong, and spiritual. We'll be able to live with both the gentle breezes and the heavy winds of life.

Prayer for the Day

Higher Power, help me believe in what I can't see. Just as I believe that the roots of a tree are there because I can see the leaves, I believe in a Higher Power because I can see the results.

Action for the Day

I will ask myself, "Which Step do I need to work on the most right now?" I will volunteer to give a meeting on that Step.

*Forgiveness is the way to
true health and happiness.*
— *Gerald Jampolsky*

We can't afford to hold grudges. We have all felt hurt by others at times. But when we stay angry at another person, it hurts *us*. It keeps our wounds open. It takes our energy away from our healing.

We can forgive now. We know that living our program of honesty and love makes us safe. We don't have to be afraid. We don't have to be angry. We don't have to let old hurts stand in our way. We let them go. We empty the anger from our hearts to clear the way for love.

Prayer for the Day

Higher Power, help me forgive the people I'm still angry with. Help me see that each of those people taught me something about myself.

Action for the Day

Am I holding on to anger and resentment? If so, I'll make a list today, and I'll talk with my sponsor about ways to let go of them.

*It's not enough to talk to
plants, you also have to
listen.*
— David Bergman

Sometimes, we find ourselves doing all the
talking. When this happens, we need to stop,
think, and listen.

When we do all the talking, we're trying to
control what happens. But when we listen, we
get better results. No one has to be in control.
What a relief!

And we're learning to listen better every
day. It's great—the care, love, and help we
find—just by listening.

Prayer for the Day
Higher Power, help me learn the "give-and-take"
of talking and listening.

Action for the Day
Today, I'll focus on listening, not only to other
people but to my Higher Power's voice.

*Anyone can blame; it takes
a specialist to praise.*
— Konstantin Stanislavski

Are we blamers? We sure were blamers
when we were using alcohol and other drugs.
Then *everything* was someone's fault. Some
of us did our blaming out loud. And some of
us blamed others silently.

It's harder to praise than to blame people.
Faults stand out like street signs, but the good
things about people may be harder to see. We
can see the good in people when we slow
down, watch, and listen.

Prayer for the Day
Higher Power, help me pay attention to people
around me. Help me praise them.

Action for the Day
Today, I'll list three people who mean a lot to me.
I'll write what I like about each of them. I'll talk
to them and tell them what I wrote.

Never grow a wishbone,
daughter, where your
backbone ought to be.
— *Clementine Pappleford*

At meetings, we meet people who have what we want. Our old way is to think these people are better or luckier than us. Our old way is to wish we were like them. But our program tells us how to work for change, not just wish for it. There is a big difference!

There are many ways to work for recovery. We practice the Steps. We attend meetings, and we help out at meetings. We welcome new members. We call our sponsor often. And we sponsor others when we're ready. It takes more than a wishbone. It takes courage and hard work, with the help of our Higher Power.

Prayer for the Day

Higher Power, help me know that wishing is lost energy. I must work at recovery. As I do today's work, guide me.

Today's Action

Today I'll do an extra bit of work on my recovery. I'll call a group member. I'll read. I'll spend extra time in prayer and meditation.

Who is the bravest hero?
He who turns his enemy
into a friend.
— *Hebrew Proverb*

In recovery we take our worst enemy, addiction, and turn it around. We were ashamed of our addiction. Over time we become proud of our recovery. We were our own worst enemy. Now we're our own best friend. We are brave people.

Being brave is about facing our fears. Often we think brave people don't get afraid, but this isn't true. Brave people learn to stay put, even when their knees are shaking. Many times in recovery, we will want to run when we should stay put. We may even think about using chemicals again. We need to remember our bravery and how we turned our worst enemy into a friend.

Prayer for the Day

Higher Power, teach me when to run and when to stay put. Help me be brave.

Action for the Day

I will claim my bravery today. I'll hold my head up high and be proud of how far I've come. I now have nothing to be ashamed of.

The lust for power is not rooted in strength, but in weakness.
— Erich Fromm

We believed alcohol or other drugs could help us control our happiness. But now we're learning to rely on faith for our happiness. Faith is about leaving things to our Higher Power's control. Instead of wanting the control ourselves, we trust our Higher Power will help us handle things that come along.

In recovery, we work at having more faith. Faith in a Higher Power. Faith in the Steps. Faith in our groups. Faith that our lives will get better, if we don't use chemicals and we work an honest recovery program. Faith makes life a lot easier.

Prayer for the Day
Higher Power, surround me with Your love. Give me strength to do hard things. Give me faith to know that I'm not alone.

Action for the Day
Today, I'll notice how I still want to be in control. I'll remind myself that it's okay to Let Go and Let God.

The reason why worry kills
more people than work is
that more people worry
than work.

— *Robert Frost*

Worry—it's a lonely activity. It puts distance between us and others. Our program is
full of ideas about what to do with worry. In
Step Three, we turn our will and lives over to
God. This includes our worry.

Our slogans also suggest what to do with
worry. One Day at a Time. Live and Let Live.
Easy Does It. Let Go and Let God. Their
main message is *stop worrying.* Trust the
program. Trust your Higher Power. Everything will be okay.

Prayer for the Day

Higher Power, I give You my worries. Teach me
how to trust again. I want to trust in You, my program, and myself.

Action for the Day

I'll write the program slogans listed above on a
piece of paper, and I'll read them over today. I'll
let myself live them today.

*Time is nature's way of
keeping everything from
happening at once.*
     — Unknown

Time always seems to pass too slowly or too quickly for us. We want the fun times to last longer. We want the boring or painful times to go faster. But time goes at just the right pace. Any faster, and we wouldn't have enough time to learn as we go. Any slower, and we'd lose interest. In our program, we learn to respect the pace of time. We let go, and we let time go at its own pace. We call this *patience.*

Prayer for the Day

Higher Power, thank-you for patience. Help me look forward to the future without rushing. Help me live fully in the here and now. Help me make today a good one by doing Your will.

Action for the Day

I'll list five ways I can use time to be more healthy—in body, mind, and spirit. Which of these five things can I do today?

He who laughs, lasts.
— *Mary Pettibone Poole*

It feels so good to laugh again! Our disease took away our sense of humor. Recovery gives it back. That's why there's so much laughter at our meetings. By seeing the funny side of things, we ease up.

A person in treatment was talking about the Higher Power he had come to believe in. The counselor asked, "Does your God have a sense of humor?" The group had fun talking about this idea for a while. The next day, the counselor came to work and found a note on her door. It read: "Of course God has a sense of humor. He made you, didn't He?"

Laughter helps us heal.

Prayer for the Day

Higher Power, help me ease up today. Let me see the funny side of things.

Action for the Day

I'll let myself laugh today.

> *A.A. states that resentment is the "number one offender" among our members, that it puts more alcoholics in their graves than any other thing.*
> — Stools and Bottles

We can get high on anger. That's why it's dangerous. We get a false sense of power from being angry. Our anger turns into resentments. Resentments turn into hate. Hate eats at our spiritual core.

We can get rid of resentments and hate through prayer and helping others. That's why we're to pray for those who have wronged us, so our hearts don't fill with hate. This way, we use our energy in a healthy way. And our serenity will grow as we see that anger no longer has so much power over our actions.

Prayer for the Day

Higher Power, help me stop using anger, resentments, and hate for control over other people and events I don't like.

Action for the Day

I'll list all the people I'm angry at. I'll say a simple prayer for each of them.

*Each day provides its
own gifts.*
— *Ruth D. Freedman*

Life is full of wonderful gifts. Recovery is
life's greatest gift to us. If we're not excited
about being sober, we need to check on ourselves. Are we keeping something secret? Is
there a sadness we need to talk about? Are
we stuffing anger? These things eat away at
our excitement for life.

Many addicts never get the gift of recovery.
Those of us in recovery are special. We've
been given a new life. There will be hard
times. But the joy of getting a second chance
will be stronger. Am I grateful that I've been
given recovery?

Prayer for the Day

Higher Power, help me see recovery as a gift. I
deserve this gift because I'm human. Help me to
always accept this gift.

Action for the Day

At the end of the day, I'll list three gifts that this
day has given me.

*Nothing is a waste of time
if you use the experience
wisely.*
— *Rodin*

When we first start our recovery, it hurts a lot to look at our past. We feel sad. It feels like our life was a waste.

But it wasn't a waste. The program promises that if we practice the Steps, we'll not regret the past nor wish to shut the door on it. Hard to believe? Just look at all the happy old-timers in AA. Their lives were just as messed up as ours.

Because of our addiction, we're now learning a *new* way to live. We are getting to know ourselves, our Higher Power, and other people.

Prayer for the Day

Higher Power, thanks for helping me into recovery. Help me learn from my addiction.

Action for the Day

I'll list three important things I've learned about life because of my addiction. I'll talk to my sponsor about them.

*If you tell the truth, you
don't need to remember
anything.*

— *Mark Twain*

One thing that's a lot easier in our life now is this—we can keep our story straight! We are learning that there's one really good way to get along with people: Keep It Simple. Just tell the truth.

It's hard to do at first. We might think, "If people see the real me, what will happen?" We might be afraid of what will happen if we don't lie or make excuses.

But telling the truth works! We find out we never did fool anyone anyway!

Prayer for the Day
Higher Power, make me honest.

Action for the Day
I'll list all the ways honesty will help me in recovery. I'll sign-up to give a meeting on honesty.

Order is heaven's first law.
— Alexander Pope

We need order in our lives. It makes life simpler for us. Life without order would be like driving in a large city without traffic signals. Our lives as addicts were like this. We lived with no plan, no order.

Now that we're sober, we can put some order in our lives. We can get up every morning. We can make our beds and be on time for work. These little things make life so much easier and nicer! We need this order. It allows us to depend on ourselves.

We now look at the Twelve Steps to bring order to our lives. The Steps follow each other as summer follows spring. Do I allow myself to follow the natural order or do I fight it?

Prayer for the Day

Higher Power, You've put order in this world. Please put order in my life. Let me flow within this order instead of being on my own.

Action for the Day

The Twelve Steps have a natural order. Today I'll take time to read each Step and think about the order found in them.

*The future is much like the
present, only longer.*
— *Dan Quisenberry*

In many ways, we don't know what the future holds. But in terms of recovery, we know
the future holds the Twelve Steps. They will
be with us for life.

We should never fall into the trap of thinking we "know" the program. We'll *never*
know all the truth and love the Steps hold for
us. "Knowing the Steps" is a project we'll
never finish. As we change, the Steps change.

The Steps are like the seasons. As the seasons come and go, the same field or the same
tree becomes a different picture.

Prayer for the Day

Higher Power, I pray for Your help as I work the
Steps and continue my recovery. Help me discover
new treasures.

Action for the Day

I will ask long-time members of my program how
they keep the program fresh and alive.

The confession of evil
works is the first beginning
of good works.
— *St. Augustine*

We started recovering the minute we admitted we were powerless over our illness. We crossed over from dishonesty to honesty.

Often, we don't see what power honesty has. Maybe we still aren't sure that being honest is best for us. It is! This is why the authors of the Big Book ask us to be totally honest from the start. Just as denial is what makes addiction work, honesty is what makes recovery work.

Honesty means self-respect. Honesty heals. Honesty lets us look people in the eyes. What comfort we'll feel as we step deeper into our program!

Prayer for the Day
I pray that I'll let go totally. I pray that I'll keep no secrets that could put my sobriety at risk.

Action for the Day
Today, I'll read the first three pages of "How It Works" in the Big Book.

*Words are sacred, we must
use them wisely. . . . They
are a gift of God.*
— *Burton Pretty-On-Top*

We can use words to bring peace to others.
We can use words to tell God and others how
much we care. Or we can use words to hurt
others. We can curse them and scare them
away. We often did this when we used alcohol and other drugs.

In recovery, we learn to use words in a kind,
wise way. We treat words as a gift from God.
We use words to build our relationships.

Do I use words in a kind way? Do I treat
words as a powerful gift from God? Do my
words make the world better or worse for
those who hear me speak?

Prayer for the Day

Higher Power, when I speak words, help me
think about their power. Help me speak to others
in a kind way.

Action for the Day

Today, I'll speak to others with respect. My words
will add a little kindness, honesty, and love to the
world today.

Beauty is a gift of God.
— *Aristotle*

In our addiction, we often went after what was ugly in life. Maybe we hung out in bad places. Maybe we saw people's defects instead of their beauty. Addiction is an ugly, painful disease. The worst part of addiction is how it doesn't let us see beauty in the world.

There is much beauty in each of us. Recovery is beautiful. Our stories are beautiful. The way we help each other is beautiful. The way we become loving family members is beautiful. But sometimes, we may still see the world as ugly. At these times, we need to turn to our program. Maybe we need to help someone by working Step Twelve. Maybe we need to ask to give the Step at our meeting. Maybe we just need to read the Big Book. Whatever we do, one thing is sure—if we turn to our program, we'll see how beautiful the world is.

Prayer for the Day

Higher Power, help me see beauty today. Help me be beautiful today.

Action for the Day

Today I'll let myself feel beautiful. I'll see recovery as beautiful.

When a man points a finger at someone else, he should remember that three of his fingers are pointing at himself.
— *Louis Nizer*

It's so easy to blame others. Others are always making mistakes we can hide behind. That's what blame is—hiding. When we blame others for our mistakes, we're trying to hide our character defects.

It's nobody else's fault that we act the way we do. It's our fault. We're responsible for our actions. And with the help of our Higher Power, we can change. We can turn over our character defects. But first, we have to know them. Then, we give up blaming others for our defects. Over time, we're not afraid to learn about ourselves—even the parts we don't like—because we want to know ourselves better.

Prayer for the Day

I pray for help in facing my character defects.

Action for the Day

I'll think about the past week. I'll list times I've used blame to hide from reality.

*But what is happiness
except the simple harmony
between a man and the life
he leads?*
— *Albert Camus*

Sometimes, we say we're getting our lives together. Together with what? With our selves. The Twelve Steps help us clean up the mess we've made. We're fixing our mistakes. We're looking at ourselves closely—at what we believe, what we feel, what we like to do, who we *are*. We're asking our Higher Power to help us to be our best.

No wonder our lives are coming together! No wonder we feel more peace, harmony, and happiness!

Prayer for the Day
Higher Power, help me remember the best harmony comes when I sing from Your songbook.

Action for the Day
Today, I'll make choices that are in line with who I am.

Hell is not to love anymore.
— George Bernanos

Someone in an AA group said, "From the first day I started this program, I felt like I had died and gone to heaven." This person had walked into a room full of love. In recovery, we are spiritual people because we believe in love. We have faith in love.

Love is respect. Love is truth with kindness. Love is being willing to forgive and help others. Love is thinking about how our Higher Power wants us to act. Love is what we do best. We have turned our will and our life over to love.

Prayer for the Day

I pray that I may love all parts of life. Higher Power, help me seek out love, not material things.

Action for the Day

Today, I'll think about what I love about recovery. I will share this with a couple of friends and my Higher Power.

*The closest to perfection a
person ever comes is when
he fills out a job
application form.*
— *Stanley J. Randall*

Trying to be perfect gets us in trouble. Trying to be perfect means we're trying to control things. We may be trying to cover up something. Maybe we aren't facing our pain. Maybe we've hurt someone and we need to make amends.

We need to practice being human. Humans aren't perfect. In Steps Six and Seven, we face our human limits and our shortcomings. We then start the lifelong job of letting them go. To accept our human limits leads us to our Higher Power. We see how we need a guide in life. Our Higher Power makes a perfect guide.

Prayer for the Day

Higher Power, help me accept that I can't be perfect. Help me be a good human being.

Action for the Day

Today, I'll list my shortcomings. I'll talk with a friend about them. I'll ask my friend to tell me what my good qualities are.

*I don't believe in the
afterlife, although I am
bringing a change of
underwear.*

— *Woody Allen*

Most of us have many questions about a
Higher Power. Sometimes we have more ques-
tions than answers. No matter how much we
believe about God, there are always questions.
Why do bad things happen if God is good?
Does God punish people?

Is God called Jesus, Buddha, the Great
Spirit? Perhaps we've chosen a name for our
Higher Power, or maybe we haven't. Yet, we
know there is some Power greater than ourselves that's helping us in our recovery.

We know what we need to know about God
for today. We know how to ask for help, and
how to accept help.

Prayer for the Day

Higher Power, help me to know You more clearly.
There's much I'm not sure about. For now, I will
act as if the help I get comes from You.

Today's Action

I'll think of three ways my Higher Power has
done just the right thing for me.

*If you don't know where
you are going, you'll
probably end up
somewhere else.*
— Lawrence J. Peter

The Twelve Steps are our plan for living. We must have a plan. Without one, we waste our energy. We react instead of think. This is what we did as an addict. We lived our lives as out-of-control people. This caused a lot of pain for us and those around us.

Recovery brings us the Twelve Steps, and each Step gives us direction and wisdom. Each Step builds on the progress we made from the Step before it. Sometimes we follow the plan well. Sometimes we think we can do better on our own. Do I believe the Twelve Steps are a good plan of living?

Prayer for the Day

Higher Power, You have shown me a new way of life, a plan for living. Thank you for leading me to the Twelve Steps. Help me follow them.

Action for the Day

Today, I'll take time out to read the Twelve Steps. Then I'll list three reasons why the Steps are a good plan for living.

Humbly asked
Him to remove our
shortcomings.

— *Step Seven*
from Alcoholics
Anonymous

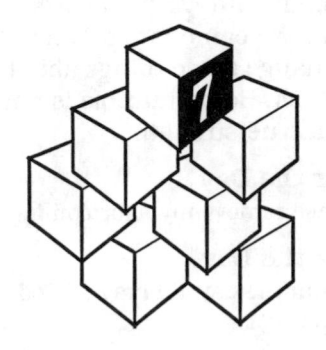

Humbly asked Him to
remove our shortcomings.
— Step Seven

In Step Six, we got ready to give up our shortcomings. In Step Seven, we ask God to remove them. There is one catch. We *humbly* ask God to remove them.

Being humble means we remember who we are: human beings who need God's help. Being humble means not pretending we're God. We admit we need God's help. Being humble means seeing ourselves as we are. We're a small but very important part of God's plan. We can change much, but only God can change some things about us. This is why we ask. Being humble is not a weakness, but a true strength.

Prayer for the Day
God, please remove my shortcomings.

Action for the Day
Throughout the day, I'll pray to God to remove my shortcomings.

I never think of the future.
It comes soon enough.
— Albert Einstein

None of us know anything for sure about the future. We don't know if we'll be sober tomorrow. But we can be sure of this moment. We get sober by moments. Our sober moments then stretch into hours, days, and years.

Our program tells us to live in the present moment. This is because we can control this moment. We can't control the past or the future. We need to have a sense of control in our life. In our illness, we were out of control. This was because we wouldn't live from moment to moment.

Each moment is filled with as much life as we can handle. Each moment is filled with enough to keep us alive, interested, and growing!

Prayer for the Day

Higher Power, help me find You in each moment.

Action for the Day

Today, I'll stop and focus on the present moment. I will work to see how much control I can have if I stay with the moment at hand.

We are only as sick as the
secrets we keep.
— *Anonymous*

It is dangerous for us to keep secrets. Shame builds, and we'll want relief. We may turn to alcohol or other drugs. True relief comes by talking about our secrets, by sharing who we really are with others. Our program helps us live a life based on honesty. Our program helps us battle shame. We don't keep secrets anymore. We start our meetings and share what we tried to keep secret before. "Hi, my name is _____, and I'm an alcoholic." "Hi, my name is _____, and I'm a drug addict." We keep telling our secret, and the shame gets less and less.

Prayer for the Day
Higher Power, I pray to live an honest life.

Action for the Day
I'll list any secrets I've been keeping. I'll talk with my sponsor about them.

I have a dream !
— Martin Luther King, Jr.

During our addiction, maybe we dreamed of joy and laughter with our family—only to find tears and anger. Maybe we dreamed of respect at our job—only to be fired. Our dreams began to feel like burdens. We had lost hope.

With recovery, the hope starts to return. We start to trust ourselves again. We start to trust others again. We start to trust in our Higher Power. Over time, we even dare to dream again. In our dreams, we are loving people. We have something to offer others. We are not scared. This is a sign that hope is returning. We fall in love again with the world, our Higher Power, and ourselves.

Prayer for the Day

Higher Power, thank-you for giving back my future. Thank-you for giving back my dreams.

Action for the Day

Today, I'll tell my dreams to a friend. Do my future dreams include improving myself through the program?

*If at first you don't succeed,
you're running about
average.*

— Ovid

Our program speaks of spiritual progress,
not perfection. We can take all the time we
need. Our bottom line is steady progress. We
can ask ourselves, "Am I a little more spiritual
than I was a year ago? A month ago?" If the
answer is yes, we're doing great. If the answer
is no, we should look at why.

Our illness pushes us to be perfect. In
recovery, we learn that we are free to be what
we are—just human. Even the world's fastest
runners are average in most other areas of
their lives. This is okay. Remember, "spiritual
progress, *not* perfection."

Prayer for the Day

Higher Power, I'll not be ashamed of how average
I am. I'll remember I'm average—and that's good.

Action for the Day

I'll list what is average about me. I'll share this
with a friend. Then I'll ask my friend what is special about me.

When fate hands us a lemon,
let's try to make lemonade.
— *Dale Carnegie*

Our illness is one big lemon, but our recovery is lemonade! None of us signed up to be drunks or druggies, but we all signed up for recovery. That's when the happiness began. Yes, there will be pain, but the joy will far outweigh the pain. The sweet joy of recovery becomes our drink—our lemonade. And, do we drink!

We have new friends. We love ourselves, our Higher Power, our family, and much more. We are creative when we give joy, love, and help to others and to ourselves. If your lemonade isn't sweet enough, add more of your program to it.

Prayer for the Day

Higher Power, it's easy to forget how much You've given me. Thank you for all the joy and love You have given me.

Action for the Day

Today, I'll write down what part of recovery I really enjoy. I will then share this list with my group or a friend.

*Be brave enough to accept
the help of others.*
— *Melba Colgrove,
Harold H. Bloomfield,
Peter McWilliams*

Often in the past, we acted like we didn't
need anyone. It takes courage to let others
help us. As we get better, our courage grows.
We invite people into our lives. We help
others, and we let others help us.

We will learn to let others help us if we work
our program. Why? Because we need others
to stay sober. When we have a problem, we
talk about it in our group. When we need a
shoulder to cry on, we call a friend or our
sponsor. Over time, our relationships become
one of the biggest rewards of recovery.

Prayer for the Day

Higher Power, help me see my need for others
as a test—a test to see if I'll be brave enough and
wise enough to ask for help when I need it.

Action for the Day

Today, I'll list four times in my life when I needed
help but didn't ask for it. I'll tell a friend about how
these times would've been different if I had asked
for help.

*Pain can't be avoided. It's
as natural as joy.*
— *Unknown*

We got into a lot of trouble trying to avoid pain. We used alcohol and other drugs to avoid pain. We didn't want to accept pain as a fact of life.

We can't avoid pain, but now we have the program. The program teaches us how to talk about our pain. The program teaches how to turn over our pain to our Higher Power.

We don't have to be alone when we face pain. We have friends to go to. Before, when we hurt, we ran to alcohol or other drugs. Now, when we hurt, we run to the comfort of our sponsor and our program friends.

Prayer for the Day

Higher Power, help me accept pain as part of life. Help me remember that You are always there to help me with my pain. I'm not alone.

Action for the Day

Today, I'll list three painful events in my life. I'll talk with a friend about them.

*First say to yourself what
you would be; and then do
what you have to do.*
— *Epictetus*

We often tell ourselves we want to be more
peaceful, more in touch with our Higher
Power. In other words, we want to become
more spiritual. Acting as spiritual people is
hard. Too often, we choose the easy way. We
make a nasty comment even if we know it'll
only make things worse.

We say we have a program for living. Are
we living our program? We'll find the answer
in our behavior. Sober people act in sober
ways. We attend meetings regularly. We study
spiritual ideas. We work to bring joy to our
lives and the lives of others. Just as we know
a good friend by the way he or she behaves,
we know a sober person by the way he or she
behaves.

Prayer for the Day

Higher Power, help me be a person whose words
and actions match up.

Today's Action

Today I'll take an inventory of my actions to see
if they are those of a sober person.

*Everybody knows that
when they're happy, then
usually the people around
them are happy.*
— George Harrison

Do we think we can't be happy until others are happy? Then nobody is happy. Our unhappy friends won't take our advice. They say, "Why should I do what you say? You are not happy either." And we answer, "I'll be okay when you're happy." We make them responsible for our happiness. What a mess!

We can only make one person happy—ourselves. How? By living as our Higher Power leads us. By working the Steps. By being grateful for the good things in our lives. By loving ourselves and others, *just as we are.*

And maybe when we're happy, our friends will learn from us. They can be happy too. But only our friends can make themselves happy.

Prayer for the Day
Higher Power, as I do my part in Your plan today, help me feel connected to You and to life.

Today's Action
Today I'll enjoy my happiness. I'll look for three ways to share it with others.

*If you would be loved, love
and be lovable.*
— *Benjamin Franklin*

We all want to be loved. And no matter how much we're loved, we always want more.

How can we be lovable? What does this mean? Should we try to be perfect? Should we act cute and helpless? No, being lovable means that we act ourselves. We let others get to know us. When others love us, we enjoy it. We tell them. We let them know that their love isn't wasted on us, that it's important to us.

We are lovable, and we are loved!

Prayer for the Day
Higher Power, help me accept the love of others today. Help me be lovable.

Action for the Day
Today, I'll list all the little things others do that show they care about me.

*Just because everything is
different doesn't mean
anything has changed.*
 — *Irene Peter*

Our life changed a lot when we stopped
drinking and using other drugs. But this is
only a start. We need to go further.

Our old attitudes can kill us, even if we
aren't drinking or drugging any more. This
is called a "dry drunk." If we're on a dry
drunk, we've changed the way we act without
changing the way we think.

Our program shows us how to change the
way we think. And we change how we treat
ourselves and others. We learn to live a new
life based on love and care.

Prayer for the Day

Higher Power, help me guard against my old
attitudes. Help me keep changing.

Action for the Day

I'll list four ways I've changed because I'm sober.
I'll list four ways I haven't changed yet.

*A brother may not be a
friend, but a friend will
always be a brother.*
— *Benjamin Franklin*

Many of us come from families that aren't
very healthy for us. Many families have lots
of love but aren't able to show it. Maybe our
parents argued or drank too much. When we
share our recovery with them, they may not
seem happy for us. They may be doing the
best they can, but they don't understand our
new way of life.

We *can* have the love we wanted, but it
might not come from our family. We can
choose healthy friends to be our new "family."
Some friends may seem like the sister or
brother we always wanted. A sponsor can give
us advice we never got from our parents. We
can have a full, healthy "family life" after all.

Prayer for the Day

Higher Power, help me choose good friends who
will help me be the best that I can be.

Action for the Day

The best way to have a friend is to be a friend.
What will I do today to be a friend?

*Most of the evils of life arise
from man's being unable to
sit still in a room.*
— Blaise Pascal

Our program teaches us to slow down. We learn to slow down by taking time out. During these time-outs, we look at our values and see if we're staying true to them.

Because of that, meditation is an important part of our program. It teaches us to slow down. Our Higher Power wants us to have fun and play. But we need to bring our Higher Power along. Remember, our Higher Power loves fun. We can have fun, but not at the expense of others.

Prayer for the Day

I pray for help so I can remember my values. Higher Power, teach me to have fun. Teach me to be true to You at the same time.

Action for the Day

Today, I'll list three times mischief has gotten me in trouble. I'll list three times mischief has been good fun. I'll talk with a friend about the difference between trouble mischief and fun mischief.

*Let there be spaces in your
Togetherness.*
— *Kahlil Gibran*

We all need time alone. Then we can get to
know ourselves better. We can get to know
our Higher Power better too.

When we were using chemicals, we were
afraid of being alone. We didn't want to think
too much. So we got high.

Now we know we're never totally alone. Our
Higher Power is with us. We can relax. We can
rest. We can think, read, meditate. We can be
our own best friend.

Prayer for the Day

Higher Power, help me use my time alone to
know myself better. Help me get to know You too.

Action for the Day

Today, I'll plan to spend two hours alone to get to
know myself better. I could take a long walk, or enjoy a park, or my garden. What will I do, and when?

*We can't all be heroes
because someone has to sit
on the curb and clap as
they go by.*
— *Will Rogers*

Humility is being thankful for the chance to watch the parade. There were days we thought that all that counted were the heroes. But our program has no heroes. It has many fine, spiritual people. . .but no heroes.

When someone is needed to make coffee or pick up after a meeting, we can be willing to do those things. Let's look at doing these little jobs as our way of looking for a good spot on the curb. . .to watch the parade. How good it feels to just sit back and watch the parade! The floats are so colorful, and the bands play so loud!

Prayer for the Day

Higher Power, help me be proud of who I am, instead of always putting myself down because I'm not who I "should" be.

Action for the Day

I will look and help someone today. Service to others is service to my Higher Power.

*Nothing in life is to be
feared. It is only to be
understood.*

— *Marie Curie*

We have many sides, some good, some bad. Maybe we're afraid to see our faults. But we don't need to be afraid. After all, we need to know our dark side before we can change it. When we see ourselves clearly, we can stop our dark side from causing trouble.

When we shine light on our fears and secrets, we'll begin to feel better about ourselves. We'll feel more safe about sharing our worries. The more honest we are with ourselves and others, the better and stronger we become. The goodness and love in us will blossom. We have a Higher Power and a program to help us.

Prayer for the Day

Higher Power, help me be brave enough to see myself clearly. Gently teach me to see who I really am. Help me know enough to stay sober today.

Action for the Day

Today, I'll look myself in the eyes. I'll spend two minutes looking into my eyes in a mirror. I'll talk to my sponsor about what I see.

*It takes twenty years to
become an overnight
success.*
— *Eddie Cantor*

Successful people make life look easy. But
it's not. Years of hard work, trial and error,
and learning probably went into each
success.

The key is this: We must choose to do what
we really *like*. If we want to be successful,
we'll have to keep working at it. We'll have let-
downs, and we'll get bored at times. But we'll
be happy because we're doing what we want,
what we know is best for us. Real success has
to do with our own happiness.

In our programs, we'll meet many successful people. They've worked hard at recovery,
and they're still learning. And they're happy
to share their success with us.

Prayer for the Day
Higher Power, thank-you for the success the program has already given me.

Action for the Day
I'll list three ways I know I am a success today.
Number one: I'm sober!

We grow small trying to be great.
— E. Stanley Jones

We dreamed of being great. Trying to be great is about *control*. We've caused a lot of trouble trying to control things. We've been afraid to just let things happen. We're not very trusting. Many of us have good reasons not to trust. Whatever the reasons, we had put our trust in getting drunk or high. We thought that was one thing we could control. What really happened? We got sick.

Recovery is based on trust. We must learn to trust that it's best for us to give up control. It will seem strange, at first. But letting go and trusting can become a way of life. The Steps, our groups, our sponsor, and our Higher Power—here, we find love and caring. We can trust them.

Prayer for the Day

I pray that day by day, I'll put more trust in my program and in my Higher Power.

Action for the Day

I'll list five reasons why I can trust my Twelve Step program.

*Living so fully, I can't
imagine what any drug
would do for me.*
— Joan Baez

When we were using alcohol and other drugs, our lives kept getting emptier. We tried to keep new things out of our lives. We were scared and tired. We saw feelings as bad. So we got high instead of feeling them.

Now we can live fully every day. We don't want to block our feelings. We aren't afraid of opening up to new things and people.

And the more we open up, the happier we are. Our feelings are free. They bounce around. They don't get stuck. We feel alive. Sure, we feel pain and fear sometimes. But we feel joy, love, and laughter too. And, more and more often, we feel alive.

Prayer for the Day
Higher Power, please help me live fully today. Help me notice my feelings.

Action for the Day
Today, I'll list five things I've enjoyed in the last twenty-four hours.

*There is no human
problem which could not be
solved if people would
simply do as I advise.*
— *Gore Vidal*

Many of us used a "know it all" act to keep people away. We kept everyone around us on edge. They were afraid of our judgments, just as we were secretly afraid of theirs. Why were we so busy with everyone else's life? So we didn't have to look at our own! We were afraid of what was happening to us. But we didn't want to see how sick we were becoming. Now we're not afraid. We don't need to keep people away. We don't need to run their lives. We have our own life to live. And we're enjoying it.

Prayer for the Day

Higher Power, You are the expert, not me. Teach me. I am Your student.

Action for the Day

Today, I'll list the ways I chased away those who cared about me. I'll work on the Steps on these items for the next week.

> . . .*for, behold, the*
> *kingdom of God is within*
> *you.*
>
> — *Luke 17:21*

We want so much to be good. Even when we used alcohol or other drugs, we wanted to believe we were good people. But we often felt we couldn't measure up. We thought we had to live by a set of rules that we could never follow.

Now we're finding the goodness inside us. Goodness isn't something we *do*. Goodness is just being what we already *are*. Our Higher Power speaks to us in many ways, including through our hearts and minds. We don't have to try so hard to be good. We just learn to relax and invite our Higher Power to be a part of our lives.

Prayer for the Day

Higher Power, You have put peace, knowledge, love, and joy in my heart today. Help me to always find these things.

Action for the Day

How's my Higher Power like a loving king or queen? How can I have a kingdom inside me? I'll talk with my sponsor about this today.

*Don't talk unless you can
improve the silence.*
— *Laurence Coughlin*

"Do I talk too much?" Most of us wonder this sometimes. There are some ways to find out.

Ask yourself these questions: "How much do I know about the people in my life?" "What do they think and feel?" "Do I listen to them?" "Do I often feel that I say too much?"

Then ask a few trusted friends these questions: "Do you think I talk too much?" "How well do you think I listen to you?"

Silence helps us listen—to ourselves, to others, and to our Higher Power.

Prayer for the Day
Higher Power, help me enjoy the silent moments in my day.

Action for the Day
Today, I'll think before I speak. What do I really want to say?

The work of adult life is not easy.

— *Gail Sheehy*

We used to look for an easier, softer way. We tried to take care of ourselves by staying clear of hard tasks. The result? We haven't known what the work of adult life *is*.

The work of adult life is this: to become spiritually centered. And to do this, we work at getting rid of our self-will. There will be many great rewards for doing this. We will wake up spiritually. We will connect with those we love. The result? We will receive self-love to replace self-will. Our work will not be easy, but it will be rewarding.

Prayer for the Day

Higher Power, help me to give it all to my recovery program. Then help me be open to the rewards this will bring.

Action for the Day

I will list the hard parts of my program. Then I'll talk about them with my sponsor, friends, family, and Higher Power.

*If the spirit within us
withers (dies), so too will
all the world we build
around us.*

— *Theodore Roszab*

This is what happened during our illness—our spirits were dying. Our relationships were dying. Our self-esteem was dying. Our love of beauty was dying. This is because addiction is death.

And recovery is life! The Steps breathe life into us. Our groups breathe life into us. We start to heal because we once again feel hope. We're less afraid of what tomorrow may bring. As our hope grows, others feel it too.

We're starting to slowly rebuild our world. We're building our world on the Twelve Steps and their message of hope.

Prayer for the Day

I give myself to life. Higher Power, work with me as I rebuild my world.

Action for the Day

I'll talk with a friend about hope. I'll see my hope as a sign of how close I am to my program.

*I was never less alone than
when by myself.*
— *Edward Gibbon*

To stay in this program, we need to *accept*
that we have an illness. We need to *accept*
that we were out of control. And we need to
accept that we need others and they need us.
At times, we won't want to accept these facts.
We will want to deny we have an illness and
our lives were out of control.

Many of us get into trouble when we don't
accept that we need others. This is why helping others is so important. It teaches us that
we need others, and others need us. By helping others, we learn about the give-and-take of
human relationships. There is no give-and-
take in addiction. There is just take. Now,
finally, we can give too!

Prayer for the Day

I pray to remember that I need other people.

Action for the Day

Today, I'll help out. I will make coffee at the meeting or offer to do the Step next week. I will let a
fellow addict know I'm glad he or she is sober.

*To enjoy freedom we have
to control ourselves.*
— *Virginia Woolf*

Freedom is a funny thing. In a way, it makes life harder. We are free to do what we want, but every choice makes a difference in our lives. Some choices make us happy, and some bring trouble.

We can make good choices. We can control our actions. We can start by having control in little ways: follow the law, pay the rent, make the bed every day. These choices put order in our lives. Eat right, exercise, and get enough sleep. These choices make us strong enough to live each day to the fullest. These kinds of choices set us free.

Prayer for the Day

Higher Power, when I was drinking and drugging, I couldn't enjoy my freedom. I had no control over the little things in my life. Help me stay sober today.

Action for the Day

Today, I'll be grateful for having some control. I will list five ways I am more free because I can control my actions.

The best leaders are those
who know how to follow.
— Anonymous

Am I a leader or a follower? The fact is, I *am* responsible for where I end up. If I choose to be a follower, I'd better follow leaders who know where they're going. And I had better know where they're going.

If I choose to be a leader, I'd better know that I'm responsible for getting myself on the right path. I also must be honest with my followers, so they can make good choices. I'm not responsible for my followers' choices, but I must give them the truth. Being a leader doesn't always mean I know where I'll end up. But it can mean that I know I'm on the right path, following the lead from my Higher Power—one step at a time.

Prayer for the Day

Higher Power, give me the faith and courage to choose good leaders to follow. When it is Your will, help me be a good leader.

Action for the Day

Today I'll list my leaders. They might be a Higher Power, a sponsor, or a friend. I'll think of why I choose to follow these leaders.

*They have rights who dare
defend them.*
— Roger Baldwin

In recovery, we regain our right to have choices, our right to have honest relationships. Do we claim these rights, or do we let them go by?

Sometimes, standing up for our rights will mean going against the crowd. It will mean turning down that drink when everyone else has one. It will mean telling your honest opinion when it's different from what others think. Being sober will mean, at times, being different. Lots of times, we find being different hard. We want to fit in. This is normal.

But we don't stand alone. We have friends who will stand with us during hard times. We have a Higher Power who will guide and comfort us. We are people with rights. Let's work hard so nothing takes away our rights.

Prayer for the Day

Higher Power, please help me keep and defend my dignity and human rights.

Action for the Day

I'll take time out to list the rights I've gotten back due to my recovery.

*Beauty may be said to be
God's trademark in creation.*
— Henry Ward Beecher

Our addiction was like a veil over our heads. We saw the world as an ugly place. We saw people as trouble. We thought our drinks and drugs were beautiful. But even they became ugly over time. Life became ugly because we had put distance between our Higher Power and ourselves.

Now we are blessed because the veil is lifted, and we are part of the healing process. We help others step into the beauty of recovery.

Our spirits are again free to seek a relationship with God and others. Through these relationships, we get our hope back. This hope helps us focus on the beauty of the world. Hope is the rain that helps our souls grow.

Prayer for the Day

Higher Power, the world is both beautiful and ugly. For too long I only saw the ugly. Help me focus on the beauty.

Action for the Day

Today, I will keep an eye out for the beauty recovery holds for me. Throughout the day, I'll pray for this.

Less is more.
— *Mies Vander Rohe*

Our program is simple. It has four equal parts: sobriety, fellowship, service, and faith.

Sobriety means we don't use alcohol or other drugs anymore. *Fellowship* means we let people into our lives. We work at having a life that's rich with friends. *Service* means we help when we see a need. It means knowing we have much to offer. *Faith* means we believe in a loving, caring Higher Power. It means using our Higher Power as a guide in life.

Ours is a simple, easy program. Just remember sobriety, fellowship, service, and faith.

Prayer for the Day
I pray that I may keep my program simple. I pray for sobriety, fellowship, service, and faith.

Action for the Day
Throughout the day, I'll remind myself that less is more.

Made a list of all persons we had harmed, and became willing to make amends to them all.

— *Step Eight*
from Alcoholics
Anonymous

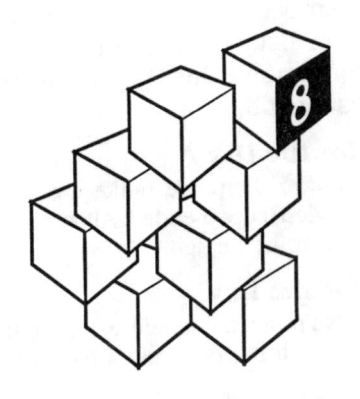

*Made a list of all persons
we had harmed...*
— First half of Step Eight

By the time we get to Step Eight, we're ready to work on our relationships. We start by making a list of all the persons we've harmed. We look at where we have been at fault. We own our behavior.

Now we're healing, and we must help others heal too. Our list must be as complete as we can make it. As our recovery goes on, we'll remember others we have hurt. We add them to our list. By doing this, we heal even more. Remember, this Step is for us. It is to help us stay sober.

Prayer for the Day

Higher Power, help me make a complete list. Help me to keep it open-ended. Allow me and those I've harmed to be healed.

Action for the Day

Even if I've made a list before, I'll make another one today. I will list *all* those I have harmed.

> *. .and became willing to*
> *make amends to them all.*
> *— Second half of Step Eight*

We have made our list of persons we've harmed. Now we look at how willing we are to make amends. We might find that we aren't ready and willing to make amends to everyone. Maybe they have wronged us more than we have wronged them. Maybe we're afraid they'll get angry with us. Maybe we're afraid they'll put us in jail.

We get ready to make amends by listening and talking to others in our group—and to our sponsor. We pray for help to be willing to make amends. Becoming willing does not just happen. We have to work at it. We need to be willing to let go of the past.

Prayer for the Day

Higher Power, help me become willing. Help me see my part. I know "my part" is the only part I can change.

Action for the Day

I will take time to go over my list. To whom am I not yet ready to make amends? I will take time to read the Serenity Prayer.

*Alcoholism isn't a spectator
sport. Eventually the whole
family gets to play.*
— Joyce Rebeta-Burditt

One of the biggest lies addicts can tell themselves is, "I'm not hurting anyone but myself." This is just another way we don't see how important we are to others. During our using, love was a burden. When anyone showed love for us, we turned away. They hurt. And we hurt.

In recovery, when ready, we try and help our families heal. We listen as they speak of how our illness has hurt them. We comfort them as they tell their stories. Remember, our illness hurt them. Remember, our recovery will help them heal.

Prayer for the Day
Higher Power, help me face the pain my illness has brought to others. Let me know their pain. Let it help me stay sober.

Action for the Day
I will list all persons my illness has hurt. I will say a prayer for them, even if they have harmed me.

*Let him that would move
the world, first move
himself.*

— *Socrates*

Before recovery, most of us were big talkers.
The Twelve Steps are for doers, not talkers. In
the Steps we find action words: *admitted,
humbly asked, made direct amends, continued to take personal inventory.* All of
these words speak of action, of doing. Recovery is about action. It's for doers. An action
may be very simple. Such as going to a meeting early to set up chairs. Or it could be helping a neighbor. The program teaches that
spirituality is action. By being spiritually active, we grow and change.

Prayer for the Day

Higher Power, give me movement. Give me
spiritual movement. Help me be a doer, not just
a talker. Teach me to work my program.

Today's Action

Today I'll remember that words and action go
together.

*You're only human, you're
supposed to make
mistakes.*

— *Billy Joel*

Listen to the kind voice inside. Listen to the voice that tells you you're good enough. Listen to the voice that tells you it's okay to make mistakes—you'll learn from them. Listen to the voice that tells you to go to your meeting even though it's cold outside and you're tired. Listen, and let this voice become more and more clear. Listen, and welcome it into your heart. Talk with this voice. Ask it questions and seek it out when you need a friend. This voice is your Higher Power. Listen as your Higher Power speaks to you. Listen as your Higher Power tells you what a great person you are.

Prayer for the Day

I pray to the gentle, loving voice that lives in me. Higher Power, You've always been kind to me. You've always loved me. Help me to remember You're always there—inside me.

Action for the Day

I will take time from my busy day to listen and talk with the loving voice that lives inside me.

*Fear of people and
economic insecurity will
leave you...*
— *Alcoholics Anonymous*

We don't have to fear people. They can't wreck our spirit. We don't have to fear money problems. We won't starve to death. Our Higher Power will lead us on a safe path through life.

Our Higher Power wants us to be safe, happy, and wise. Our Higher Power wants us to feel loved. We'll learn to trust our Higher Power. And we'll learn to trust the happiness we find in our new way of life. People may still hurt us, but there will be much more love to carry us through.

Prayer for the Day

Higher Power, I know You protect me and care for me. Help me stop worrying.

Action for the Day

Today, I'll list four fears I have. I will talk with my sponsor about how to turn these over to my Higher Power.

*True enjoyment comes from
activity of the mind and
exercise of the body.*
— *Humboldt*

In recovery, we work at taking better care
of ourselves. We care for our mind and our
body. Often, during our drinking and drugging, we ignored our mind and body. We probably ate poorly, and we pushed our body to
the limit.

But now, we are to recover... *totally!* We
are to care for our mind and body as we care
for our spirit. Our illness is an illness of mind,
body, and spirit. So let's care for all three. In
recovery, we learn to care for and love *all* of
who we are.

Prayer for the Day

Higher Power, help me care for my mind and
body as I recover. You love all of me. Help me to
respect and care for *all* of me.

Action for the Day

I will write down how much time I've spent caring for my mind and body in the past two weeks.
Is it enough?

Adventure is not outside a
man; it is within.
— David Grayson

Sobriety. It's an exciting adventure. It's a spiritual adventure. We look inward. We find where our Higher Power lives: within us. We then reach outward. We share our joy with others. Not with words and preaching, but by trying to help others. Sobriety is faith turned into action.

Sobriety. It's an adventure in coming to know one's self. At times, we'll have to face our fears. But we'll also find just how much love we have for life.

Sobriety. It's as if we're on a trip. Our Higher Power holds the map. Our job is to listen. And we go in the direction we're told.

Prayer for the Day

I pray to be an adventurer. Higher Power, I pray to follow Your direction.

Action for the Day

I'll ask some friends to tell me about an adventure their Higher Power has taken them on.

If there is no wind, row.
          — Latin proverb

At times, staying sober will be easy; at other times, it will be hard. But we must do what is needed to stay sober. Having a hard week? Go to extra meetings. Feeling alone? Call a friend and ask if you can get together. Feel like drinking? Go to a safe place until the urge passes.

We have no choice. We must row when there's no wind. If not, we'll fall back into our addiction.

If we work hard, we'll stay sober. Plus we'll grow as spiritual people. Hard times test us and make us better people. But this will only happen if we keep our Higher Power and our program close to our heart.

Prayer for the Day

Higher Power, help me remember that I grow during hard times. I pray that I'll accept and use what You've given me each day.

Action for the Day

Today, I'll list five things I learned from my program in hard times.

*There are times we must
grab God's hand and walk
forward.*
— *Anonymous*

Sometimes we struggle with being part of
the problem, instead of being part of the
solution. Inside we know this, but somehow
we can't Let Go and Let God.

To let go takes faith that the outcome will
be okay. When we have faith, we know our
Higher Power believes in us and will guide us.
When we have faith, we believe in ourselves.
When we let go, we let go of our need to
always be right. Letting go first takes place on
the inside. Letting go allows us to change how
we view what's happening. Often, all we really
need is this change of attitude. This is the
beauty of faith: it allows us to see the same
thing in different ways.

Prayer for the Day

Higher Power, permit me to let go. Let me see that
believing in You must also mean believing in myself.

Action for the Day

I will review my life since entering the Twelve
Step program. I will work at seeing what good partners my Higher Power and I make.

The trouble with the rat
race is that even if you win
you're still a rat.
— *Lily Tomlin*

Alcoholism is a rat race. Drug addiction is a rat race. We were always trying to keep one or two steps ahead of the cat. We were always sneaking around, and everyone was disgusted with us.

Our goal in recovery is to stop acting like a rat and join the human race again. Recovery teaches us sayings like Easy Does It and One Day at a Time. Our sayings remind us to pace ourselves. Our sayings remind us that healing takes time.

We live by human values: honesty, respect for others, fairness, openness, self-respect. We work at just being ourselves. We learn that this is enough. We are enough.

Prayer for the Day
Higher Power, help me accept my humanness. I am part of the human race, not the rat race.

Action for the Day
Just for today, I'll pace myself. I'll list ways I often go too fast for my own good. I'll ask friends how they pace themselves.

> *Fairness is what justice*
> *really is.*
> *— The late Supreme Court*
> *Justice Potter Stewart*

Some of us get hung up on what's fair. We might feel, because we've worked hard to stay sober, we should be rewarded. We might keep score of what we get and what others get. And we complain if it's "not fair."

Maybe we should be *glad* life isn't fair. Why? Most of us caused a lot of trouble we've never had to pay for. And we've hurt a lot of people who haven't gotten even. Would we really want life to be fair?

Our Higher Power isn't fair either. That is, our Higher Power doesn't keep score. Our Higher Power doesn't try to get even. Our Higher Power is loving and forgiving, no matter what. Our Higher Power has the same love and help for everyone.

Prayer for the Day
Higher Power, give me the wisdom to stop keeping score. Help me want the best for everyone.

Action for the Day
I'll list five times I've been unfair to others. Do I need to make amends?

Once it [a spoken word]
flies out, you can't catch it.
— *Russian proverb*

We've said many mean words. Our words most often hurt the people we love. We can never really take back those words. But we're learning now to speak with care. We know that words have a lot of power.

What do we say when we're angry? When we want something? When we're trying to be kind? Now, think about this: people will remember our words. If we're honest and careful in our speech, people will respect us. But if we say things to force our will, we may be sorry later.

Prayer for the Day

Higher Power, speak through me today.

Action for the Day

Today, I'll ask one question of the person I love the most: "How have my words hurt you in the past?" Then I'll talk with my sponsor about this.

The best side of a saloon is the outside.

— Anonymous

We need to stay away from places where we used to drink or use other drugs. Sometimes we need to stay away from our old using friends. But some days it's hard to stay away. We remember the fun times. Or we want a quick fix for our problems. When we feel like this, we know something is wrong. We can call our sponsor and talk about it. And get to a meeting. We need to remember how much better our lives are now. We don't want our old lives back.

Prayer for the Day

Higher Power, help me stay away from trouble. Thanks for keeping me sober today.

Action for the Day

Today, I'll make a list of places that mean trouble for me—places I need to stay away from.

*We know what we are, but
know not what we may be.*
— *Shakespeare*

We are addicts. We suffer from an illness.
We go to Twelve Step meetings because we
know who we are. We have a sponsor because
we know who we are. We ask friends for support because we know who we are. We know
why we need our Higher Power to guide us.
Recovery is a spiritual journey. In this journey,
we are followers, not guides. It's a journey that
will change us. We don't know how recovery
will change us, but we know it will. Is my faith
strong enough for my journey? Part of how we
get strong for our journey is by knowing who
we truly are: addicts.

Prayer for the Day
I pray to remember who I am, so I'll learn to
respect the power of my illness.

Today's Action
I'll take time to remember my past, both good
and bad. I'll also take time to think about who I
am now. How far have I come?

> *The strongest rebellion*
> *may be expressed in quiet,*
> *undramatic behavior.*
> —Benjamin Spock

In recovery, we each rebel against our disease. Each day we fight for the freedom to stay close to our Higher Power, friends, and family.

It's mainly a quiet battle. It's fought daily. We fight and win by acting in a spiritual way. We fight and win every time we help a friend, go to a meeting, or read about how to improve our lives.

We move slowly but always forward. Rushing will only tire us out. Our battle will go on for life. We are quiet fighters, but we're strong, for we do not fight alone. And we know what waits for us if we lose.

Prayer for the Day

Higher Power, help me stay free. When I want to give up, help me realize this is normal. Help me to keep fighting at these times.

Action for the Day

Today, I'll be a rebel. I will go to an extra meeting, or I'll talk with my sponsor. I'll find a way to help someone without the person knowing.

*Words that do not match
deeds are not important.*
— *Ernesto Ché Guevara*

What we do can be much more important than what we say. We tend to talk about things we *want* to do. We need to also be people who do the things we talk about. We are not spiritual people unless our actions are spiritual.

Many of us used to be "all or nothing" people. That made us afraid to tackle the big projects. But now we know we can get things done, if we take one step at a time. We're not "all or nothing" people anymore. We're people who are changing and growing a little every day. And each day our deeds match our words a little better.

Prayer for the Day

Higher Power, help me live fully today. Help me to not just talk about what I want to do. Give me the gift of patience, so I can be pleased with my progress.

Action for the Day

Today, I'll list the things that I say I'd like to do. What is one thing I can do today to make each of them happen? I'll take one step today to match my life to my dreams.

*The Master doesn't talk,
she acts. When her work is
done, the people say,
"Amazing: we did it, all by
ourselves!"*

— Lao-tzu

Our Higher Power works like the Master. Quietly. In fact, we usually take the credit ourselves!

We're like a child who bakes cookies for the first time. Mother found the recipe, bought the ingredients, and got out the bowl and pans and spoons. She told us what to do, and finished when we got tired. Then she cleaned up after us. We proudly served our cookies, saying, "I made them all by myself!"

In recovery, our Higher Power helps and teaches us every step of the way, just like a loving parent.

Prayer for the Day

Higher Power, *thank-you*—for my life, for my recovery, for love, for hope, and for faith. Thank-you for teaching me how to live in a better way.

Action for the Day

I'll list five ways my Higher Power has acted in my life.

*The future is made of the
same stuff as the present.*
— *Simone Weil*

We found we didn't need magic to recover—
we needed a miracle! Now we are walking
miracles. Part of our miracle is that we see
how important today is. We can't change our
future unless we change today. So we live One
Day at a Time. By living today well, we make
our future better. There is comfort in knowing that the program will be there. Friends
will be there. Hope will be there.

Old-timers say sobriety is easy if we go by
one simple rule: don't drink and go to meetings. Life can get simpler for us. The rules of
life are simple; they don't change much. Staying sober will be easier for us over time.

Prayer for the Day

Higher Power, help me keep my sobriety simple.
Help me accept the rules of life.

Action for the Day

I will list three things that will be there for me
tomorrow and the next day, because I'm working
on them today.

*Heaven and hell is right
now. . .You make it heaven
or you make it hell by your
actions.*

— *George Harrison*

We used chemicals to feel better, but we started feeling worse. We were out of control. Life seemed like hell.

Now we have a program that tells us how to make life better. Some days, it even feels like heaven! But we have to work our program to make our own heaven.

Working the program isn't too hard. And it makes us feel so good. So, why don't we do it all the time? Maybe we're a little afraid of heaven. It's time to learn to love having a better life!

Prayer for the Day

Higher Power, help me work my program each day, so each day has a little bit of heaven in it. Help me get used to having a better life.

Action for the Day

Tonight, I'll think about the moments of kindness, joy, hope, and faith that put a little bit of heaven into my day today.

Beauty is not caused. It is.
— *Emily Dickinson*

Probably, there have been many times when we thought we weren't beautiful. We thought we were ugly. We thought we were bad people. This is a natural part of addiction. Our program tells us we're good, we're beautiful. Do we believe this? Do we accept this part of our program?

Beauty is an attitude, just as self-hate is an attitude. We need to keep the attitude that we're beautiful. We owe it to ourselves and to those around us. And, yes, it's true that you must love yourself before you can love others. Remember, ours is a selfish program. We have to love and see ourselves as beautiful, before we try to give to others.

Prayer for the Day
Higher Power, help me claim my beauty. Help me to see that, sometimes, I have to be selfish to grow.

Action for the Day
Today, I'll work at falling in love with myself.

It's a rare person who
wants to hear what he
doesn't want to hear.
— Dick Cavett

We only want to hear good things. That
we're nice people. That our loved ones are
healthy. That we did a good job. We don't
want to hear that anyone is angry with us, or
that we made a mistake. We don't want to
hear about an illness or troubles.

But life isn't just happy news. Bad things
happen. We can't change that. As we live our
recovery program, we learn to handle the
hard things without running back to our addiction. We choose the path of life. We need
to know all the news, good and bad. Then we
can deal with life as it really is.

Prayer for the Day

Higher Power, help me listen—even when I don't
want to. Gently help me deal with both the good
and bad. All the help I need is mine for the asking.

Action for the Day

I will ask my sponsor and three friends to tell me
about my blind spots.

*Where there is no vision, a
people perish.*
— *Ralph Waldo Emerson*

Working our program teaches us to see
things more clearly. We learn to look at who
we really are. At first, we're scared to see ourselves. But it turns out okay. We have others
to remind us that we're okay, even though
we're not perfect.

We also begin to see others more clearly. We
see good in people we don't like. And we see
faults in people we thought were perfect. But
we don't judge people anymore. Nobody is
perfect. Just as our program friends accept
us as we are, we learn to accept others.

Prayer for the Day

Higher Power, sometimes I don't like what I see.
Help me to believe Your way will work for me. Help
me have vision.

Action for the Day

I will use my new way of seeing things to avoid
trouble today.

*To love oneself is the
beginning of a lifelong
romance.*
— Oscar Wilde

There's a big difference between being self-centered and having self-love. We're self-centered when we think we don't need people. We might think, "I'm more important than others." Being self-centered ends up hurting us. It makes us lonely. It keeps us from our Higher Power. Addiction is about being self-centered.

Recovery and the Twelve Steps are about self-love. If we love ourselves, we'd say, "We're all equal and in need of each other." Self-love includes having good relationships. It includes trusting that we'll do what is best, with the help of our Higher Power. We must believe in ourselves to trust others.

Prayer for the Day

Higher Power, help me love myself as You love me. Help me take good care of myself.

Action for the Day

Today, I'll list three things I like about myself. I'll talk with a friend and share these things. I'll ask my friend what he or she likes about me.

In every real man a child is
hidden that wants to play.
— *Friedrich Nietzsche*

All of us have a child inside. We may see that child as a friend or as an enemy. Many of us were taught that growing up meant doing away with our inner child. It was as if being a child was bad and being an adult was good. If we try to be only an adult, the child cries, "Let me run free and show you the beauty of the world." If we try to be only a child, we find the adult in us saying, "It's time to grow up."

Let's find a balance. Remember, the adult needs the wonder found in the eyes of the child. Remember, the child needs the loving care of the adult. The child lives where we find our spirit. Our Higher Power is the perfect balance of the two.

Prayer for the Day
Higher Power, help me be both the child and the adult. I need both.

Action for the Day
Today, I'll make time to be a child and to be an adult.

THINK
— *Alcoholics Anonymous
slogan*

Now that we're recovering, our minds are free. We can think. When we are faced with problems or choices, we can do this:

- Ask, "What is the problem?"
- Make a list of what we can do to work on the problem.
- Decide which of the actions on our list might work.
- Pick the action that seems the best so far.
- Ask ourselves, "Can I do it? *Will* I do it?" If not, it's not a good plan.
- Talk to our sponsors if we need help thinking it out.
- Do it.
- Look back on it. Did it work? If not, go back and try something else.

Prayer for the Day

Higher Power, help me to think well. Help me to see things clearly.

Action for the Day

Today, I'll use the points listed above to help me think about a choice I have to make.

Things do not change, we do.
— Henry David Thoreau

There are still as many bars as there were when we were drinking. There are still lots of drugs around. The world hasn't changed. What's changed is that we now live a different way of life. We've learned that, for us, alcohol and other drugs are poison.

For us, there are now two worlds: the world we left behind, and our new world of recovery. In our old world, we'd try to get everyone else to change. We had to be right. In our new world, we look for ways we can change for the better. In our new life, we're willing to change.

Prayer for the Day
I pray that I may be like a mighty river, always changing.

Action for the Day
I will list changes I need to make in my new life.

*The saints are the sinners
who kept on going.*
— *Robert Louis Stevenson*

The saints are what our program calls the "winners." We're told to "stick with the winners." Saints are just proven winners. They keep on believing in their Higher Power even when things get hard.

There will be times when we'll want to give up. We may want to stop going to meetings. We may want to get high. We may want to stop working the Steps.

To be winners in this program, we need to follow the example of the saints. This means we live a spiritual life. We need to keep on going. One Day at a Time.

Prayer for the Day

I pray that I'll be a winner in this program. Higher Power, be with me in the easy times and the hard times. Help me keep going.

Action for the Day

I'll list people who are winners in this program. I'll ask one of them how he or she keeps going in tough times.

*This day I choose to spend
in perfect peace.*
— A Course in Miracles

Today, let's be gentle and kind. Let's talk to ourselves with love and respect. Let's be gentle with others too.

Today, let's be clear in how we think, speak, and act. And if we start to get mixed up, let's stop thinking and listen for our Higher Power's voice.

Today, we know that we have just a small job to do. It is to live today with love in our heart. We can't take care of every problem in the world. But we can make our actions today part of the answer instead of part of the problem. Let's Keep It Simple.

Prayer for the Day

Higher Power, help me find Your calmness and peace in my heart today.

Action for the Day

Do I believe that peace starts with me? Today, I'll listen to the simple voice of peace inside of me. And I'll Keep It Simple.

*Love is something if you
give away, you end up
having more.*
— *Malvina Reynolds*

Service is how we give love away. It's the "self" of self-help. Service is not a duty; it's a gift that's been given to us. We help ourselves by helping others. It's how we make sure the program will be here tomorrow. We "carry the message." It's just one way we see how important we are to others. The world needs us. The world needs our love.

Prayer for the Day

I pray for help in making service a big part of my program. Higher Power, help me to "carry the message."

Action for the Day

Which people could use a kind word and a little love? I will go visit them or give them a call.

*One must never, for
whatever reason, turn his
back on life.*
— *Eleanor Roosevelt*

We're going to have tough times. Maybe we don't get a pay raise. Maybe we get fired. Whatever happens, don't use alcohol or other drugs. Whatever happens, keep working the program. Our program will never turn its back on us. When tough times come, we can always turn to our meetings and sponsors. We're lucky because we don't have to face hard times alone. We have no reason to give up because our program will never give up.

So, pull closer to your program when times get tough. Call a friend and talk about your problems. Take in an extra meeting. All of this keeps us from turning our backs on life.

Prayer for the Day
Higher Power, help me believe that tough times are a chance to get closer to You.

Action for the Day
The program will always be there for me in tough times. Today, I'll make a list of what I'll do to stay sober when tough times come. I'll put the list in my Big Book.

September

***M**ade direct amends
to such people
wherever possible, except
when to do so would injure
them or others.*

— *Step Nine*
from Alcoholics
Anonymous

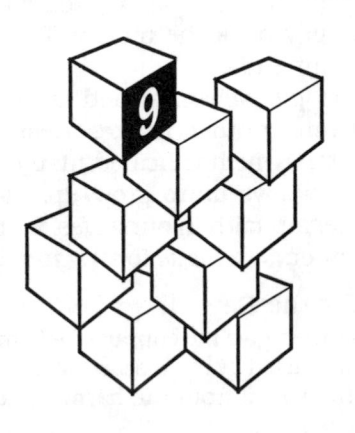

*Made direct amends to such
people wherever possible...*
— *First half of Step Nine*

In our illness, we harmed people. In Step Nine, we are to make amends. Making amends is about asking people we have harmed what we need to do to set things right. But making amends is more than saying, "I'm sorry." If you ran a store and someone had stolen five dollars, you wouldn't want them to just say, "I'm sorry." You'd want the person to pay back the money. The same is true with amends.

Many people we've harmed ask only that we don't repeat our mistakes. Respect their wishes. Step Nine has healed many wounds. Step Nine allows us to grow up. Step Nine helps us regain faith in ourselves. Remember, the best amend we make to all is to stay sober.

Prayer for the Day

Higher Power, give me courage. Help me to face the trouble caused by my disease. Make me ready to help others heal from the harm I've caused.

Action for the Day

Today, I'll pray that those I've harmed will heal. I will be responsible for my actions.

*. . .except when to do so
would injure them or others.*
— *Second half of Step Nine*

We have to be careful when we make amends. We must think about people's well-being. Can we help them heal by being direct with them? Or would this hurt them again?

At times, this means not making *direct* amends. Sometimes, it's better to make some other kind of amend. If you're not sure how to make amends to someone, ask for advice from your sponsor and your group. And pray. Over time, you'll know if making direct amends is the right thing to do. Remember, Step Nine means we're responsible for our actions. In recovery, our actions can be healing. Healing takes place when we love ourselves and others. And love is what heals us.

Prayer for the Day

Higher Power, I've hurt people in the past. Please use me now to help those people heal. Give me good judgment, courage, and good timing.

Action for the Day

I will never be able to make *direct* amends to some people. I will think of other kinds of amends I can make to them. I can pray daily for their healing.

*You will not regret the past
nor wish to shut the door
on it. . .*
— *Alcoholics Anonymous*

As we work the Steps, we fix our broken life. Many things in our life have been painful. Our addiction to alcohol or drugs made it all worse. But if things hadn't gotten so bad, we might not have gotten into recovery.

We have changed so much! We have learned so much! Why? Because we have to learn so much about life, our Higher Power, and ourselves in order to fix our lives. We can't act like nothing in the past matters. It does matter, because it brought us to this new life. And it's better already!

Prayer for the Day

Higher Power, help me face my past and heal the wounds—my wounds and others' wounds.

Action for the Day

Today, I'll list three things I'm ashamed of. How can I make amends for them when I work Step Nine? I will call my sponsor if I need help.

*In my view, we of this
world are pupils in a great
school of life.*

— *Bill W.*

Our addiction has taught us much. It has taught us how far we can get from ourselves, our Higher Power, and those who love us. Hopefully, we've learned we can't go it alone. Do I allow myself to learn from the bad things that happened?

Recovery has much to teach us too. We need to be students of life. We need to be open to learning. Our spirits can grow if we're willing to do three things: First, we listen. Second, we think about what we've learned. Third, we turn what we've learned into action. Listening, combined with thought and action, will help us learn life's best lessons.

Prayer for the Day

Higher Power, You'll test me so I can learn. Help me accept the tasks You give me. And help me learn from them.

Action for the Day

I will view today as a class. I will do three things—listen, think, act.

*I have never seen a greater
monster or miracle than
myself.*

— Montaigne

We know we've hurt people. We've heard our family cry out from the pain we've caused them. Because of alcohol and other drugs, we acted like monsters.

But we now live surrounded with love. We now work hard to make this world better. Recovery is a miracle. The rebirth of our spirit is our miracle.

It's no wonder we love life the way we do! We've been given a second chance. Our joy is overflowing. Our Higher Power must love us very much!

Prayer for the Day

Higher Power, help me with the monster that lives within me. I pray that it will never again be let out.

Action for the Day

Today, I'll see myself as a miracle. I'll be grateful for my new life.

*Addiction is answering the
spiritual calling inside us by
going to the wrong address.*
— Chris Ringer

Where can we go to feel better, to feel
spiritually alive? Not to alcohol or other
drugs. Not to compulsive spending, gambling, or sex. Not to overeating or overwork-
ing. When we turn to these things to feel
better, we're trading one addiction for
another, we're going to the "wrong address."

What is the right address? Our inner needs.
Our Higher Power. Our recovery program. Our
friends. Soon, we become part of a network
of "safe addresses."

Prayer for the Day

Higher Power, keep me on the right path. I don't
want to go to the wrong address anymore.

Action for the Day

Today, I'll make sure I have at least three "right
addresses" in my wallet or purse. I'll list names
and day and evening phone numbers of people
who will love and help me.

*A liar needs a good
memory.*
— *Quintilian*

Many of us wasted a lot of energy trying to keep track of whom we had told what. For example, we'd tell our boss one story and our family another. Then we'd work hard to make sure they never met.

How wonderful to be done with that way of life! We now have a life based on honesty. We can now be ourselves wherever we go.

Our program tells us that to get sober, we must live a life of strict honesty. Honesty is our first rule to get and stay sober. Life is much more simple this way. We can relax and think of the happy details of life.

Prayer for the Day

Higher Power, help me to live honestly. Being honest brings me closer to You. Help me become closer to You.

Action for the Day

Today, I'll read the first three pages of Chapter Five in *Alcoholics Anonymous* (Third Edition). Here, I'll learn why honesty is so important to my recovery.

*I have an intense desire to
return to the womb—
Anybody's!*
— *Woody Allen*

Some days the world just doesn't seem safe. Maybe a friend died and you are hurting. Maybe you argued with a loved one. You just want someone to take care of you. You want to feel safe and warm.

Turn to the spiritual part of the program. Let your Higher Power hold you with warm, loving care. Pray. Pray to feel the program's love. If you do this, the love of the program will find you. Why? Because you've opened your heart to recovery. To be loved, you have to open up to love.

Prayer for the Day

I pray for an open heart. I pray that the love of the program will find me and comfort me. Higher Power, I need Your love as a child needs the love of parents.

Action for the Day

Today, I'll list three times the world has felt unsafe. I'll meditate on how things would have been different if I had turned to my Higher Power for comfort.

One of the best ways to persuade others is with your ears—by listening to them.
— *Dean Rusk*

We hate being told what to think. We like to make up our own minds. It helps to talk things out with another person who listens to us. Someone who cares what we think.

We can give this respect to others. We can listen to their point of view. We can try to understand them and care about what they think.

When we do this, others start to care what we think too. We share ideas. The ideas get a little more clear. They change a little. We get a little closer to agreement. We both feel good.

Prayer for the Day

Higher Power, help me know when to listen and when to talk today. Work for me and through me. Thanks.

Action for the Day

Today, I'll look for chances to listen to others when I really want to talk. I'll say, "Tell me more about that." And I'll listen.

*If you want a thing done
"right," you have to do it
yourself.*

— *Anonymous*

We addicts can be very picky. We think there's only one way to do things. It's *our* way, but we call it the *right* way. When we think like this, three things happen. First, we put down other people. Second, we end up doing all the work. Third, everyone feels bad. The other person feels hurt that we don't respect him or her. And we feel angry because we "had" to do all the work.

We need to know that there are many ways to do things. It's okay when others don't do things our way. Their way probably works just fine for them. If they want our advice, they'll ask for it.

Prayer for the Day

Higher Power, help me accept other people and their ways.

Action for the Day

Today, I'll watch how other people do things. Maybe I'll learn a better way to do something.

*This above all: to thine
own self be true.*
— William Shakespeare

What does this saying mean: "To thine own self be true"? Hadn't we thought only of ourselves before recovery? The answer is no. That wasn't the real us. Each of us lost touch with our real self because of our addiction. We lost our goals, our feelings, our values. We chased the high. In this way, we lost our spirit. We became addicts.

With sobriety, we find ourselves again—and it feels great! We stop playing a role and become ourselves—and it's wonderful. We follow our dreams and beliefs, not some addictive wild goose chase. We are again free to be ourselves. Thank you, Higher Power.

Prayer for the Day

Today, I pray to be myself, to know all of me. I can trust myself because my spirit is good.

Action for the Day

Today, I'll pray: "To thine own self be true."

*When angry, count to ten
before you speak; if very
angry, a hundred.*
— *Thomas Jefferson*

Sometimes we just want to yell. Maybe a family member or a friend messed up, and we want to "set them straight." Start counting. Maybe we got chewed out at work and we want "to get even." Start counting.

We can get drunk on anger. We may feel powerful when we "set someone straight." But like an alcohol high, an anger high lasts only a short time and can hurt others. We must control our anger. This is why we count. Cool down. Think out what you need or want to say. Use words that you'll not be ashamed of later. Learning how to respect others when we're angry is a sign of recovery.

Prayer for the Day
Higher Power, teach me to respect others when I'm angry.

Action for the Day
Today, when I feel angry I'll count. I'll work at not controlling others with my anger.

*People seldom improve
when they have no model
but themselves to copy.*
— *Oliver Goldsmith*

If we had to get well by ourselves, we'd be in trouble. We've already tried this route. We need to learn a new way to live, not the old way we already know.

That's why we have sponsors in Twelve Step programs. Sponsors are one of the best things about our recovery program. We pick people who are happy and doing well in recovery. Then we copy them. We copy them because sponsors are special people who have what we want. They have sobriety. They have happiness. They have common sense. They have peace and serenity. And they will help us get those things too. We learn a new way to live from them.

Prayer for the Day

Higher Power, help me pick good models. Help me copy what works for them.

Action for the Day

If I don't have a sponsor now, I'll work today on getting one.

*You must look into people,
as well as at them.*
— *Lord Chesterfield*

When we were using alcohol and other drugs, we only looked *at* people. We treated them like objects. Often, we could only see how they helped us get high, or how they got in our way.

Now we can see others as people. We look *into* them. We learn about their feelings and thoughts. We care about them. What a wonderful change! We are fully human again. We can have relationships.

When we look into others, we see life. We see beauty, courage, hope, and love. We see bits of ourselves and our Higher Power. What a miracle life is!

Prayer for the Day

Higher Power, help me be fully human today. Help me see You in others.

Action for the Day

Today, I'll look into someone. I'll do this by having a talk with a friend. And I'll *really listen.*

*Often the test of courage is
not to die but to live.*
— *Vittorio Alfieri*

What brave people we are! We have chosen life. Okay, maybe we had a little push, maybe a big push from our family, police, or the pain of our disease. But still, we've chosen recovery. We choose daily to let our Higher Power run our lives. What trust! What faith! What courage!

We work hard at recovery. We do our readings. We go to meetings. We pray and meditate. We look for ways to serve others. Each one of us is building a miracle. We can be proud of this.

Prayer for the Day

I pray that I'll have the courage to love myself. Higher Power, teach me to pat myself on the back when I deserve it.

Action for the Day

I will list three ways I am brave in recovery and share them with my group.

*Here's my Golden Rule: Be
fair with others but then
keep after them until
they're fair with you.*
— *Alan Alda*

Often, in our illness we were ashamed, so
we let people take advantage of us. We acted
as if we had no rights. In recovery, we work
hard to be fair with others. And we deserve
to be treated with fairness too. If people are
mean to us, we talk with them about it. If people cheat us, we ask them to set it right. In
recovery, we live by our human rights.

Prayer for the Day

Higher Power, help me to stand for fairness. Help
me respect myself and others.

Action for the Day

Today, I'll list people who have wronged me. I will
make plans to talk to those with whom I feel will
listen. I will let love, not shame or fear, control my
actions.

It is better to be wanted too much than not at all.
— *Anonymous*

It may seem that so many people want our time and love. Parents say we don't call often enough. Children demand our time. Our partner says we're gone too much. Our sponsor tells us to check in more often.

When we feel off balance by all these people, we need to stop and rest. We need to remember how lonely we were when we were using. No one wanted our time and love then! Now we're important to others again.

You can handle all this by giving people what they need and ask for, within reason— not what *you* think they need, which may be way too much. Maybe you need Al-Anon, too, to learn to love others while still taking care of yourself.

Prayer for the Day

Higher Power, help me put my time and energy to best use today. Help me find the balance I need between work, play, loving others, and self-care.

Action for the Day

When I feel I have to give too much today, I'll stop and ask my Higher Power for guidance.

*We feel that the elimination
of our drinking is but a
beginning.*
— *Alcoholics Anonymous*

Giving up alcohol or other drugs is just the
start. Even if we give up chemicals, can we
be happy if we have our old life back in every
other way?

We have to do more. We have to see how our
illness has changed us. To do this, we turn to
the Steps. Our program teaches us to become
new persons. We will change. And the
changes will make us happy. That's the best
part of recovery—change.

Prayer for the Day
Higher Power, make me open to changes that
will heal me. Help me see I'm *not* cured just because I've stopped drinking or using other drugs.

Today's Action
Today I'll choose one thing about myself I want
to change.

*When we look back, we
realize that the things which
came to us when we put
ourselves in God's hands
were better than anything
we could have planned.*
— *Alcoholics Anonymous*

We can't control the present by looking into the future. We can only look back at the past. The past can teach us how to get more out of the present. But the past is to be learned from, not to be judged.

As we look back, we see the trouble caused by addiction. But we also see recovery. We see how our lives are better. We see our Higher Power's work in our lives. If we honestly look at our past, we learn.

Prayer for the Day

Higher Power, help me learn from the past. With Your help, I'll stop judging my past, just as I wouldn't judge those who have gone before me.

Action for the Day

Today, I'll remember my life before I got sober. Do I still hang on to attitudes or behaviors that might make me start to use alcohol and other drugs again?

*The best way to cheer
yourself up is to try to
cheer somebody else up.*
— *Mark Twain*

Sometimes it does no good to try to "deal" with our feelings. For the moment, we're stuck. We can only see things one way. No matter what anyone says, we're closed up. For the moment. But this puts our sobriety at risk.

How do we stop self-pity? Focus on someone else. When we really want to help someone else be happy, we'll ask our Higher Power's help. Then things start to change, because our good deeds come back to us. Remember, service will always keep us sober.

Prayer for the Day

Higher Power, sometimes I get stuck in my old ways. Help me change my focus at those times. Help me stay sober.

Action for the Day

I will think of a time when I was stuck in bad feelings. How did I get out of that spot?

*Love doesn't make the
world go round. Love is
what makes the ride
worthwhile.*
— Franklin Jones

Before recovery, anger, self-pity, and sadness often filled our hearts. The world went
on. We came to hate the ride.

In recovery, love fills our hearts. We begin
to love life. Love is really caring about what
happens to other people. Love is what makes
the ride worth it.

We find much love in our program. People
really matter to us. We really matter to others.
For many of us, we learn how to love in our
meetings. The program teaches love because
the program is love.

Prayer for the Day

I pray that I'll welcome love into my heart and
others into my life. Love brings me closer to my
Higher Power.

Action for the Day

I'll list all the people I love and why they matter
to me.

One Day at a Time.
> — *Program slogan*

This slogan means we are to take with us *only* the joys and problems of the present day. We don't carry with us the mistakes of days gone by. We have no room for them. We are to work at loving others today. Just today.

It's crazy for us to think we can handle more than one day at a time. During our illness, we lived everywhere but in the here and now. We looked to the future or punished ourselves with our past. One Day at a Time teaches us to go easy. It teaches us to focus on what really means anything to us: the here and now.

Prayer for the Day
Higher Power, help me turn the slogans of my programs into a way of life. Help me to live life moment by moment, One Day at a Time.

Action for the Day
Today, I'll practice living in the present. When I find myself living in the past or in the future, I'll bring myself back to today.

> *. . . he who finds himself*
> *loses his misery.*
> — *Matthew Arnold*

We have lost a lot of misery. In its place inside us, a spirit grows. . .as love is added. Especially self-love. In our illness, we came to hate ourselves. It was really our illness we hated. We couldn't find ourselves. All we saw was what others saw—our illness.

In recovery, we've found ourselves again. We've found we're good people. We've also come to love the world around us. We see we have something to offer this world—ourselves. Why? Because we have found ourselves.

Prayer for the Day

I'm so glad to be alive. At times life hurts, but, in living, I've found You. Thank-you, Higher Power. I pray that we may always be close.

Action for the Day

I will list ten great things I've discovered about myself in recovery.

Martyrs set bad examples.
— *David Russell*

Sometimes we call people "martyrs." We think of them as victims. They suffer, but sometimes not for a cause. They play "poor me." They want people to notice how much they suffer. They are afraid to really live. These are the people who set bad examples.

True martyrs died for causes they believed in. We remember them because they were so full of energy and spirit.

We can also live a life full of energy and spirit. Recovery helps us live better. Let's go for it!

Prayer for the Day
Higher Power, thanks for giving me energy and for healing my spirit. Help me live fully by putting my life in Your care.

Action for the Day
What kind of example do I set? Does my life reflect joy for life and recovery?

*To speak ill of others is a
dishonest way of praising
ourselves.*

— *Will Durant*

Sometimes we say bad things about others.
When we do this, it makes us look bad too.
Our friends worry what we might say about
them behind their backs. They're afraid to
trust us. We become known as gossips.

The things we say about other people tell
a lot about *us*. We are kind or unkind. We gossip or we don't. This doesn't mean we have
to say everyone is wonderful all the time. As
we work our program to see ourselves better,
we begin to see other people more clearly too.
We see their strong points and their weak
points. But we can know these things without
gossiping about them.

Prayer for the Day

Higher Power, help me see others clearly, and in
their best light. Let me bring out the good in others.

Action for the Day

Today, I'll list the people I'm closest to at work,
school, and home. I'll think of how I talk about
them to others. Am I kind?

*The distance doesn't
matter; only the first step is
difficult.*
— Mme. Marquise du Deffand

During our addiction, we were on a path leading to death—death of our spirit, mind, and body. On that path, we tried not to think about where it would lead. We didn't want to get there. We just followed the path toward death, with one drink, pill, snort, or toke at a time.

Now we've chosen a new path for our lives. Making that choice was hard. We knew only the old path. We were afraid to change. But we did it! That was the hardest part.

We are excited to follow our new path. We know it leads to good things. We can follow the map—the Twelve Steps—and enjoy the trip. It will last as long as we live, and the map will guide us.

Prayer for the Day
Higher Power, thanks for helping me choose the path of life.

Action for the Day
Today, I'll study the map for my life by reading the Twelve Steps.

Honesty is the first chapter
of the book of wisdom.
— Thomas Jefferson

Honesty is the backbone of our recovery program. Honesty opens us up. It breaks down the walls we had built around our secret world. Those walls made a prison for us. But all of that is now changed. We are free.

Honesty has made us wise. We aren't sneaking drinks anymore. We don't have a stash to protect. People who didn't trust us now depend on our honesty. People who worked hard to avoid us, now seek us out. Self-honesty *is* the greatest gift we can give ourselves.

Prayer for the Day
Higher Power, You are truth. I pray that I may not turn away from the truth. I will not lie. My life depends on honesty.

Action for the Day
For twenty or thirty minutes, I will think about how learning to be honest has changed my life.

*The gift we can offer others
is so simple a thing as
hope.*
— *Daniel Berrigan*

Our actions and beliefs affect others. As we grow and change, we feel better. We view the world with more positive eyes. We must share this with others. We were quick to share our beliefs when we thought life was mixed up and crazy. We need to be just as quick to share our hope.

Each time we tell our story, we must be sure to tell what it's like now. We must tell about our hope for the future. But we must not just *speak* of hope. We must also put our hope into action. We need to become hope—not just for ourselves, but for those who still drink and use, and suffer.

Prayer for the Day
In my hope, I find You. Higher Power, help me to share my hope freely.

Today's Action
If I get stuck today, I'll first reach for the hope found in my recovery. If I see someone who is stuck, I'll share my hope with that person.

*Al didn't smile for forty
years. You've got to admire
a man like that.*
— *From the TV show,
"Mary Hartman, Mary
Hartman"*

Remember how we used to live? We were always trying to cover up some lie or mistake. We were all like Al. Our energy was going into our illness, not into living.

Gratitude is a key word in the program. Gratitude is being thankful for the program. Gratitude is being thankful for getting to know our Higher Power. Remember what it was like to not smile for all those years?

Recovery has given us back our smiles. What a relief! We can relax and enjoy our new life.

Prayer for the Day

I pray that I'll always remember what it was like when I was using. I pray that I'll not take my recovery for granted. I pray for gratitude.

Action for the Day

I will list all the things the program and recovery have given me. I will smile about them today.

*Rarely have we seen a
person fail who has
thoroughly followed our
path.*
— *Alcoholics Anonymous
"The Big Book"*

If we follow the Twelve Steps, we'll leave failure behind. We may have tried and tried to be sober, good people, but failed if we were doing it our own way. Now is the time to stop listening to ourselves and to start listening to the pros, those who have gone before us.

When we follow their lead, exciting changes happen. First, we stay sober. We regain self-respect. We meet people we respect and become friends. Our families start to trust us again. And why? Because we gave up doing it our way and listened. We listened to the experts.

Prayer for the Day

Higher Power, allow me to become an expert listener.

Action for the Day

Today, I'll find someone I respect and ask how they work their program. I'll ask them to share their wisdom.

October

*C*ontinued to take personal inventory and when we were wrong promptly admitted it.

— *Step Ten*
from Alcoholics
Anonymous

Continued to take personal
inventory. . .
— First half of Step Ten

Step Ten tells us to keep looking at who we are. We ask ourselves, "Is what I'm doing okay?" If it is, then we take pride in the way we're acting. If not, we change our behavior. Step Ten keeps us in the right direction.

Throughout time, wise persons have told us to get to know ourselves. Step Ten helps us do this. We become our own best friend. A true friend tells us when we're doing right and when we're messing up. Step Ten is our teacher. Even when we want to pretend we don't know right from wrong, Step Ten reminds us that we do know. Step Ten is our daily reminder that we now have values— *good* values.

Prayer for the Day

Higher Power, Step Ten is a lot of work. Keep me working. Help me form a habit. Let this habit be called "Step Ten."

Action for the Day

Today, I'll continue to take a personal inventory. I will list what is good about me today and what I don't like.

. . .and when we were
wrong promptly admitted it.
— *Second half of Step Ten*

We are human. We make mistakes. This is
half the fun of being human. Step Ten clearly
tells us what to do when we are wrong: *admit*
it. This keeps us honest. It keeps us from hiding secrets that could cause us to use alcohol
or other drugs again.

Trust is a gift we get from Step Ten. When
we admit our wrongs, people start to trust us
again. We feel good, and people feel good
being around us. Even when they don't like
how we act, they can trust us to run our lives.
No one will ever be perfect. The closest we get
is that we admit it when we're wrong. This
is as good as it gets.

Prayer for the Day

Higher Power, help me admit my wrongs. Help
me earn the trust of others by being honest about
my mistakes.

Action for the Day

I will list any wrongs I've done today. That way,
I'll start tomorrow fresh and without any burdens
from today.

That which is called
firmness in a king is called
stubbornness in a donkey.
— *Lord Erskine*

"Rigid" is a fancy word for "stubborn." We addicts can be rigid, stubborn. We act this way because of our fear. When we're afraid, we hang on to what we're used to doing. Our illness had us so scared, we were afraid of new ideas and new people. The only thing that didn't scare us was using alcohol or other drugs.

We also were stubborn when anyone tried to help us. We thought we knew what was best. How silly our stubborn actions made us look! How lonely they kept us!

But our stubborn behavior can teach us about our fears. We need to be aware of our stubbornness. Then we'll be able to find out what we're afraid of—and do something about it.

Prayer for the Day

Higher Power, help me know when I'm stubborn.

Action for the Day

Today, I'll work at accepting my stubbornness. I will use it to learn about what I am afraid of today.

Your three best doctors are
faith, time, and patience.
— From a fortune cookie

Only a short time ago, we were very sick. Getting sober made us so much better. At first, when we stopped drinking and using other drugs, we thought we were fixed. Then we began to see that we were not all that well.

No doctor can fix us. To get well, we need to keep on living by the Twelve Steps and the slogans of our program. We need to keep on trusting that our Higher Power will heal us. One Day at a Time, day after day, we get stronger and happier. And it never has to stop. Each day, we know ourselves a little better.

Prayer for the Day

Higher Power, You are my best doctor. Help me remember that.

Action for the Day

Today, I'll do what the "doctor" suggests. I will talk with my sponsor about Step Ten today.

*It is often easier to fight for
one's principles than to live
up to them.*
— *Adlai Stevenson*

It is easy to talk about our values. But when
the clerk at the store gives us extra change by
mistake, those values get put to the test. It
feels good to read about spirituality in a comfortable chair at home. But when we get stuck
in a traffic jam, it's hard to live by our values.

That's why practicing our program *daily*
helps. Practice prepares us for the tough
times. Maybe we'll only feel like drinking or
using other drugs once a year. Maybe we'll
only get the wrong amount of change once
a year. But if we live our values daily, we'll be
ready when the hard times come. Remember:
"It's not enough to talk the talk. You have to
walk the walk."

Prayer for the Day

Higher Power, help me live this program each
day. Help me "walk the walk."

Action for the Day

Today, I'll do a Step Ten. Taking an inventory tells
me if I'm living up to my values.

*If you do not tell the truth
about yourself, you cannot
tell it about other people.*
— *Virginia Woolf*

Working the Twelve Steps helps us learn the truth. As we struggle with Step Four, we learn the truth about ourselves. We learn even more about ourselves by doing Steps Eight and Ten. When we admit the truth about ourselves, things come into focus. Big changes happen.

As a result, we can see other people more clearly. We see bad sides in people we thought were perfect. We see good sides in people we hated. We start to know that everyone has to work hard to find what's right for them. No one knows all the answers.

In short, we begin to trust others who also are looking for the truth.

Prayer for the Day

Higher Power, help me clearly see myself and others.

Action for the Day

Today, I'll think about how doing Step Ten keeps me clear about what's going on in my life.

*We never thought we could
get old.*
— *Bob Dylan*

Here we are, no longer children. Yet we're
not quite grown up either. At least, we don't
always *feel* grown up. Our program helps us
accept the stages of our life. We're children
in our hearts all our life. And the child in our
heart is getting happier. In some ways, we feel
younger every day.

We're also starting to feel older and wiser.
It feels good. We're not so afraid of the world,
because we're learning better ways to live in
it. We can learn by having friends who teach
us to stay young at heart.

Prayer for the Day
Higher Power, help me be the best I can be, at
the age I am today.

Action for the Day
Today, I'll call an older friend and ask him or her
this question: "What's the most important thing
you've learned about life since you were my age?"

Just Say No.
— *Nancy Reagan*

We addicts were great at saying *no*. Our spouse asked us to help around the house, but we said *no* and went drinking. Friends tried to care, but we said, "No, mind your own business!" Our parents or our kids begged us to stop drinking, but we said *no*.

We were also good at saying *yes*. We always said *yes* when asked if we wanted to have a drink or get high. Addiction really mixed us up. When we said *no*, we should've said *yes*. And when we said *yes*, we should've said *no*.

In recovery, we do things better. We say *yes* when others ask for help. We say *yes* when someone wants to give us love. We say *no* to alcohol and other drugs. We finally answer *yes* or *no* the right way—the right way and at the right time for *us*.

Prayer for the Day

Higher Power, help me to always say *yes* to You, even when I'm tired or angry.

Action for the Day

In today's inventory, I'll ask myself if there are any ways I'm still saying *no* to my program and Higher Power.

A man should never be
ashamed to own he has
been in the wrong...
— *Jonathan Swift*

In the past, we felt a mistake was a crisis. We thought we had to be perfect. Our old way was to try to hide our mistakes. We were ashamed. We thought making mistakes meant we were bad.

Mistakes are normal. We can learn from our mistakes. They can teach us. They can guide us. The Tenth Step directs us to *promptly* admit when we're wrong. Then, over time, we start to see mistakes as normal life events. As we face and correct our mistakes, shame is washed away. We feel lighter. We know it is normal to make mistakes.

Prayer for the Day
Higher Power, help me see that mistakes are normal life events. Help me promptly admit when I'm wrong.

Action for the Day
Today, I'll talk to my sponsor about the mistakes I've made the past week. I'll not act ashamed of my mistakes.

*The foolish and the dead
never change their opinions.*
— *James Russell Lowell*

We need to stay fresh in our program. We need to be open to new ideas. We need change. The ways we work the Steps should change for us as the years go by. And as we grow, more of the fog of our denial clears away. Then we see the world and our program in different ways.

We need to allow this to happen. At times, it's scary to give up old ways and old opinions, but this is what allows new growth. Every day, we wake up to a new world. Being alive means change. Being alive in our program will also mean change. Opinions and ideas are like a strong tree: the base is strong, but the leaves change with the seasons.

Prayer for the Day

Higher Power, help me stay fresh and alive. Help me stay open to new ideas and attitudes. Help me to not become rigid.

Action for the Day

Today, I'll ask two friends to tell me how I may be rigid. I will listen to what they say.

*May you live all the days of
your life.*
— *Jonathan Swift*

The truth is, life is hard. Accepting this fact
will make life easier. Remember how well it
worked in Step One? Once we admitted and
accepted that we were powerless over alcohol
and other drugs, we were given the power
to recover. It works the same with life's
problems.

We can spend a lot of energy trying to avoid
life's hardships. But our program teaches us
to use this same energy to solve our
problems. Problems are chances to better
ourselves and become more spiritual. We
have a choice: we can either use our energy
to avoid problems, or we can face them. When
we stop wasting energy, we start to feel more
sure of ourselves.

Prayer for the Day

Higher Power, life is to be lived, both the easy and
the hard parts. Help me face and learn from it all.

Action for the Day

I'll work at not complaining about how hard life
is. I'll take the same energy and use it to solve
problems I may face.

*Trust only movement. Life
happens at the level of
events, not words.*
— *Alfred Adler*

Being sober is an event. Being sober also means movement. We *go* to meetings. We *find* and *meet* with a sponsor. We *talk* with friends. If we don't act in these ways we're not sober.

Our actions also tell us if we're leading a spiritual life. What do you *do* when you see someone in need? Spirituality means helping. It's not just kind words.

In Steps Four and Ten, we check out our actions, not our words. Our actions will tell us if we're on the recovery path.

Prayer for the Day

Higher Power, help me to not hide in my words. I pray for the strength to take the right action. Help me walk a sober path.

Action for the Day

Today as I work Step Ten, I'll focus only on my actions. How have I *acted* sober today?

Self-pity is one of the most dangerous forms of self-centeredness. It fogs our vision.

— *Kathy S.*

Sometimes, we get stuck in our own way of seeing things. We may feel as if everything that happens, happens to us or for us. If it rains, we may think about our ruined picnic and not about the dry fields that need rain. We need to focus on the big picture. This keeps us from becoming self-centered. If it rains, we'll gather indoors and be glad for the farmers. When we do our part, things go well. When we don't, we feel it. Everyone else feels it too. Self-pity keeps us from doing our part.

Prayer for the Day

Higher Power, help me see myself as part of a big picture. My job is just to do my part.

Action for the Day

Today I'll think about how I fit in with my Higher Power, my family, the place I work, my community. Do I do my part?

*A baby is God's opinion
that the world should go on.*
— *Carl Sandburg*

Recovery is also God's opinion that the world should go on. But when we used alcohol and other drugs, there were days when even the sight of a newborn baby couldn't bring hope into our hearts. We were spiritually dead. We didn't care if the world went on. We didn't care about anything but getting high.

Through recovery, our souls come alive. The beauty of a fall day can reach our hearts. We can see the miracle found in a baby's eyes. We can see the beauty of the world. We can feel how much we're loved by our Higher Power and by others. This is how we know we're alive. Hope fills our minds and love fills our hearts.

Prayer for the Day

Higher Power, now that I again believe the world should go on, have me work to improve it. Have me be a person who makes the world more beautiful.

Action for the Day

Today I'll notice the children and babies around me. I'll notice how alive they are. I'll try to be as alive as they are.

Not to decide is to decide.
— *Harvey Cox*

We are winners, because every day we decide to stay sober. Every day we decide to listen to our Higher Power. We win by making active choices. We've stopped acting as if we have no choice. Our old way was to pretend that everything happened to us by accident. Not true. We pretended we had no power. Also not true. We lost our power over alcohol and other drugs, but we still had the power to ask for help. Each time we used chemicals was a decision, just as to stay sober each day is a decision.

It feels great to know we aren't victims. We like ourselves again. We smile as we hear the strength in our voices. We walk as proud and sober men and women who know how to make decisions.

Prayer for the Day

Higher Power, thanks for giving me choices. I will not run from them. Help me make good choices. Help me decide every day to listen to You.

Action for the Day

Not for one minute will I pretend I am a victim. I'll face my choices squarely and decide.

*To err is human, but when
the eraser wears out ahead
of the pencil, you're
overdoing it.*
— Josh Jenkins

It's okay to make mistakes. But we shouldn't live a life of excuses. We shouldn't slide over our mistakes; we should learn from them.

Excuses keep us apart from ourselves and others. People don't trust us if we won't admit and accept our mistakes. Relying on excuses dooms us to repeat the same mistakes.

In recovery, we admit and accept our behavior. We do this by continuing to take an inventory of our lives. We do this so we can learn from our mistakes. "Owning" our mistakes helps us grow.

Prayer for the Day

Higher Power, help me own my mistakes. Thank-you for Step Ten and the growth it holds for me.

Action for the Day

Today, I'll list my five favorite excuses. I'll think of the last time I used each of these. What was I trying to avoid?

Every child is an artist.
The problem is to remain
an artist once you grow up.
— Pablo Picasso

We each have colorful ideas waiting to be shared. We're alive inside. But do we let this side of us show? Our disease stole much of our childlike openness. Many of us were taught that growing up meant denying the child within us. Many of us grew up in homes where it wasn't safe to act alive and creative. Whatever the reason, it's time to claim the child, the artist, in each of us. Each of our programs is different, and each has its artistic touch. When we tell our stories, we share our lives. And our lives are unique and alive. The more alive we become, the more color we bring to others and ourselves. Let's not be afraid to add color to our lives.

Prayer for the Day

Higher Power, help me claim the child inside of me. Joy is a choice. Help me choose it.

Action for the Day

Today, I'll work at not hiding myself from others. I'll be alive, and I'll greet everyone I meet with the openness of a child.

*If God wanted us to be
brave, why did he give us
legs?*
— Marvin Kitman

Many of our problems are caused by taking
an unwise stand. We end up being stubborn.
We need the courage to know when to take a
stand, and the wisdom to know when not to.
Our program has taught us not to stand up to
our drinking and other drug use, but to walk
away from it. It beats us every time we stay
around it. When we walk away we can get help.
By walking away, we stay sober and we win.

Step Ten can help us learn when and where
not to take a stand. If we take a stand just to
be stubborn, we must surrender and admit
this is wrong. That way, we learn how to take
a stand for good reasons.

Prayer for the Day

I pray that I may stand for recovery. I pray that
I'll surrender when I'm just being stubborn.

Action for the Day

Today, I'll list how I get stubborn. I'll list what
Steps help me to surrender to my Higher Power
and to the program.

*A wise man changes his
mind, a fool never will.*
— *Seventeenth century
proverb*

We addicts used to be stubborn. Once we got an idea in our heads, we wouldn't change it. We didn't listen to other ideas. We almost seemed to say, "Don't tell me the facts. I've already made up my mind."

But lately, some new ideas are making sense to us. We are starting to change our minds. Maybe we *are* good people, after all. Maybe we *do* deserve to be happy. Maybe other people *can* help us. Maybe our Higher Power *does* know best.

We're not acting like fools any longer. We're learning to change our old ideas.

Prayer for the Day

Higher Power, when I hear a better idea, help me change my mind.

Action for the Day

When I hear or read a new idea today, I'll really think about it. If it fits, I'll try it.

*We lie loudest when we lie
to ourselves.*
> — *Eric Hoffer*

When we're not honest with others, we're not being honest with ourselves. In recovery, we're taught how to heal our hearts. We admit we're wrong, and we do it quickly. We let our spirit speak out. We listen to our spirit. We let our spirit have the loudest voice. This way, lies lose power over us. We find a way to be true to our spirit.

Prayer for the Day

Higher Power, You have a soft, quiet voice inside of me. Help me, through meditation, to hear You better. Yours is the voice I want to follow.

Action for the Day

I'll listen to my Higher Power. I'll list any lies I've been telling myself and others lately. Then I'll find someone I trust and tell that person what I've lied about.

Even a stopped clock is
right twice a day.
— *Anonymous*

Nobody's always wrong. Nobody's all bad. And that includes us.

Sometimes, we really get down on ourselves. When we do Step Four, we sometimes see only our faults. When we make our Step Ten checkup, we see only our mistakes. We can't afford to do this. We need to see our strengths too. But even our faults have a good side. Are you stubborn? Good—be stubborn about staying sober. If you're stubborn, you know how to hang on to feelings. So, hang on to the good feelings instead of the bad ones.

Each of us is good and wise. What's good about us got twisted by our disease. But now we can get the kinks out. We are sober, and we have a program to help us.

Prayer for the Day

Higher Power, help me to see the good in myself and others.

Action for the Day

I'll take another look at my faults today. How can I use them in good ways?

*Life is what happens to us
while we're making other
plans.*
— *Thomas LaMance*

What happened to our years of drinking
and using other drugs? They seemed to pass
so quickly with so little to show for them. We
had plans, but we didn't get where we wanted
to go. There was always "tomorrow."

What a difference today! Now we work a
program that helps us really live each day.
We're not losing time out of our lives anymore. Now every day is full of life: sights,
sounds, people, feelings—those things we
used to miss out on. We have the help of a
Higher Power who makes every day important.

Prayer for the Day

Higher Power, help me do Your will for me today.
I place this day in Your care.

Action for the Day

Be on the lookout today for signs of life!

It's not dying for faith that's so hard, it's living up to it.
— *William Makepeace Thackeray*

We may ask, "Do I have to do an Eighth or Ninth Step?" "Do I really need a sponsor?" "Hmm . . . can I get by without going to so many meetings?" Having faith means putting our questions aside. So . . . what *do* we do? We work the program. We accept that those who've gone before us were right. We accept the idea that we need others. Faith is knowing that others love and care for us. Faith is also about action. The main way we know that we have faith is by looking at our behavior. Ask yourself this: "Are my actions those of a person with faith?"

Prayer for the Day
Higher Power, help me remove the questions that get in my way. Help me act like a person with faith.

Action for the Day
I'll list four parts of my program that I have faith in, such as, "I believe honesty is important to my sobriety."

Sin has many tools, but
a lie is the handle that
fits them all.
— Oliver Wendell Holmes

Lying, above anything else, brings us close to getting crazy again. Lying is what addicts do. In our addiction, our whole life was a lie.

Lying creates danger because it creates secrets. Secrets keep us from others. To stay sober, we need to stay close to people. We can't make it on our own.

Lying creates danger because it creates shame. A lie, like a drink, may make us feel good for the moment. But in the long run, it creates shame.

Do we still lie to deal with the world? Why? There is no such thing as a small lie. Lies are like drinks—one leads to another.

Prayer for the Day

Higher Power, help me to live today free of lies.

Action for the Day

For the next twenty-four hours, I will tell no lies. If I do, I'll go back and do Step Ten. I will remember that lies can lead to relapse.

*Love thy neighbor as
thyself, but choose your
neighbor.*

— *Louise Beal*

In our program, we learn a lot about loving ourselves. Then we start to see how this helps us love our neighbors. We learn to love ourselves honestly, seeing our strengths and our weaknesses. We learn to see others honestly. We learn how much to trust ourselves, and when to get extra help. We learn how much to trust others too. We learn to love ourselves with a love that's honest and challenging. We learn to love others this way too. We learn to care about others without losing our common sense. We learn to protect our spirit from harm.

Prayer for the Day

Higher Power, help me see others clearly. Help me love them. But help me choose carefully who I trust.

Action for the Day

Today, I'll list three people I trust the most, and I'll write down why.

*Nobody can give you
freedom.*

— *Malcolm X*

We were not free. We were prisoners of our
illness. What our illness wanted, we gave it—
our dignity, our self-respect, even our families. Our prison walls were made of denial,
false pride, and self-will run riot. Now we
know that brick walls don't have to stop us.
We don't have to bang our heads on them.

Slowly, we're learning about freedom. We're
learning that freedom comes from within. It
comes when we think clearly and make our
own choices. It comes when we follow a better
way of life. It comes when we take care of ourselves. It comes when we take responsibility.
The key to freedom is in loving our Higher
Power. Do you choose freedom?

Prayer for the Day

Higher Power, show me how to walk away from
a wall or go around it. But teach me to stop and
think when I get to a wall. Maybe it's there for my
safety.

Today's Action

Today I'll think about all the freedom I have given
myself by living a sober way of life.

*An excuse is worse and
more terrible than a lie.*
— *Alexander Pope*

Excuses. They're lies. We use excuses to hide from ourselves. Maybe we don't want to be honest about our anger. So we say someone else made us angry. Maybe we don't want to admit how mean we can be. So we pretend we have no part in what happens.

Excuses keep us from ourselves. They keep us from our Higher Power. A lot of our program is about looking at ourselves. Steps Four, Five, and Ten tell us to be honest about our excuses. We can be honest because we are good people. We are loved.

Prayer for the Day

Today, I'll say the Serenity Prayer: God grant me the serenity to accept the things I cannot change, the courage to change the things I can, and the wisdom to know the difference.

Action for the Day

I'll list my five most often used excuses. Then, I'll share them with my friends, family, and sponsor. I'll ask them to tell me when I make excuses.

*I wish you the courage to
be warm when the world
would prefer you to be cool.*
— *Robert A. Ward*

Our program and the Steps have warmed
us—warmed us from the inside out. Just as
a bonfire warms those who stand around it,
the Steps take away the chill we have felt for
so long.

At times, we'll be tempted to move away
from the Steps. At times, we'll get tired of
looking at our behavior and attitudes. We are,
by nature, controlling people. We'll want to
"prove our point" about something when our
program tells us to let it go. We need to stay
close to the Steps and the warmth they hold.
Remember the chill of our disease.

Prayer for the Day

I need to remember that the Steps and the fellowship of the program keep me sober, not me
alone.

Action for the Day

Today, I'll think about what the Steps have done
for me. I will think of how they have kept me warm.

*Each morning puts a man
on trial and each evening
passes judgement.*
— *Ray L. Smith*

In many ways, the Tenth Step is very natural. We continue to take a personal inventory. And when we're wrong, we promptly admit it.

At the end of each day we ask ourselves, "How did my day go?" As we think about our day, we bring order to our life. The Tenth Step teaches us about order. It also teaches us how to correct mistakes. We do this by admitting our wrongs. This way, we have no backlog of guilt. It's good to start each day fresh, free from guilt. Admitting our wrongs is a loving thing to do. It's another way the program teaches us to love ourselves.

Prayer for the Day

Today, I'll face many choices. Higher Power, be with me as I choose. When the day is done, remind me to think about how I lived today. This will help me learn.

Action for the Day

Tonight, I'll list three choices I made today. Would I make the same choices again?

*The universe is full of
magical things waiting for
our wits to grow sharper.*
— *Eden Phillpots*

How nice to have the fog lifted! Sobriety lets our wits grow sharper. We can go after our dreams and ideas. We can listen to music and sing. We are part of the magic of the universe. At times we may not feel very magical, but we are. Our spirits hold much magic. Sobriety is magic. We work at making the world a better place. In doing so, we get magical powers. Powers that heal and comfort others. Powers to understand things that before we could not. Powers that let us see the world as we've never seen it. Enjoy the magic and use your powers wisely!

Prayer for the Day

Higher Power, let Your magic enter and fill my heart.

Action for the Day

I'll list four magical powers I have from being sober.

*A man who has committed
a mistake and doesn't
correct it is committing
another mistake.*
— *Confucius*

Step Ten tells us that when we are wrong, we must "promptly" admit it. We aren't used to admitting our mistakes. We defend ourselves or blame others. This is called *denial*.

Denial is bad for two reasons. First, it keeps us from learning from our mistakes, so we keep making them. Second, we don't listen to others, so we close off ourselves and become lonely.

What a relief it is to admit our wrongs! We don't have to keep trying to do things the hard way. We can learn new ways to think and act that will work better for us. We can let other people be our teachers.

Prayer for the Day

Higher Power, help me out of denial, so I can see the changes I need to make.

Action for the Day

Today, if I disagree with someone, I'll promptly admit it when I'm wrong. If I'm right, I'll be gentle. I don't have to prove anything.

*S*ought through prayer and meditation to improve our conscious contact with God as we understood Him, praying only for knowledge of His will for us and the power to carry that out.

— *Step Eleven*
from Alcoholics
Anonymous

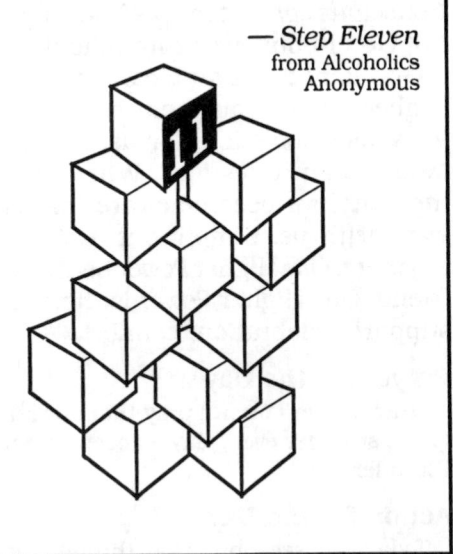

*Sought through prayer and
meditation to improve our
conscious contact with God*
as we understood Him . . .
— *First half of Step Eleven*

Through Step Eleven, we develop a lasting,
loving relationship with our Higher Power.
Conscious contact means knowing and sens-
ing God in our lives throughout the day.

God is not just an idea. We talk with our
Higher Power through prayer. As we meditate,
we sense God's love for us, and we get answers to our questions. When we pray and
meditate, we become aware that God is always with us. Simply put, we're not alone
anymore. Our Higher Power becomes our best
friend. Our Higher Power is there for advice,
support, celebration, comfort.

Prayer for the Day

Dear Higher Power, I pray that our relationship
grows stronger every day. I accept the friendship
You offer me.

Action for the Day

Today, I'll seek out God through prayer and
meditation.

. . . praying only for knowledge of His will for us and the power to carry that out.
— *Second half of Step Eleven*

Step Eleven teaches us how to pray. We pray for God's will to replace ours. Our will got us in trouble. God's will guides us to simple serenity. We pray for power to live a spiritual life. This is important, for it takes much strength and courage to live a spiritual life.

The sober path is not always easy. It takes self-discipline. We have to say no to our self-will. We follow God's will for us. The rewards are great. We get sobriety. We get serenity. We get friendship. We regain our family. We get a deep, loving relationship with a Higher Power who wants peace and joy for us and for the world.

Prayer for the Day

Dear Higher Power, I pray the words of Step Eleven. I pray to know Your will for me. And I pray that I have the power to carry out Your will.

Action for the Day

I will examine my life. I will look to see how my will gets in the way of God's will.

*Words are the voice of the
heart.*

— *Confucius*

What does my heart have to say today? Am
I happy? Or am I troubled? We will find this
out if we slow down and listen to our words.
We can also hear our spirit in the tone of our
words.

We are to meditate. Meditation is about
slowing down so we can hear what our spirit
is trying to tell us. Meditation is listening. Our
spirit is but a quiet whisper inside us. To hear
it we must quiet ourselves.

Slowing down allows us to find our center.
As we find our center we find our spirit and
our Higher Power. Do I take the time needed
to slow myself down? Do I take the time to
listen—to listen to my heart?

Prayer for the Day

Higher Power, teach me to slow down. Teach me
to listen. Teach me to hear Your whispers as well
as Your yells.

Action for the Day

Today, I will take a half hour to slow down and
listen. I will find a place to relax and listen to my
heart and my words.

*Each day comes bearing its
gifts. Untie the ribbons.*
— *Ruth Ann Schabacker*

How full life can be! We can untie the ribbon on this gift by keeping our spirits open. Open to life. Open to how much our Higher Power loves us.

Who knows what gifts the day may bring? Maybe it brings a solution to a problem. Maybe it brings the smile of a child. Maybe we'll find a new friend. Whatever gifts the day brings, we must be able to receive them. How do we do this? We keep our spirit open and lively through prayer and meditation. Then we'll be awake to see the beauty and the wonders life holds for us.

Prayer for the Day
Higher Power, remind me to pray to You often. Remind me to stop and listen to You. Remind me that You love me very much.

Action for the Day
At the end of the day, I'll take time to list the gifts I've been given today. This will be first on my list: I am sober.

*Acceptance and faith are
capable of producing 100
percent sobriety.*
— *Grapevine*

Acceptance and faith are the most important parts of our recovery. If we boil down
Steps One and Two, we'll find acceptance and
faith. *Acceptance* means we see the world as
it is, not as we want it to be. We start to see
ourselves as humans, not as gods. We are
good, and we are bad. We need to fit in the
world, not run it.

Acceptance also guides us toward faith.
Faith is believing. We start to believe that
someone or something will take care of us.
Faith is about giving up control of outcomes.
We learn to say to our Higher Power, "Thy will
be done."

Prayer for the Day

Higher Power, help me accept my illness. Give
me the faith to know that You and I, together, will
keep me sober.

Action for the Day

Throughout the day, I'll think of the Eleventh
Step. I'll pray to my Higher Power, "Thy will be
done, not mine."

*That suit is best that best
suits me.*
— *John Clark*

How much time do we spend trying to "fit in"? Many of us used to care so much what other people thought about us—our clothes, our ideas, our work. Did we drink the right brand, drive the right car, listen to the right music?

In our program, we still have to watch out for fads and peer pressure. We have to ask ourselves if we're really in touch with our Higher Power. Are we searching for a sponsor who has inner peace and direction? Or do we look for people who are like our old using friends? As we learn to find our own way of following our Higher Power, we need to be okay with being different.

Prayer for the Day
Higher Power, help me be the best me I can be today.

Action for the Day
Today, I'll work to be me—honestly me—to everyone I meet.

*Telling the truth is a pretty
hard thing.*
— *Thomas Wolfe*

Often, we get scared to tell the truth. We wonder, "What will happen? Will I get in trouble? Will someone be mad at me?" These things could happen. But good things could happen too.

Sometimes we want to lie. We don't want anyone mad at us or unhappy with us. We want people off our back. So we lie. And it comes back to haunt us. We must believe that the best will happen in the long run if we tell the truth.

Our program tells us that we can stay sober if we're honest. Telling the truth takes faith. We must have faith in the program. We must be honest. Our sobriety and our life depend on it.

Prayer for the Day
Higher Power, help me remember that I'm doing things Your way when I tell the truth.

Action for the Day
I will think about what I say today. I will be as honest as I can be.

*Any man may make a
mistake; none but a fool
will persist in it.*
— *Cicero*

The way we face life's challenges is what
gives meaning to our lives. If we run from our
mistakes, they follow us. If we stand up and
work with them, we learn.

Facing our mistakes teaches us wisdom
and courage. Our self-respect grows. Spiritual
growth means asking, "How would my
Higher Power want me to deal with this
mistake?" Then we listen for the answer and
do what is needed.

The better we get at facing our mistakes,
the better we become at learning from them.
Native American culture teaches us that all
mistakes in life are gifts. The gift is that we
are given a chance to learn.

Prayer for the Day

Higher Power, help me face the mistakes of life
and find the lessons that lie within them.

Action for the Day

When I make a mistake, I'll stop and ask, "What
does my Higher Power want me to learn from
this?"

*He who can take advice is
sometimes superior to he
who can give it.*
— *Karl von Knebel*

In recovery, we learn that we don't know everything. We had stopped listening. Most of us had been asked by family, friends, doctors, and employers to stop drinking and using other drugs. But, we didn't listen. If we had listened, we would've been in this program long ago. Addiction did something to how we listen. We heard only what we wanted to hear. Do I still hear only what I want?

In recovery, we learn to listen. We listen to our groups. We listen to our sponsor. We listen as we read. The better we listen, the better our recovery.

Prayer for the Day

Higher Power, open my ears and eyes to this new way of life. Allow me to hear Your wisdom in the Twelve Steps. Allow me to be someone who takes advice, not just gives it.

Action for the Day

Today I'll try to listen. Today I'll seek the advice of others. I'll ask my sponsor how I may better my program.

*Even if you're on the right
track, you'll get run over if
you just sit there.*
— *Will Rogers*

The greatest adventure ever is recovery. And action is what's important in recovery. That's because the Twelve Steps are full of action. The whole world has now opened up to us. At times, this will scare us. But we aren't alone. Our Higher Power is there to help us. All we have to ask ourselves is, "Would this action keep me in touch with my Higher Power?" If the answer is yes, then we take action. If the answer is no, then we don't.

In recovery, we'll be busy. We admit our wrongs. We take inventories. We seek answers. We ask for help. We are to get as much as we can out of life. We can't sit and watch; we have to get out and live life.

Prayer for the Day
Higher Power, You gave me a second chance at life. Help me use it and not let my fear stop me.

Action for the Day
Today, I'll list five things I want to do but am afraid to try. I'll talk to someone I trust about how I can do these things.

Have the courage to live;
anyone can die.
— *Robert Cody*

Living means facing all of life. Life is joy *and* sorrow. We used to be people who wanted the joy without the sorrow. But we can learn from hard times, maybe more than we do in easy times. Often, getting through hard times helps us grow. When things get tough, maybe we want to turn and run. Then, a gentle voice from within us says, "I am with you. You have friends who will help." If we listen, we'll hear our Higher Power. This is what is meant by "conscious contact" in Step Eleven. As this conscious contact grows, our courage grows. And we find the strength to face hard times.

Prayer for the Day

I pray for the strength and courage to live. I pray that I'll never have to face hard times alone again.

Action for the Day

I'll list two examples of "conscious contact" in my life.

*It may be those who do
most, dream most.*
— *Stephen Leacock*

Daydreaming gives us hope. It makes our world bigger. Daydreaming can be part of doing Step Eleven. As we meditate, we daydream. Through our daydreaming, we get to know ourselves, our spirit, and our Higher Power. What special work can we do? Our dreams can tell us.

There is time to work and time to dream. Daydreaming helps us find the work our Higher Power wants us to do.

Prayer for the Day

Higher Power, please speak to me through my daydreams.

Action for the Day

I'll set aside time to daydream. I will look into a candle flame, at a picture, or out a window, and let my mind wander.

*Write down the advice of
him who loves you, though
you like it not at present.*
— *Anonymous*

We addicts often learn things the hard way.
In the past, we found it very hard to take advice from anyone. It's still hard to take advice,
but it's getting easier every day. We know now
that we can't handle everything in life by ourselves. We've come to believe there is help for
us. And we're learning to ask for help and
advice.

Sometimes we don't like the advice we get.
We don't have to use it. But if it comes from
people who love and understand us, we can
try to listen. Write it down. Think about it. It
may make sense another day.

Prayer for the Day

Higher Power, please work through people who
love me. I need Your advice. Help me listen to it.

Action for the Day

I will make notes to myself, writing down things
that seem important. I will read them once in a
while.

*Make it a point to do
something every day that
you don't want to do.*
— *Mark Twain*

Self-discipline is a key part of living a sober life. We need it to get to our meetings regularly. We need it to understand the Steps. We need it to work the Steps.

And we get much in return. With self-discipline, we learn to trust ourselves. We learn to do what is most loving and caring for ourselves. What a great relief! One of the worst parts of our illness was that we couldn't count on ourselves. We didn't know what we'd do next. Self-discipline heals this part of our illness.

Prayer for the Day
Higher Power, You have given me much. It's only right that I give You part of my day. I will pray and meditate on Your wonders.

Action for the Day
I will list areas of my program where I lack self-discipline. I will share the list with my group and sponsor, and I'll let them know in a month how I'm doing.

*The best way to know God
is to love many things.*
— *Vincent Van Gogh*

Now that we're in recovery, we're learning to love people. We're learning to love nature. We're learning to love new ideas about life. The result? We love the way we feel now that we're taking care of ourselves.

Is our Higher Power really so close? Can we really find our Higher Power just by loving many things? Yes! When we love, we wake up that part of us that is part of all creation—our spirit. We really come to life when we love!

Prayer for the Day

Higher Power, remind me that You are near when I love someone or something. The energy of love comes from You.

Action for the Day

I will list three things I love that help me know my Higher Power is near me.

*Pray for powers equal to
your tasks.*
— *Phillips Brooks*

Our task is to stay sober and to help others who still suffer from addiction. We will need patience and understanding. We will need much love. Most of all, we'll need to work a strong program.

Pray that you come to know the Steps well. Pray that you'll want to help others—always. Pray for courage and wisdom. Pray for these things, and you'll have a strong program. In the program, we learn that prayer works. We see prayer change our lives and the lives of those around us. We came to know the power of prayer.

Prayer for the Day
Higher Power, I pray for knowledge of Your will for me and the power to carry it out.

Action for the Day
Today, I'll admit my needs by praying for help from my Higher Power.

Mishaps are like knives,
that either serve us or cut
us, as we grasp them by
the blade or the handle.
— *Herman Melville*

We have hung on in hard times. We made it through our addiction. Some of us have lived through abuse. We've felt like our hearts were broken. But we've proven *we are survivors*. Now we're learning that we can *heal*.

Being in recovery doesn't mean things will be easy. But we have a Higher Power to help us. We have friends who listen to us, care for us, and help us through the pain. Because of our recovery program, we're able to keep hope and love in our lives—One Day at a Time.

Prayer for the Day

Higher Power, help me through the hard times. Help me trust in Your love and care.

Action for the Day

Today I'll plan ahead with my sponsor. What will I do now so that I'll have strong support when hard times come?

Life is short: live it up.
— *Nikita Khrushchev*

We won't stay sober for long unless it's more fun than using chemicals. The truth is, using chemicals wasn't fun anymore. It was work. We just *told* ourselves it was still fun.

So live it up! Try new things. Meet new friends. Try new foods. Taking risks and having adventures are a basic human need. So go for it. Sobriety is fun. Living a spiritual life is fun. Get out there and live!

Prayer for the Day

Higher Power, teach me to play. Teach me to have fun. Teach me to live!

Action for the Day

Today is for fun. I'll try something new. I'll see how many people I can get to smile. And I'll celebrate the fact that I'm sober.

*What we don't live, we
cannot teach others.*
— Day By Day

Remember—we don't carry the message to
others until we get to Step Twelve. We must
first learn to live in a sober way. Sobriety takes
time. We have to stop using alcohol and other
drugs, but this is only the start.

Just as it takes time to build a home, it
takes time to build a new way of life. We talk
with friends and sponsors about the Steps.
We try using them in our lives. Then we talk
about how the Steps work for us. We talk
about where we get stuck with the Steps.

All this takes time. We aren't in a hurry. We
have a lifetime ahead of us. Remember—
the better we live our program, the better
we help others.

Prayer for the Day
Higher Power, You'll let me know when I'm to
carry the message. Until then, be with me as I
build a new way of life—a sober way of life, a
spiritual way of life.

Action for the Day
I'll take time to think over where I'm at with my
program. I'll talk about it with a friend.

*A man is too apt to forget
that in this world he
cannot have everything. A
choice is all that is left him.*
— *H. Mathews*

Sobriety is about choice. Each day we choose to stay sober, we teach ourselves how to make better choices.

Life is about choice. To be spiritual people, we must make spiritual choices. Honesty is a spiritual choice. And working the Steps is a spiritual choice.

Our life is the sum total of our choices. We owe it to ourselves to choose wisely. We can do that now, thanks to the program.

Prayer for the Day
Higher Power, help me choose a spiritual way of life. Help me to see choice as my way to a better relationship with You.

Action for the Day
Today, I'll be aware of the many choices I make. At the end of the day, I'll think about all the choices I've made. Am I proud of my choices?

*To love others, we must
first learn to love ourselves.*
— *Anonymous*

Sometimes we think our life would be fine if that dream person showed up. But loving someone isn't easy. Our bad habits cause problems. We have to change. Sometimes we aren't ready to have one special person. We need to have a group of people—our recovery group—to love and help us get healthy. We must learn to trust, to be honest, to give help, and to love others. The truth is, no one person can make our life wonderful—except us. We hold happiness inside of us. It's in our spirit. Look no further.

Prayer for the Day
Higher Power, help me love myself.

Action for the Day
I'll list five ways I will love myself today.

*We are healed of a
suffering only by
experiencing it in full.*
— Marcel Proust

We must never forget our past. We need to remember the power that our illness has over us. Why? So we can remember how our recovery began. So we can remember we're not cured. So we can tell our stories.

We must remember how we acted. Why? So we can look at our behaviors every day. So we don't act and think like addicts. Most of us had poor relationships with friends, family, and ourselves. We need to remember how lonely we felt. That way, we'll make our recovery grow stronger One Day at a Time.

Prayer for the Day

Higher Power, help me always remember how my illness almost destroyed me. Help me face the pain of these memories.

Action for the Day

I will talk about my past life with those who support my recovery. I will tell them what it is that I must remember about my past.

*Let me listen to me and not
to them.*
— *Gertrude Stein*

Often, we try to please everyone around us.
But this may not make us happy, and so we
get angry. We feel taken advantage of.

We may be kind to others, but first we must
love ourselves. How? By learning to listen to
ourselves. To our dreams. To our Higher Power.
By doing this we'll be more happy. And those
around us will probably be more happy too.

As our AA medallions say, "To Thine Own
Self Be True."

Prayer for the Day

I pray that I'll listen to that gentle, loving voice
inside me. Higher Power, help me make my "conscious contact" with You better.

Action for the Day

I will write four reasons why I need to be true
to myself.

Freedom is not enough.
— Lyndon B. Johnson

We are free of alcohol and other drugs. We've been given a second or third chance. For that, we thank our Higher Power. We've started a new life. But to keep this life, we need to change. We need new friends. We need to let a Higher Power guide our hearts, minds, and bodies. We need to learn new values and how to stand up for them. We need to learn how to give and to receive.

Freedom from dependence is not enough. We also want to be happy, and to do something with our lives. So each day we keep learning, we keep growing. Each day without alcohol or other drugs is a gift, a gift from God.

Prayer for the Day

Higher Power, You set me free. Now teach me to stay free. Guide me, for keeping my freedom is a big task.

Action for the Day

I will meditate on my freedom. I will take time to list all the ways I am now free.

Love is the reward of love.
— Johann von Schiller

When we used alcohol and other drugs, we shared as little as possible. There was little love in our hearts. We had become selfish. This caused us to be lonely.

Then something happened to change all of that. Remember the first time you walked into a meeting? You were met by people who shared. Maybe they shared a smile, their story, or just a cup of coffee with you. The sharing that goes on in a Twelve Step program is great. We learn that the more we give, the more we get. We get well by giving to others. Helping others is a great way to hold on to sobriety. Love is the reward of love.

Prayer for the Day

I pray that I will be there when others need me. I pray that service will become a big part of my program.

Action for the Day

Today, I'll think of friends who could use my help. I'll talk to them and offer to be there for them.

*It's gonna be a long hard
drag, but we'll make it.*
— *Janis Joplin*

Some people start each day with a groan.
They act like staying sober is no fun at all.
They may have turned over their illness to
their Higher Power. But they haven't yet
turned over their *will* and their *life*. They
don't see that a loving Higher Power can
change them into happy people.

Maybe they don't want to change. They just
want to feel better. After all, that's one reason
we all took drugs—to feel better without
changing. The program asks us to be willing
to *change*. That's how we become happier
people.

Prayer for the Day

Higher Power, help me listen to Your voice. Teach
me that following Your directions will make me
happy.

Action for the Day

Today, I'll list three things in my life that I haven't
yet turned over to my Higher Power. Why are these
things so important to me? What can I do to turn
them over?

*Life is not lost by dying; life
is lost minute by minute, day
by day, in all the thousand,
small, uncaring ways.*
— Stephen V. Bénet

Our Twelve Step program promises us a new way of life. But most of us won't just wake up one day with a new attitude. We only gain this new way of life if we get involved.

The Twelve Steps are *tools* to build a new life. The more we use a tool, the easier it is to use. The same goes for the Twelve Steps. We need to depend on the Twelve Steps, just as carpenters depend on their tools. If we only wait for the new way of life, it'll never come. The quicker we get involved, the quicker we'll get fixed.

Prayer for the Day
Higher Power, help me get involved. Help me build a new way of life.

Action for the Day
Today, I'll look for ways to use the Twelve Steps. If I have a problem, I'll first stop and think of how the Twelve Steps can help me solve it.

*The purpose of freedom is
to create it for others.*
— *Bernard Malamud*

Sobriety is freedom. With this freedom, we have a responsibility to help other addicts who still suffer. The program tells us this in Step Twelve. We do this by telling our stories and offering hope.

We must be ready to care, to give of ourselves. This is what spirituality is about. When we help others, we prepare the road for those who enter the program after us.

Tradition Five of the Twelve Traditions says, "Each group has but one primary purpose—to carry its message to the alcoholic who still suffers." It means we get better by helping others.

Prayer for the Day

Higher Power, help me create more freedom. Bring me to where I'm needed. Help me carry the message well.

Action for the Day

Today, I'll think of ways I can help the addict who still suffers. Then I'll choose one way I can be of help. I'll talk with my sponsor about it, and I'll follow through with my plan.

One is happy as the result
of one's own efforts.
— George Sand

Happiness is not an accident. It comes from following the spiritual voice found in each of us. This isn't always easy. Sometimes, the voice tells us to do things we're afraid of. For example, if we're lonely and the voice tells us to call someone on our phone list, we may make excuses to not do it. Again, the voice may say, "Just make the call. It will be okay." If we follow the voice, we'll find happiness.

The spiritual voice inside us speaks of care and love. It will never tell us to hurt others or ourselves. It is our Higher Power's voice. It's what Step Eleven calls "conscious contact." If we follow this guiding voice, it will lead us to happiness.

Prayer for the Day
I pray that I'll come to know my Higher Power by listening to the spiritual voice in me.

Action for the Day
Today, I'll meditate and listen to my Higher Power's gentle voice within.

*There is no fear in love, but
perfect love casts out fear.*
— 1 John 4:18

Love is allowing another person to be part
of you. When we love someone, we feel the
person inside of us. Spiritual love is letting
our Higher Power become part of us. We feel
our Higher Power inside of us. This is what
is meant by "conscious contact" in Step
Eleven.

When we were drinking and drugging, we
kept others on the outside. Inside we felt bad,
and we didn't want anyone to be close to us.

We are now asked to open ourselves up to
love and its healing power. Part of the joy of
love comes from letting another person know
us. You may even wonder, "Will people stick
around if they really know me?" Love will
answer, "Yes."

Prayer for the Day

Higher Power, let me trust Your love. Then I can
give up my fear.

Action for the Day

Today I'll invite my Higher Power into my heart.
I will practice conscious contact.

Having had a spiritual awakening as the result of these steps, we tried to carry this message to alcoholics, and to practice these principles in all our affairs.

— *Step Twelve*
from Alcoholics
Anonymous

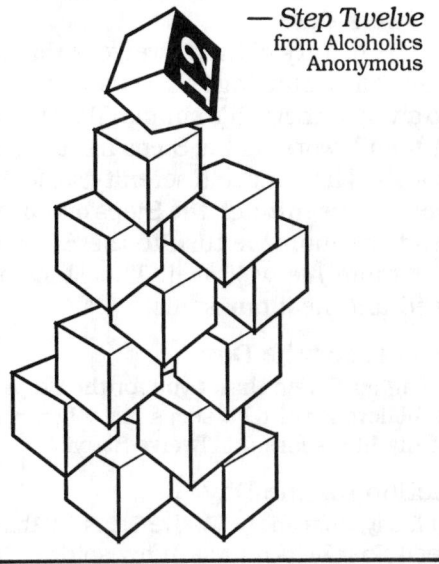

*Having had a spiritual
awakening as the result of
these steps. . .*
— First part of Step Twelve

We are awake! Our spirits are alive. We are part of the world. Our addiction no longer clouds our vision. How? Step Twelve answers this.

The beauty of Step Twelve is that if we feel our spirits starting to go dead, we know how to awaken them. It's simple. Turn to the Steps. After all, working the Steps has awakened our spirits. The hope and serenity we feel are gifts given to us through the Steps of our program. And the more we turn to the Steps for help, the more life we'll feel. The Steps are what feed and heal our souls.

Prayer for the Day

Higher Power, thank you for the Steps. If I start to believe it is I who keeps me sober, remind me of my life before the Twelve Steps.

Action for the Day

Today, I'll read the Twelve Steps. I'll think of how each Step helped awaken my spirit.

. . .we tried to carry this
message to alcoholics. . .
— Second part of Step Twelve

In this part of Step Twelve, we carry the message of hope. But it's not up to us if anyone accepts the message or not. This keeps us from playing God. We just gently deliver the message. We don't force the program down people's throats.

In general, Step Twelve tells us, "Be helpful to those we can help." When a neighbor is sick, mow her lawn. When a friend is in the hospital, visit him. Step Twelve reminds us that we make a difference. We have hope to give the world. And hope is what we stand for to the addict who still suffers. Hope is what we stand for to the addict's family. How beautiful to stand for hope! Remember when our lives stood for despair? What a change!

Prayer for the Day

Higher Power, help me shine brightly as a symbol of Your hope.

Action for the Day

Today, I'll help someone in need. It may be an alcoholic or other drug addict, or just someone in need. I'll help make the world a better place.

DECEMBER 3

*. . .and to practice these
principles in all our affairs.*
— Third part of Step Twelve

This is a statement about us. We are now people with values. These values reflect our spiritual growth. We know how to help others. We know how to admit our wrongs. We know how to look at ourselves and change our defects. We know how to live an honest life. Step Twelve tells us, "Go use these tools for better living. Go be all you can be. Enjoy life and live a life you can be proud of."

Step Twelve also tells us about how to have loving relationships. By the time we complete Step Twelve, we make or regain many relationships. The most important one is with our Higher Power. As we grow in the program, we realize all our relationships are spiritual gifts.

Prayer for the Day
Higher Power, I now have one face instead of many masks. Help me be a person who will stand before You with pride, not shame.

Action for the Day
Today, I'll talk with a friend and talk about my new values. I will talk about how much my life has changed.

DECEMBER 4

The measure of a man's real character is what he would do if he knew he would never be found out.
— Thomas Macaulay

We must live our new life all the time. This is what the Twelfth Step means by practicing "these principles in all our affairs." We try to be honest all the time. We don't cheat, and we tell the truth when asked a question. We learn that even if we can get away with something, we can't get away from ourselves.

This makes our lives so much easier. Our relationships, and our spirituality, get built on solid ground. We also come to trust in ourselves. We depend on ourselves to do the right thing—and we do. How nice it is to count on ourselves!

Prayer for the Day
Higher Power, make me strong enough to practice the Twelve Steps in all my affairs.

Action for the Day
Have I done anything that's bothering me? If so, I'll set a time to talk about it with my sponsor. The two of us can figure out how to solve it.

*Each day, somewhere in
the world, recovery begins
when one alcoholic talks
with another alcoholic,
sharing experience,
strength, and hope.*
— *Alcoholics Anonymous*

All over the world, recovering men and
women use the same Twelve Steps to live
their lives. Our fellowship keeps on growing.
The bigger it gets, the faster it grows. Why?
Because the program brings our spirits back
to life. All over the world, many of us were dying, and now we're full of life and love. We are
bringing our world back to life. As we share
our experience, strength, and hope, we help
others join us in coming back to life.

Prayer for the Day
Higher Power, help me stay sober today. Guide
me and all others who are doing Your will today.

Action for the Day
Today, I'll think of three things I can do to help
spread the message of A.A. and N.A.

The strongest of all
warriors are these two—
Time and Patience.
— *Leo Tolstoy*

One of the first things we learn about in recovery is time. Before, we may have tried to control time by pushing it along. We tried to hurry everything and everybody. We wanted our "quick fix." But the program tells us to slow down. Easy Does It.

We probably couldn't picture ourselves staying sober for the rest of our life. So we were told to just work at staying sober today. We learned to work our program One Day at a Time. We were being taught that time can be our friend. Time is our Higher Power's way of not having everything happen at once.

Prayer for the Day

Higher Power, You are my teacher. You are in charge of the lesson. Help me accept this. Teach me how to use my time wisely.

Action for the Day

Today, I'll list five ways I use my time in ways that aren't helpful to me. I'll work at making time my friend.

> *We are here to add what*
> *we can to, not to get what*
> *we can from, Life.*
> — *Sir William Osler*

Service is a word we hear in our recovery program. *Service* means *work we do for others*. It's the backbone of our program. The reason is simple. Service to our Higher Power and to others breaks down our wanting to be self-centered.

Service brings us back into the world. We really are part of the group when we pitch in to make coffee, set up chairs, or talk in meetings. We really feel like part of the family when we run errands and help with meals and housework. We really connect with our Higher Power when we pray, "Use me today to help others." Service breaks down the feeling of being alone that being self-centered brings.

Prayer for the Day

Higher Power, help me to be of service to You and others. Show me what is needed.

Action for the Day

Today will be a service day. I'll look for where my skills are needed. I'll see how valued I am. I'll give to others, knowing that I, too, will receive.

*When I was about twelve, I
used to think I must be a
genius, but nobody's noticed.*
— *John Lennon*

We all have secret ideas about ourselves.
How often we have said to ourselves, *If only
they knew* . . . But if we watch others, we see
that many of their ideas are not so secret. We
can often guess how they see themselves by
the way they act. We all act out our secrets.

Faith means trusting our Higher Power
with our secrets. Faith in others means trusting them with our secret feelings.

Why share these secrets? When we were using alcohol or other drugs we lived too much
in a secret world. We need to give up the
secrets that keep us from others. We need
others in our lives. Our spirits *need* to be close
to others.

Prayer for the Day

God, help me to live in ways I'm not ashamed
to tell others. Allow me to meet you and others, free
of shame.

Action for the Day

Today I'll share one of my secrets with a loving
friend.

There is no stronger bond
of friendship than a
mutual enemy.
— *Frankfort Moore*

A.A. is a fellowship united against the same enemy—alcoholism. Our bonds give us strength to recover. We may not even know each other's last name, but we'll do anything to help each other stay sober.

Our illness has taken much. But it has also given us much. We have millions of new friends. Almost anywhere in the world, we can find a member of our fellowship. Our new way of life depends on the strength of the fellowship. We should do nothing to weaken it.

When you don't feel like going to a meeting—go, not only for yourself but for the sake of the fellowship. It truly needs you.

Prayer for the Day

Higher Power, You have given me A.A. Now help me to keep it going. A.A. needs me, just as I need A.A. Help me give even when I don't want to.

Action for the Day

Today, I'll give back to the program. I'll call a new member, volunteer to put on a meeting, or make the coffee.

*Kindness in giving creates
love.*

— *Lao-tzu*

In our illness, we were *takers*. Now, we've changed this around. We are now *givers*. Giving is a big part of recovery. Our word for it is *service*. Our program is based on care, respect, and service. Our program tells us to "practice these principles in all our affairs." No matter if it's getting to our meeting early to put on the coffee, or going on a Twelfth Step call, we are giving of ourselves. We give so that we know we can make a difference. We give so that we can know how to love better. The healing power of recovery is love. As we give love and kindness to others, we heal. Why? Because people grow by giving kindness and love to others.

Prayer for the Day

Higher Power, with Your help I'll be a kind and loving giver. I'll look for ways to share Your kindness.

Action for the Day

Today, I'll list five ways I can be of service to others. I'll put at least one of these ways into action today.

When patterns are broken,
new worlds emerge.
> — *Tuli Kupferberg*

Recovery has happened to us. We stopped drinking or using other drugs and, like magic, a new world appeared. Being sober sure shakes up a person's life!

It's good to shake up our world every now and then. This way, we see there's not just one "world," but many. We grow each time we step into a new world and learn new things. Of course, the addict's world was new and exciting to us at one time. But we got trapped and couldn't find our way out. Our Higher Power had to free us.

We need to try new worlds, but we always need to take our Higher Power with us—into worlds where there's honesty, love, and trust.

Prayer for the Day
Higher Power, lead me to new worlds where I'll learn more about living fully.

Action for the Day
I'll list three ways I can step into a new world today. For example, I could read something new, go to a museum, or eat a new food.

*God gave us memory that
we might have roses in
December.*
— *James M. Barrie*

Do you remember what it was like to not have sobriety? Remember the shame? Remember the loneliness? Remember lying and wishing you could stop? Remember the powerlessness?

Do you remember, also, how it felt when you began to believe you had an illness? Your shame was lifted. Remember what it was like to look around at your meeting and know you belonged? Your loneliness was lifted. Remember when your family started to trust you again? Your dishonesty had been lifted.

Sobriety gives us many roses. Our memory will help to keep them fresh.

Prayer for the Day

Higher Power, never let me forget what it was like. Why? Because I'm only one drink or pill away from losing You.

Action for the Day

I'll find a friend I trust. I'll tell that person what my life was like before sobriety. I'll also talk about how I got sober.

Live and Let Live.
> — *AA slogan*

In our addiction, we didn't *care.* We didn't care about other people, even though we wanted to. We just didn't come through for them in ways that mattered. We didn't care for ourselves. We let bad things happen to us. And we didn't care about living. We set no goals, had no fun, smelled no flowers.

In our recovery, we do care. We care about others, ourselves, and life. Our spirits are on the move again. There's life in our hearts. Our bodies are getting well. And we're daring to dream.

We're living!

Prayer for the Day

Higher Power, put some life and energy into me today. Help me love my new life.

Action for the Day

Today, I'll focus on being alive. As I breathe in, I'll gather more and more life energy from nature.

*Hold fast to dreams for if
dreams die, life is a broken
winged bird that cannot
fly.*

— *Langston Hughes*

Many of our dreams died as our addiction
got worse. We felt the loss but couldn't speak
it. With recovery, we regain our ability to
dream. Dreams of sharing our lives with
family and friends return. They push out
thoughts of getting high. Dreams of pride and
self-respect reappear. They replace the awful
feeling of shame.

Like the quote above says, "Hold fast to
dreams. . . ." Our dreams are our wishes for
the future. They hold a picture of who we
want to be. In our dreams, we let our spirits
soar. Often, we feel close to God, others, and
ourselves. Thank God, we can dream again.

Prayer for the Day

Higher Power, thanks to you, my wings have
been mended. Guide me as I fly.

Action for the Day

Today, I'll take time out to dream and share my
dream with those I love.

*An ass is beautiful to an
ass, and a pig to a pig.*
— English proverb

When we see someone drunk and out of control, can we see the beautiful person inside them? If we can't, who will? Step Twelve reminds us that we have to help the alcoholic or other drug addict who still suffers.

This task has been given to us because we, most of all, should be able to look past the drunkenness and see the person. We were there. We know what it's like to be trapped in a world without meaning. If these memories have faded, we may need to go back over Step One. We may find ourselves angry with the practicing drunk or other drug addict. This is a sign that we have gotten too far from our past. Remember, "But for the grace of God ..."

Prayer for the Day

Higher Power, help me remember my past and what it's like now. This helps me care about the person who still suffers.

Action for the Day

Today, I'll respect my illness. I'll look for the beauty inside every drunk and other drug addict.

*Charity sees the need, not
the cause.*
— *German proverb*

Charity is not just giving money to good causes. Charity is having a heart that's ready to give. Charity is helping a friend at two in the morning. Charity is going early to the meeting to put on coffee without being asked. *Service* is how Twelve Step programs refer to "charity." Service and charity are a lifestyle. We see a need, so we try to help. Our values and our heart will guide us in how we help.

Service is a big part of our program. Service helps us think of others, not just of ourselves. We stop asking, "What's in it for me?" The act of helping others is what's in it for us. Sobriety is what's in it for us. Serenity is what's in it for us.

Prayer for the Day

Higher Power, You have given me many talents. Help me see how my talents can make the world a better place. Giving of myself is believing in You and myself.

Action for the Day

Today, I'll list my talents and I'll think of ways I can use them to help others.

The rose and the thorn,
and sorrow and gladness
are linked together.

— Saadi

When we were drinking and drugging, we didn't have to deal much with feelings. We turned them off. Then, when we let go of the alcohol and other drugs, we started to come back to life. Now—we have feelings again!

But even now, in recovery, we're scared of too much happiness. It's true—we don't want sadness and pain at all. Yet, feelings—the good and the bad—keep on coming.

And we have to handle them. We *are* learning to handle our feelings. We're getting strong enough to deal with them. With the help of our friends in the program, and our Higher Power, we're ready for life.

Prayer for the Day

Higher Power, I want to be fully alive, but I'm a little scared. Help me know what to do with my feelings today.

Action for the Day

Today, I'll be open to feelings. I'll enjoy my good feelings and share them. I'll ask for help with hard feelings by praying, and by calling my sponsor.

The only thing we have to
fear is fear itself.
— *Franklin D. Roosevelt*

As addicts, we had lots of fear. Some of us were afraid of failure. So we didn't try to do much. Or else we tried too hard all the time. We used alcohol and other drugs to forget our fear, but it didn't go away. It got worse.

Now we know we don't have to be afraid. When our lives are in the care of our Higher Power, we're safe. Faith is the cure for our fear.

But still, fear keeps creeping back inside us. That's okay. It's normal. There is so much that's new in our sober life! We don't know what will happen next. It's hard to always remember to trust our Higher Power. It's hard to always do what our Higher Power says. It's hard to always have faith. We have to practice turning our fear over to our Higher Power.

Prayer for the Day

Higher Power, be with me when I'm afraid. Help me remember to have faith to believe in You, even when my fear tells me not to.

Action for the Day

Today, I'll notice my fear and pray each time I get afraid.

*The truth is more
important than the facts.*
— Frank Lloyd Wright

Before recovery, we relied on false facts about addiction. We said things like: "I can quit anytime I want." "If you had my family, you'd drink too." The truth is, we were out of control. We couldn't manage our lives. We were sick. We were scared. When others pointed out this truth to us, we denied it.

Honesty, the backbone of our program, is about *truth*. We even start our meetings with the truth about who we are. "Hi, my name is _____, and I'm an alcoholic," or "Hi, my name is _____, and I'm a drug addict." The truth frees us from our addiction. The truth heals us and gives us comfort. It's like a blanket on a cold winter night.

Prayer for the Day

Higher Power, help me be an honest person. I pray for the strength to face the truth and speak it.

Action for the Day

Today, I'll list three ways I have used facts in a dishonest way.

There are two ways of spreading light: to be the candle or the mirror that reflects it.

— *Edith Wharton*

Our Higher Power is the candle. And our hearts, like a mirror, reflect a warm, loving glow.

But when we used alcohol and other drugs, we tried to be the candle. We wanted to have control. Many of us acted like this to hide how out of control we felt. We never thought we could be happy by admitting we were out of control.

In recovery, we accept that it's okay to be the mirror. We accept that our Higher Power is the candle that guides us. We want to be the mirror that reflects how much our Higher Power loves us.

Prayer for the Day
Higher Power, thank-you for the light and warmth You give me.

Action for the Day
Tonight, I'll light a candle and place it in front of a mirror. I'll study how they work together to light the room.

*Don't give your advice
before you are called upon.*
— *Desiderius Erasmus*

If someone wants your advice, the person will ask for it. That's one reason why in Twelve Step programs we don't go around trying to talk people into joining.

But people will ask us for advice. They'll see how we've changed, and they'll want what we have. All we have to do is tell them where we found it—in AA, NA, or another Twelve Step group. We don't tell them what to do. We tell them our own story—what it was like, what happened, and where we are now.

And we invite them to join us.

Prayer for the Day
Higher Power, help me carry the healing message of the program to those who ask for my advice.

Action for the Day
I'll make a decision to spend time with the next person who asks for my help.

*It is possible to be different
and still be all right.*
— *Anne Wilson Schaef*

Each of us is special. In some ways, we're
all different. It's a good thing too. We'd be
bored if we were all the same.

Sometimes, though, we try to hide the special things about us. We don't want to be
"different." But the ways that we're different
make us special. Some of us have a good
sense of humor. Others have a knack of fixing
things. Some of us make beautiful art. Others
are great with kids. Our Higher Power made us
as different, as unique, as beautiful snowflakes.

Prayer for the Day

Higher Power, help me use my special gifts the
way You want me to. Help me be thankful that You
have given me something special to share with
others.

Action for the Day

I'll think of one thing about me that's special.
I'll talk with my sponsor about it.

*We not only need to be
willing to give, but also to
be open to receiving from
others.*

— *from* On Hope

Many of us took so much from others during our addiction that now we may not want to ask for anything. We may be afraid to ask for help, so our needs go unmet. In fact, many of us would now rather give than receive.

In recovery, we need to understand the difference between *taking* and *receiving*. Giving to others is important. So is receiving from others. As we grow spiritually, we learn to accept gifts. The gift of sobriety teaches us this. We need to accept the gifts the world gives us without shame. We are entitled. God loves us and will give us much if we're willing to receive it.

Prayer for the Day

Higher Power, help me be receptive to Your gifts. Help me see and believe that I'm entitled to all the happiness of the world.

Action for the Day

I'll think of what a friend has given me. I'll thank this friend.

*We must all hang together
or we will hang separately.*
— *Benjamin Franklin*

We didn't get ourselves sober. And we don't keep ourselves sober. Our program does this. This is why the Twelfth Step is so important. We must be willing to give service to our program *whenever* it's needed. When a friend calls and says he or she feels like using, we don't just say we're sorry. We go get our friend and take him or her to a meeting. Our survival depends on this kind of action.

We are to carry the message. We carry the message by deeds, not words. We are part of a fellowship based on action. A fellowship guided by love. It is not words that keep us sober—it is action.

Prayer for the Day

Higher Power, help me be ready whenever there's a need. Help me be ready to put my self-will aside. Give me strength.

Action for the Day

I will think of my group members. Who could use a supportive call or visit? I will call or visit those who need my help.

*To love is to place our
happiness in the happiness
of another.*
— *Gottfried Wilhelm
von Leibnitz*

Now that we're getting well, we feel the need for love more than ever. We tried to avoid love by using chemicals to feel good. But it didn't work. Addiction cut us off even more from people.

How do we fill our need for love? We can think about this fact: People give us love all the time. Only we just haven't seen it. Every time someone comes to a meeting to get well with us, that is love. Love isn't all-or-nothing. Little gems of love are all over. Watch for them. Enjoy them. Give them to others.

Prayer for the Day

Higher Power, love comes from You. Help me see it, feel it, and give it.

Action for the Day

I'll look three persons in the eye today and send them love in my smile.

*To be emotionally
committed to somebody is
very difficult, but to be
alone is impossible.*
— *Stephen Sondheim*

Let's face it, relationships are hard work!
But we are lucky! Recovery is *about* relationships. We learn how to set limits. We learn
how to listen to and talk to others. In Step
One, we begin a new relationship with ourselves. In Steps Two and Three, we begin a
relationship with our Higher Power. In later
Steps, we mend our relationships with family
and friends.

In our relationship with our sponsor, we
learn about being friends. And our past relationship with alcohol and other drugs is being replaced by people and our Higher Power.

Prayer for the Day

Higher Power, thank-you for all my new relationships. Thank-you for teaching me how to feel
human again.

Action for the Day

Today, I'll make a list of all the new relationships
I have now, due to my sobriety.

*Reading is to the Mind,
what exercise is to the
Body.*

— *Joseph Addison*

Good ideas are the seeds that start our growth. We hear things at meetings. We listen to our sponsor. Maybe we listen to program tapes. And we read.

Reading is special, because we do it when we're alone. We read in quiet times, when we can think. We can read as fast or as slowly as we want. We can mark special words and come back to them again and again. We'll figure things out in our own way, but we need help to get started. That's why we read. It gives us good ideas to think about.

Prayer for the Day
Higher Power, speak to me through helpful readings and help me learn at my best pace.

Action for the Day
Reading is easier the more I do it. Today I'll feel proud that I've read program ideas to get my mind thinking in a healthy way.

*If you will walk with lame
men you'll soon limp
yourself.*
— *Seamas MacManus*

Before recovery, we kept company with people who were as sick as us, or worse. We got angry and made fun of people who were trying to improve their lives. They scared us. They were like mirrors that reflected how spiritually lost we were becoming.

Now we walk in the crowd we avoided. Now we have values. We have spiritual beliefs. Living up to these values and beliefs can be hard. We need to be around people who live by their values.

In recovery, we learn that we need others. Remember, the first word in Step One is *we*. We need good people in our lives. We need friends who will not just tell us what we want to hear, but what we are doing wrong.

Prayer for the Day

Sometimes I act like I need no one. Help me pick my friends wisely, for my life is at stake.

Action for the Day

Today, I'll pick one friend, and we'll talk about how we can better help each other.

*Many people are living in
an emotional jail without
recognizing it.*
— *Virginia Satir*

Our disease was our jail. We felt so bad that
we were sure we must have done something
awful. But we didn't cause our disease. We
have done nothing to deserve our disease. We
aren't responsible for the fact that we have a
disease.

But we *are* responsible for our recovery. We
have been granted probation. The terms of
our probation are simple: don't drink or use
other drugs, and work the Steps. If we follow
these simple rules, we'll be free. And it will
be clear to us that only a Power greater than
ourselves could give us this freedom.

Prayer for the Day

Higher Power, help me to stay free. For this next
twenty-four-hour period, take from me any urge to
drink or use other drugs. With Your help, I'll be free.

Action for the Day

Today, I'll think about my disease. I am not
morally weak. I have a dangerous illness. What can
keep me free from my disease?

Keep It Simple.
> — *AA slogan*

Addiction messed up our thinking. We know that from taking Step One. We forgot things. We had blackouts. We made excuses, and we even started to believe them. We were mixed up. We couldn't figure things out. We decided to get high and forget about it.

Now, our minds are clear. We can keep thinking clearly if we work our program and Keep It Simple. Don't drink or use other drugs. Go to meetings. Work the Steps. Be yourself. Ask for help. Trust your Higher Power.

Two thoughts will always mess us up if we let them in. They are "Yes, but . . ." and "What if?" Don't let them in. Keep It Simple.

Prayer for the Day
Higher Power, thanks for recovery. Help me stay sober and clean today.

Action for the Day
Today, I'll take one thing at a time and Keep It Simple.

*May you live all the days of
your life.*
— *Jonathan Swift*

Tonight, at midnight, a new year will begin.
None of us know what the new year will hold.
But we can trust ourselves to hold on to the
spirit of recovery as we go through the year.
As a new year is about to begin, we can rejoice in our new way of life. We can give our
will and our life to our Higher Power. By doing
these things, we'll be ready for the new year.

Prayer for the Day
Higher Power, I pray that I'll start the new year
safe in Your loving arms. I pray that I'll keep working my program.

Action for the Day
Tonight, at midnight, I'll say the Serenity Prayer.
I will think of all the others who have read this
meditation book and who will join me in my prayer.
We are a recovering community.

THE TWELVE STEPS
OF ALCOHOLICS ANONYMOUS*

1. We admitted we were powerless over alcohol—that our lives had become unmanageable.
2. Came to believe that a Power greater than ourselves could restore us to sanity.
3. Made a decision to turn our will and our lives over to the care of God *as we understood Him.*
4. Made a searching and fearless moral inventory of ourselves.
5. Admitted to God, to ourselves, and to another human being the exact nature of our wrongs.
6. Were entirely ready to have God remove all these defects of character.
7. Humbly asked Him to remove our shortcomings.
8. Made a list of all persons we had harmed, and became willing to make amends to them all.
9. Made direct amends to such people wherever possible, except when to do so would injure them or others.
10. Continued to take personal inventory and when we were wrong promptly admitted it.
11. Sought through prayer and meditation to improve our conscious contact with God *as we understood Him,* praying only for knowledge of His will for us and the power to carry that out.
12. Having had a spiritual awakening as the result of these steps, we tried to carry this message to alcoholics, and to practice these principles in all our affairs.

---

*The Twelve Steps of AA are taken from *Alcoholics Anonymous* (Third Edition), and published by AA World Services, Inc., New York, N.Y., 59-60. Reprinted with permission.

THE TWELVE TRADITIONS OF ALCOHOLICS ANONYMOUS*

1. Our common welfare should come first; personal recovery depends upon A.A. unity.
2. For our group purpose there is but one ultimate authority—a loving God as He may express Himself in our group conscience. Our leaders are but trusted servants—they do not govern.
3. The only requirement for A.A. membership is a desire to stop drinking.
4. Each group should be autonomous, except in matters affecting other groups or A.A. as a whole.
5. Each group has but one primary purpose—to carry its message to the alcoholic who still suffers.
6. An A.A. group ought never endorse, finance, or lend the A.A. name to any related facility or outside enterprise lest problems of money, property and prestige divert us from our primary purpose.
7. Every A.A. group ought to be fully self-supporting, declining outside contributions.
8. Alcoholics Anonymous should remain forever nonprofessional, but our service centers may employ special workers.
9. A.A., as such, ought never be organized, but we may create service boards or committees directly responsible to those they serve.
10. Alcoholics Anonymous has no opinion on outside issues, hence the A.A. name ought never be drawn into public controversy.
11. Our public relations policy is based on attraction rather than promotion; we need always maintain personal anonymity at the level of press, radio, television and films.
12. Anonymity is the spiritual foundation of all our traditions, ever reminding us to place principles before personalities.

---

*The Twelve Traditions of AA are taken from *Twelve Steps and Twelve Traditions,* published by AA World Services, Inc., New York, N.Y., 129-87. Reprinted with permission.

THE SERENITY PRAYER

God grant me the serenity
To accept the things I cannot change,
The courage to change the things I can,
And the wisdom to know the difference.

INDEX